Dedicated To
William Grignard Pecau
Vessel of Grace and Exemplar of Social Teachings

SOCIAL TEACHINGS IN THE EPISCOPAL CHURCH

Robert E. Hood

MOREHOUSE PUBLISHING
Harrisburg, PA • Wilton, CT

Morehouse Publishing

Editorial Office
78 Danbury Road
Wilton, CT 06897

Corporate Office
P.O. Box 1321
Harrisburg, PA 17105

Library of Congress Cataloging-in-Publication Data

Hood, R.E.
   Social teachings in the Episcopal church/R.E. Hood.   p.   cm.
   Includes bibliographical references.
   ISBN 0-8192-1533-3
   1. Sociology, Christian. 2. Episcopal Church—Doctrines. 3. Anglican Communion—Doctrines. I. Title.
BX5930.2.H66   1990   90-31394
261-8'08823—dc20   CIP

Printed in the United States of America
by
BSC LITHO
Harrisburg, Pennsylvania 17105

Contents

Acknowledgments vii

Introduction ix

1. What Do Social Teachings Look Like? 1
   Early Christian Social Teachings: Ernst Troeltsch 6
   Roman Catholic Social Teachings 11

2. What Do Anglican Social Teachings Look Like? 33
   Roots of Classical Anglican Social Thought 33
   Lambeth Conferences and Social Teachings 50

3. Beginnings of Episcopal Church Social Teachings 65
   The Civil War and the First Social Teachings 65
   Industrialism and the Second Social Teachings 66
   Episcopal Social Teachings in the
      Late Nineteenth Century 72
   Episcopal Social Teachings in the
      Late Twentieth Century 73

4. Pictures of an Exhibition: Episcopal Social
      Teachings I. 77
   War and Peace 77
   Peace and War 84
   Commentary 90

5. Pictures of an Exhibition: Episcopal Social
      Teachings II. 101
   Race and Racial Affairs 101
   Commentary 126

6. Pictures of an Exhibition: Episcopal Social
   Teachings III. 135
   Marriage and Family.. 135
   Sexuality.. 144
   Commentary 154

7. Pictures of an Exhibition: Episcopal Social
   Teachings IV. 163
   Economic Issues.. 163
   Commentary 174

8. The Authority of Social Teachings:
   Do They Have Teeth?.. 183

Appendix A 195

Appendix B... 223

Appendix C 239

Selected Readings 247

Index.. 251

Acknowledgments

I wish very much to acknowledge the industry and diligence of my former student assistants at the General Theological Seminary. They did a great deal of work collecting and analyzing documents, raising pertinent theological and historical questions, and suggesting possible interpretations. It helped a great deal that all of them had been trained as lawyers in their former life before going to seminary: Thomas O'Dell, who brought much intellect, imagination, and enthusiasm to his research, and for which I am most grateful; King McGlaughon, his successor who was a keen researcher of journals, minutes, and other texts with able and analytical skills; Ann–Marie Boylan, a Roman Catholic graduate student who uncovered important data and documents about church statements on the family that hitherto had been neglected.

I also owe a great deal of gratitude to the Reverend Earl Neil, D.D., Executive of the National Mission to Church and Society at the Episcopal Church Center, whose creative financial skills made possible a grant funding a research assistant and research during my sabbatical.

Introduction

Does the Episcopal Church have *social teachings*? If so, why are they not better known? Are they a body of particular theological doctrines or directions that identify the Episcopal Church? The Episcopal Church has created official social *policies* and *programs*. Are they intended to implement social teachings or do the teachings grow out of the policies and programs in the Episcopal Church?

These are the times that try souls in matters of morality, Christian social ethics, and church identity in the midst of an increasingly secular, diverse American society that esteems individual autonomy. One of the things about which liberal, moderate, and conservative Christians—Protestants, Catholics, black churches, and Fundamentalists—agree is that Christians should be more audible and visible in public discussions about public policy and public issues. Conservatives and Fundamentalists stridently call for a "revival of spiritual righteousness," whereas moderates like Richard Neuhaus complain that the lack of the religious voice in public dialogue and the formation of public policy has led to a nakedness in the public square.[1] In such times, Episcopalians, indeed all Christians, bombarded with conflicting moral and ethical claims appearing with laserlike speed, yearn for light in the midst of an ethical labyrinth overshadowed by single-issue groups. Many search for some reliable and authoritative body of theologically-grounded social teachings that allows them to find their way rather than simply to tread water. Is there a distinct core of Episcopal social teachings informed by a theological understanding or theological models of society that can empower, comfort (meaning to strengthen), and enliven the laity as well as the ordained when confronted by and addressing so many different social issues and concerns?

And if there is such a body of social teachings, what difference would or should they make in the very lives of these people and the public dialogue, the larger world and ecumenical circles? What kind of authority do they have? Would they be expected to have the same impact as Catholic social teachings in influencing attitudes, behavior, and positions of bishops, clergy, and laity as well as shaping the very existence and identity of Catholics in a pluralistic society?

Furthermore, given the importance of individualism, private choice, individual autonomy, and single-issue constituencies in American democracy, can Episcopal clerics and members be held accountable in some moral way without coercion by the Episcopal Church for the *duty* of upholding or violating such teachings? What is the degree of elasticity and obligation connected with obeying or acknowledging the authority of such teachings for a people shaped by and living in the midst of American pluralism? Is social *policy*—meaning establishing social goals in a program and budget[2]—to function like social *teachings* in the Episcopal Church? Do statements and Pastoral Letters from the House of Bishops and the interim Pastorals of the Presiding Bishop have an "official" and therefore authoritative character over against or alongside the statements and actions of the General Convention when addressing social and political matters? Are statements of the House of Bishops only binding for the bishops or also authoritative for the entire Episcopal Church?

What about the classic social teachings and methodology of the Church of England as found in F.D. Maurice, John Ludlow, and the nineteenth century Christian Socialist movement in Britain and their influence? Is the content and method of Episcopal social positions influenced by this classical period of Anglican social thought? If so, in what way? Is the Episcopal Church as a part of the Anglican tradition even under any kind of duty and theological obligation to consult these classical teachings and their methodology when formulating its own social teachings and addressing social matters?

Moreover, what is the relationship and authority of the Church's Teaching Series to these official statements or *magisterium* of the church in matters social and political? (That series does not claim to be the definitive teaching of the Episcopal Church but, presumably with the imprimatur of General Convention, bears some heavy responsibility for furthering the Episcopal social and moral teachings, if such exist, as well as critically addressing those teachings.)

These and many other questions occur when considering whether the Episcopal Church has social teachings and, if so, what their authority is in the life of the various bodies and agencies of the church and in the behavior, thinking and actions of its individual bishops, clergy, and lay people. The task of deciphering such teachings is made more difficult because the Episcopal Church, in spite of its language about *tradition,* does not in fact have a tradition of systematizing or codifying even its social statements and policies, let alone a deliberate tradition or codex for social teachings. To try to get at these questions as well as discover in its pronouncements a pattern that allows or disallows us to identify either a consistent or persistent coherent body of social teachings, I propose to look at such documents as Pastoral Letters, social policy statements, resolutions, and the parliamentary motions of General Convention and Executive Council in four areas: (1) peace and war, (2) race, (3) marriage and family life, and (4) the economy.

At the same time, the changing historical contexts that influenced the content of these teachings will be dealt with briefly as well. But more importantly, their theological character and impact will be examined to get at some of the questions raised above. By so doing, I hope to move the development of social thought in the Episcopal Church a step forward for the church, its individual members, and the larger religious and secular communities wanting to learn the church's mind about some social issues. Very little work has been done on the social teachings of the Episcopal Church, thereby causing a vacuum in which a confusion of social policy with social teachings by clergy and laity alike has occurred or a lack of knowledge about both has prevailed.

The issue of early Episcopal social teachings prior to the Civil War has been addressed in a limited historical way by Robert Bruce Mullin.[3] Mullin maintained that after the 1776 war, the leadership of the Protestant Episcopal Church shifted from the South, where the previously established Anglican Church was in disarray, to the mid-Atlantic colonies, and, in particular, to New York. There Bishop John Henry Hobart and other High Churchmen held reign with sufficient numerical and financial resources to be used in assuming leadership in the now orphaned young Anglican Church. After the war, for example, one fourth of

American Anglicans resided in New York state. With this population base and the economic strength of Trinity Church in New York City, Hobart with his High Church theology of the church and the episcopate assumed leadership of the demoralized Episcopal Church struggling to gain national trust by becoming more of an indigenous American church. Hence, Mullin said, the church's basic theological attitude toward society and social thought was shaped by Hobart and the High Churchmen reacting negatively to Calvinism and an evangelical America. They deliberately and consciously embodied British mistrust of and impatience with strict Protestant confessional principles in forming social thought, although they did not articulate this so openly due to the political conditions of the times. As a result, whenever the young church under Hobart's influence spoke theologically about society or the state, it had these Tory and Anglo-Catholic models in mind.

But I think this hypothesis is not quite on target, for while Hobart and the High Churchmen developed a theological method and attitude toward society, such did not lead to a coherent body of social teachings grounded in theological and ethical or moral reasoning. Rather they were social statements about events and trends often grounded in piety, polity, and churchmanship polemic rather than theology and ethical reasoning. Furthermore, as Mullin himself pointed out, these statements were not considered authoritative or binding. Instead they reflected a prevailing view that the state was "society" as imaged largely in the Episcopal Church's aesthetics: its beautiful architecture, wonderful music, solemn and dignified worship, as well as the continued belief that the Episcopal Church was an established surrogate guardian in matters of a national faith and morals in America. This was well caricatured in the testimony of one Episcopal gentleman of means several decades later: "As to creeds [my father] knew nothing about them, and cared nothing either; yet he seemed to know which sect he belonged with. It had to be a sect with a minimum of nonsense about it; no immersion, no exhorters, no holy confession. Since he was a respectable New Yorker he belonged to the Episcopal Church."[4]

Sources of Episcopal Church Social Teachings

The first place to look for Episcopal Church social teachings is the

Pastoral Letter, the oldest device bearing canonical authority for expressing the church's mind. Historically, as it is already known but may be worth repeating, the bishops of the Episcopal Church from the inception of the House of Bishops were clear that they did not wish to have anything resembling an archbishop or a metropolitan who might function as a central authority in the church (even though many want the current office of the Presiding Bishop to act like an archiepiscopate). When the House of Bishops was constituted after the consecration of White and Griswold, the canons of 1799 also made it clear that the senior bishop of the church was only to be the presiding administrative officer calling and presiding at General Conventions. Thus, it was not their intention that there be an official spokesman of the church in public, social, and theological matters.

But there was to be a corporate public voice when addressing the faithful or the state on matters of crucial importance that was institutionalized in the Pastoral Letter. The first Pastoral Letter was written and issued in 1808.[5] No doubt a carryover from the New Testament "pastoral letters" or epistles (the most notable of which are 1 Timothy, 2 Timothy, and Titus), the Pastoral Letter eventually became a formal letter written by the diocesan bishop to his people about doctrinal, disciplinary, or devotional affairs. Soon, national Pastoral Letters, written by the entire synod of bishops, were addressed to the whole church. In the Roman Catholic Church they presently function similarly like encyclicals, except the latter are written by the Pope either to his bishops or to the faithful with expected obedience and assent.

The Pastoral Letter in the Protestant Episcopal Church was written originally by the most senior bishop, acknowledged as the "Presiding Bishop" of the church, in consultation with other bishops, who presided at meetings of the House of Bishops and General Convention. However, eventually it became the responsibility of the entire House of Bishops. The Pastoral was (and continues to be) a means of addressing and indeed summoning the entire church in matters considered of religious urgency and importance. Pastoral Letters therefore have a particular authority in the development and evolution of the church's social thought, underscored by the fact that canon law since 1820 has required that all Pastoral Letters be read in parish churches during worship. Still, one would be hard put to say how binding their authority is in terms of assent and conformity because of the division of authority in the Episcopal Church—indeed in the Anglican Communion—between synodical governance and episcopal governance. Bishops and theologians have coined a jargon phrase for this that they call *dispersed authority*. The first Pastoral dealing explicitly with theology about social matters was that of 1862 during the national crisis of Southern secession and the resulting Civil War.[6]

Pastoral Letters command public acknowledgment of the episcopate's historical teaching and guardianship of the faith of the church. Decisions, statements and social policy of General Convention are authoritative, as we shall see, but there is no canonical requirement that they be read or even announced to Episcopal congregations either within a required period of time or indeed at all. Of course, there is no penalty for not reading the bishops' Pastoral Letter to the congregation. It is simply thought to be a duty incumbent upon the priest having charge of the congregation, *period*. Indeed, a case might be made that the Episcopal Church in the new 1979 Prayer Book thought it necessary to emphasize this teaching function of the episcopate. In the catechism ("An Outline of the Faith") in that book, the question is asked about the character of the ministry of a bishop. The reply includes the words "to guard the faith, unity, and discipline of the whole Church." That is, a bishop is expected to guard the active tradition of the Christian faith as inherited and enlarged by the Episcopal Church in its internal and external life. No other part of the three-fold ministry in this catechism is assigned this grave responsibility.

A second source for Episcopal social teachings and thought is the official reports to General Convention and House of Bishops that are approved or incorporated in a pronouncement by General Convention. These reports come from several authorized bodies: (1) committees, (2) joint commissions, and (3) standing commissions. As civil unrest and secession by Southern states over the issue of slavery generated the emergence of social teachings via the Pastoral Letter, so was it also the occasion for written reports supporting these "teachings."

We notice this first in the report of the Board of Missions to the 1868 General Convention, which established the Freedman's Commission "to educate a race suddenly elevated to political power and equality in the midst of their ignorance and in-experience."[7] This commission, which was given an initial funding of $85,000 for the welfare of some 5500 former slave children under its care, was actually authorized at the 1865 Convention as a sub-commission of the Board of Missions. It was renamed at the 1868 Convention and mandated to look after the social welfare of the emancipated slaves. Such a commission was not peculiar to the Episcopal Church. In fact it and a number of other Protestant denominations were simply imitating the model of the federal government, which created the Freedman's Bureau in March 1865 under General Oliver O. Howard, to aid, educate, and rehabilitate emancipated slaves.

The report of the Episcopal Church's Freedman's Commission was both a program and a theological declaration about (1) the church's ministry to the marginalized and needy, presented as a social service program, and (2) the ethnic diversity of the church's mission, chiefly executed through the establishment of schools and racial congregations for blacks. It also commended the work of the American Colonization Society (organized 1816-17 in Washington, D.C.) and similar programs whose expressed purpose was to encourage, finance, and organize transport for slaves and freed blacks to return to Africa. Many white Episcopalians, particularly in the South, supported the ACS. But many black Episcopalians in the North opposed it, led by the Reverend Peter Williams, first rector of St. Philip's Church, New York City. Williams, called a "timid man" by one of the leading black theologians of his day and an Episcopal priest, Alexander Crummell (1819-98), was subsequently censored and reprimanded by his bishop, Benjamin Treadwell Onderdonk, because of his active opposition to such programs.[8]

Yet the eclectic character of Episcopal social teachings was illustrated by the issuance of another committee report at that same Convention, the report of the Committee on Canons, which portrayed what H. Richard Niebuhr calls a "Christ against culture" position. This report, possibly the church's earliest statement on dissent within and loyalty to the state, recom-mended the adoption of a new canon saying "it is the sense of the Protestant Episcopal Church...that it is incompatible with their duty, position, and sacred calling, for the clergy of this Church to bear arms." The proposed canon excluded military chaplains and instructors in military academies because their teaching was considered a civil duty rather than a military one.[10]

The church approved this position without any reference to the bishops' previous theological position in 1862 about loyalty and obedience to the U.S. Constitution as recognition of the state's divine mandate given in Romans 13.   Accordingly, the 1862 Pastoral said that because of this mandate, the state could legitimately use force against evil and deploy dutiful citizens in the militia to carry out that mandate when necessary.   The General Convention and the House of Bishops simply lacked, as they still do, a tradition or historical awareness of being accountable to previous teachings and statements in matters of social concern.

In addition to committee reports as sources for social teachings are reports of joint commissions, initially a kind of task force with joint membership from bishops, priests, and laity in both houses established by General Convention to address a particular social problem.   The first was the Joint Commission on Relations of Capital and Labor, established in 1901 during all the turmoil between the early trade union movement and business. In its first report in 1904, the joint commission defined the role of the Episcopal Church as a reconciler of opposites.   The church

> stands [on the one hand] as a friend of Capital to give it opportunity to fulfill its giver's will, not to forget to do good and to distribute.... She stands [on the other hand] as a friend of Labor, that Labor may recognize that, when rightly directed, it is the fulfillment of duties put upon man by his Creator and that such labor is blessed by man's Maker. She stands to be the friend of Capital and Labor in all the sorrows, the griefs, the vicissitudes of life of them both.[11]

The joint commission asked that the church's engagement be exemplified through its members studying the goals and purposes of the labor movement as well as the causes of industrial strife. This would equip them to understand their theological task of reconciling opposite factions "with a view to bringing about mutual reconciliation and harmony in the spirit of the Prince of Peace." "The capitalist and the laborer alike are sons of the Church.... The voice of the Christian religion reaches both capital and labor. The Church helps remove the moral cause of industrial strife when she brings these different members of her family into better acquaintance."[12] The report also supported organized labor, noting that it was important for protection of the interests and well-being of the laborers "in the face of a prejudice and an hostility."[13]

The 1910 Convention replaced the commission with a new Joint Commission on Social Services to study and report on the social and industrial conditions as well as to coordinate the activities of the various church organizations in this area, now called "social service." The final report of the Labor and Capital commission affirmed the teaching of the 1908 Lambeth Conference which upheld private property as a gift to the owner for his or her benefit and that of the community. Investments conferred a mutual responsibility for the entire community and not just the individual.

Joint commissions were canonically supplemented by standing commissions, created in 1967 by General Convention. They were mandated to meet between conventions and submit reports and recommendations to the General Convention on major subjects of concern to the church. Provided a budget for their meetings and consultants, the membership of each standing commission consists of bishops, clergy, and laity who meet periodically during the triennium. Presently, they are (1) Health Affairs and Health, (2) Church in Small Communities, (3) Constitution and Canons, (4) Ecumenical Relations, (5) Metropolitan Areas, (6) World Mission, (7) Church Music, (8) Liturgical, (9) Structure of the Church, (10) Stewardship and Development, and (11) Peace. The Joint Commission on Human Affairs and Health is charged to report on "the theological, ethical, and pastoral questions . . . in such aspects of human affairs as human health, sexuality and bioethical problems."[14] Here can be uncovered a sheath of social teachings and thought, even if theologically imprecise and occasionally too blurred.

The third source for Episcopal social teachings is a bit more diffuse and complicated, namely, the resolutions, motions, memorials, and other parliamentary devices approved at General Convention and, after 1926, the Executive Council (originally called the National Council until 1967), which is authorized to speak for the church between General Conventions. All of these since 1967 have been organized and codified by the Executive Council.

A fourth but less important source is the resolutions and teachings coming out of the Lambeth Conferences and occasional papers produced by the Public Issues (Affairs) Office at the national church headquarters. Sometimes the Lambeth texts have been incorporated into a particular resolution of General Convention, at other times they have been adopted as written by Lambeth. The Public Issues papers are not definitive position papers but rather are intended to arouse discussion about issues and different, often opposing, points of view with the aim of moving the church toward some kind of consensus. They have included such topics as family life, South Africa, migration, aging, capital punishment, and the criminal justice system. Nevertheless both of these documents have had some influence on shaping the text in some of the other sources of the church's social teachings mentioned above, which will be examined in more detail later.

Thus, the Episcopal Church, with some exceptions, deals with social issues through General Convention parliamentary devices, such as resolutions, motions, budget programs, and policy statements, in addition to occasional Pastoral Letters from its bishops and reports of its commissions and committees. Such is not inappropriate. But for a church proud of its ecclesiastical tradition and theological legacy via the Church of England, it is all the more surprising that even the theological social thought and thinkers coming out of nineteenth century Anglicanism have seldom been points of reference for shaping and critically examining Episcopal social teachings. Likewise, for a church claiming to be the heir jointly of the ancient Catholic tradition and the reforms of the Protestant tradition, it offers little evidence of utilizing either of those great traditions as well.

Much of the reason may lie in the fact that, generally, the Episcopal Church when meeting in synod (General Convention and diocesan conventions) relies on predilection rather than recollection. Furthermore, in the case of General Convention, which has its own nomenclature, processes and politics, more than 30 percent of the delegates (deputies) are new, as are many bishops. Hence, there is an episodic, transient character even in its social policies, with a noticeable absence of sustained theological debate and discussion. Some might describe such a dynamic as being flexible and relevant; others might see it as an inclination to be trendy and insubstantial. Likewise, its synods separate its seminary theologians from its corporate manager-pastors, i.e., the bishops, whose inclinations tend toward programs, crisis management, and action rather than careful deliberations and time-consuming, considered discussions about social teachings for the church. The haste and shallowness with which the synods frequently deal with social issues by program and budget reminds some of the adage quoted often by foreigners to illustrate American impatience with deliberations and weighty questions of theological substance in general: afterall, *instant* coffee did come from America.

Nevertheless, these Pastoral Letters, official reports of the various committees and joint commissions, resolutions, policy statements, and texts of Lambeth Conference do provide a font of information about theological substance and models as well as methods utilized within the Episcopal Church in dealing with culture and social issues. The fact that they are documents from official and authorized bodies gives them an authority as social pronouncements. The task is to determine their theological substance as social teaching.

Notes

1. Richard J. Neuhaus, *The Naked Public Square: Religion and Democracy in America* (Grand Rapids, Mich.: William B. Eerdmans Publishing, 1984).

2. See the definitive study by M. Moran Weston, *The Social Policy of the Episcopal Church in the Twentieth Century* (New York: Seabury Press, 1964).

3. Robert Bruce Mullin, *Episcopal Vision/American Reality: High Church Theology and Social Thought in Evangelical American* (New Haven: Yale University Press, 1986).

4. Ibid., p. 92.

5. See Appendix A.

6. See Appendix B.

7. *Journal of the General Convention, 1868*, p. 370.

8. Apparently there was some ambiguity in Peter Williams' opposition to the American Colonization Society program of black emigration to Africa. See Wilson Jeremiah Moses, *Alexander Crummell: A Study of Civilization and Discontent* (New York: Oxford University Press, 1989), pp. 13, 24-25.

9. H. Richard Niebuhr, *Christ and Culture* (New York: Harper, 1951), pp. 45-82.

10. *Journal of the General Convention, 1868*, pp. 90-1.

11. *Journal of the General Convention, 1904*, p. 417. See committee's report in Appendix C.

12. *Journal of the General Convention, 1904*, pp. 95-6.

13. Ibid., p. 97.

14. *Constitution and Canons for the Government of the Protestant Episcopal Church in the United States of America*, 1982, p. 16.

Chapter 1
What Do Social Teachings Look Like?

What do we mean by *social teachings*? A fairly recent term historically and theologically, social teachings were really established as a concept by the very active Pope Leo XIII (1810; Pope: 1878–1903), the same Pope, coincidentally, who in his 1896 Bull *Apostolicae Curae* declared that, as Anglican clergy were not ordained to the historic apostolic ministry followed by Catholics and Eastern Orthodox, their ordination could not be accepted and recognized as a valid priesthood and ministry. Ernst Troeltsch (1865–1923) made the term a part of the Protestant tradition with his classic *The Social Teaching of the Christian Churches*. Therefore, some attention must be given to what Roman Catholics, who popularized the concept, and Troeltsch intended.

Social teachings are the theological ideas and models formulated by the church's hierarchy intended to govern and influence the shaping of public policy, private conduct, and private thinking in the social arena. As Christians and the institutional church interact with the forces, powers, and policies of the state, the community, and the larger world, the human community is formed and reformed under the influence of many forces, powers, and policies. Because the church considers all which affects human life (and therefore touches human dignity) to be a part of morality and ethics and therefore its proper concern, acting through its bishops and councils, the church in its social teachings seeks to portray a theological vision and to establish boundaries and limits from a Christian perspective as to what can be called legitimate public and private conduct for Christians, or at least, for Catholics, in their moral formation and citizenry in the state. To this extent, Christian identity is very much, but not totally, bound up with social teachings. Social teachings, therefore, could be said to act as the public relations voice and visionary recall of the church in public policy and discourse as well as in private realms of society.

While the early patristic Fathers and medieval theologians sometimes made statements about social matters, it was Pope Leo XIII who established a systematic corpus of social doctrines concerned with Catholic identity and theories of society amidst the smorgasbord of ideologies and social ideas making the rounds in the nineteenth century. Actually, more than anything else, it was the French Revolution and its ushering in of the democratic state, socialism and the rise of the modern trade union movement among the working classes, and the final disestablishment of the Church's controlling influence on intellectual thought by emerging secularism and pluralism that impelled the church toward some hard systematic thinking about its social vision.

Historically, the Roman Church initially resisted and was suspect of these new emerging visions of society, including American democratic thinking. Partially as a result, the American Catholic Church remained a mission of the Vatican's Congregation for the Propagation of the Faith until 1908. In fact, Cardinal Gibbons of Maryland was the first American allowed to vote for a Pope, which he did in 1903 in the election of Pius X, successor to Leo XIII. Fearful of the threats and appeals engendered by these modern political and cultural movements, the Roman Catholic Church set out the sources of its social teachings to be (1) revelation, meaning the word of God both in Scripture and the Catholic tradition; (2) natural law, that is, the moral principles that can be known through natural reason by everyone; (3) the magisterium, the divinely given teaching authority of the bishops and, more particularly, the Curia at the Vatican in matters of faith and morals; and (4) the Pope, entrusted by God as Peter's successor to have charge of the church and to be God's top representative in speaking for the church to society and the world at large. Catholic social teachings and thought, therefore, try to establish Catholic norms for shaping and judging personal relations and judgments as well as social relations between people, between people and the state, and between institutions and the state or society.

As can be imagined, for a church such as the Episcopal Church —born in a society imbued with the tenets of John Locke and the Enlightenment about individual freedom and sovereignty; which more often than not appeals to people largely for its dignified and solemn worship, well-sung music, and lovely architecture; where the creeds are frequently only liturgical acts, but not particularly pertinent or important for shaping personal belief and attitudes; and systematic theological thinking about issues is relegated to academics—such orderly thinking in the social arena appears almost antediluvian and unappealing. This characteristic led a critic in the late 1970s (in fact a descendant of the first Episcopal Bishop, Samuel Seabury) to criticize the Episcopal Church for relying in its social pronouncements more on trendiness than thoughtout theology. Therefore, we may appropriately ask, are there Episcopal norms or an Episcopal particularity in forming criteria that govern individual and social relationships in society? Should these norms differ from other codes of social morality? What are the sources informing Episcopal teachings or statements about such relationships, if such teachings exist? For whom are these teachings or statements intended? To repeat the initial query, does the Episcopal Church in fact have social teachings or a theological corpus for dealing with social concerns that is distinctive and not *ad hoc* and trendy?

Although the concept *Christian social teaching* as a theological and ethical category is a fairly recent development in the Christian tradition, the church from early times through its bishops, synods, and theologians felt compelled to announce its interpretation of certain biblical and doctrinal views on social and moral issues. This was initially done for the benefit and affirmation of Christians as they encountered structures and forces of the larger society. Bryan Wilson, the British sociologist of religion, points out that the claim of exclusivity about Jesus Christ and monotheism was maintained primarily by the clerics and bishops in their own self-interest. They considered themselves the divinely sanctioned agents of God and successors of the apostolic teachings. Their objective was to maintain and further the institution called the church as well as protect its prerogatives and their own turf. Consequently, when they perceived a threat to their status, which for them was inseparable from defense of the faith and the church, a strategy of separation and "total annihilation" was devised under the rubric of heresy and anathema:

Monotheism . . . provided the basis for a clearly formulated system of morality which overrode all local peculiarities and distinctions. Since there was but one god, his will, and thus his law, must be unambiguous, and hence intellectually consistent and coherent, and against it no local departures could be tolerated. . . . The logic of monotheism reinforced the aspects of Christianity which made its influence so strong throughout western society.[1]

Much of this is a legacy from the days of the early or primitive church, where groups of Jewish-Christians made conflicting claims based on their understanding of Scripture. Hence, such groups as the zealous Essenes, bent on resisting the state, proved awkward to the religious Establishment with its ideas of how to get along with imperial Rome, which occupied the land and circumscribed traditional religious authority in Palestinian society. Other less militant groups included the embryonic Christian movement, described by some New Testament scholars as the "Jesus movement." Thought to have risen as a renewal movement within Palestinian Judaism centered around Jesus and his teachings, even this movement could not avoid the arm of the state and had to weigh the issue of accommodating Jesus' teachings to the claims and conditions of Roman Palestinian society. For example, the claim in Luke 19:26 that those who have shall receive more, whereas those who have not or have little shall be deprived, may not have been so much a justification of the doctrine "the rich deserve to get richer and the poor poorer," as a cryptic observation by Jesus about the economic conditions of his day. In first century Palestine under Herod, there was a great concentration of wealth in the hands of a few through confiscation of lands, trade, and exports. Without actually attacking these conditions head-on, the story still posits a judgment about those conditions.[2]

> The Jesus movement, too, was connected with the socio-political tensions in Palestine. Its proclamations of the imminence of the kingdom of God could only find a ready echo in a country where no satisfactory solution had been found to the problem of government. Outside Palestine, in the earliest Hellenistic Christianity, the kingdom of God almost ceased to be mentioned.[3]

This particular movement had all the characteristics of what Ernst Troeltsch, one of the first theologians to systematize the theological and sociological traits of early Christian social thought, would identify as a "sect-type" of development. But it is clear from the New Testament that as Christianity moved from a renewal movement in the Palestinian world to fixed local communities and churches in the urbanized Roman Hellenistic world, Christian views of the relationship to the state and society also underwent some change. This is most apparent in the Acts of the Apostles, which chronicles how the Jesus movement began to attract people outside the cohesive Jewish community (the Gentiles, as well as other Jews who were prepared to abandon the tradition for the teachings of Jesus Christ), and in the Epistles, especially those of St. Paul. Sprouts of Christianity sprang up in urban areas, such as Damascus, Antioch, and Corinth, which had a different social and intellectual environment than Jewish Palestine. In fact, cities of the Roman Empire are thought by some scholars to be the key to the hellenization of the Roman Empire as well as the spur for more inclusiveness and accommodation of urban social and political forces within the Jewish renewal movement called Christianity. Not only did these new forces include more economic wealth gained from trade and land, a more educated citizenry, and a life surrounded by many religions, but also a more structured social class system held together by patronage, feudal relationships between Emperor and aristocracy, Emperor and the army, and a substantial intellectual class skilled in the various competing schools of philosophy and rhetoric.

Furthermore, St. Paul the convert, a fairly sophisticated, educated former Jew, brought urbanity and theological skills to the fledgling Christian movement that no doubt were influenced by his profession as a lawyer as well as his dual citizenship: he was a citizen of Tarsus, a city state in Asia Minor (Acts 21:39) and Rome (Acts 22:25). Paul was familiar with the language of the cities and the educated. He apparently knew the schools of intellectual thought current in the empire where many young Christian communities had been planted and were surviving. His letters addressed issues of church and society in concepts that drew on the nuances of the Greek language as well as Greek intellectual thought.

Thus, at no point in its life has the church or the Christian tradition been without some teachings as well as tensions in its relationship to and engagement with society, whether it meant rejecting or accommodating society. Some scholars maintain that as bishops and clergy became the divinely authorized dispensers of grace through the sacraments and more aggressively sought to protect their turf and status, the more they regarded the rest of the larger community as "the world" or a "them." Existing social institutions were identified with the old world with which Christians had to come to grips as they prepared for the new world in the Kingdom of God.

As a young Constantine (273?–337) took charge of an eroding and disorderly empire, it is significant that in order to save a crumbling social fabric, he initially employed Christian clerics to provide some coherence and order. For example, the civil courts had practically become private salons for learned debates between factions of civil servants struggling to preserve their turf and enhance their influence. Hence, judicial processes either never concluded or they took an interminable amount of time to be resolved. Constantine changed this by empowering the bishops' courts with new judicial responsibilities in civil matters because, as he so indelicately put it, "we want to oppress the incurable semen of the quarreling."[4] In the *Codex Theodosianus* he decreed that the bishops' courts were the court of appeal whose decision was final and unalterable.[5] This imperial favoritism in such weighty matters of community life as the judiciary simply made it all the more important for the development of a theology or theologies about the relationship between the Christian faith and the state and/or society.

Early Christian Social Teachings: Ernst Troeltsch

The establishing and institutionalizing of the Christian faith as the imperial church of the empire obviously had theological as well as social consequences for the Christian faith. Interesting enough, Marxists like Friedrich Engels (1820–95): *The Beginnings of Christianity*, and Karl Kautsky (1854–1939): *Foundations of Christianity*, were among the first modern thinkers to study church and state in the early church. But the German theologian Ernst Troeltsch was the first to analyze social teachings and thoughts about society systematically in the early days of the Christian faith.

Troeltsch was a native of Augsburg in southern Germany, former professor of theology at the University of Heidelberg and later professor of philosophy in Berlin, where he died in 1923. In his classic *The Social Teaching of the Christian Churches*, he said that in its attitude and relationship toward the state, the Christian faith and its social teachings developed in three directions: a *sect-type* of development, a *church-type,* and a *mystical-type.* Although some Roman Catholics object to this typology, saying that Troeltsch oversimplified the structure of the early catholic tradition,[7] nevertheless both the sect-type and church-type topologies do speak to the development of social teachings in the Anglican tradition and the Episcopal Church in the United States. Hence, we shall focus on them, since the mystical tradition has never been particularly characteristic of Episcopal social pronouncements, except possibly through some of its monastic movements, which historically and theologically have been on the fringe of mainstream Episcopal life.

Sect-type of thinking and teaching developed from the belief that the Christian Church was a voluntary association of like-minded believers who either separated themselves from society at large and renounced that society, or were hostile and indifferent to it. Moral perfection and inner renewal were important code words for the sect-type of social thinking. It also developed certain distinct sociological, spiritual, and theological characteristics that have continued to the present day in the Christian tradition.

Sociologically, sects in the early church and also in modern times draw their voluntary membership from the poor and lower or working social classes, the fringe people of society who consider themselves on the outside looking in or on the bottom looking up. *Spiritually,* they stress "spirit-filled" discipline and behavior as a sign of detachment from the world and society. They frequently refuse to participate in mainline social institutions, such as the Mennonites and Quakers resisting conscription into the military or the Jehovah's Witnesses' declining to swear an oath in court. *Theologically,* the sect-type of social teachings emphasize Jesus Christ as the supreme law-giver and the one who points to an apocalyptic vision of the world, that is, a struggle between two orders or two worlds, God and evil, in which God and good will eventually triumph. The Christian community is understood as a place of refuge, a recharging station for the elect battling the temptations and forces of the world in the heat of the day. Christian in John Bunyan's *Pilgrim's Progress* describes this blend of moral perfection and apocalyptic expectation very well. "What are the things you seek," asks Obstinate, "since you leave all the world to find them?" Christian replies,

> I seek an inheritance incorruptible, undefiled, and that fadeth not away; and it is laid up in heaven, and safe there, to be bestowed, at the time appointed, on them that diligently seek it.[8]

In counterdistinction, the church-type development, according to Troeltsch, emerged as the pattern for social teachings in the Christian community trying to be inclusive as the established religion of the Roman Empire in the fourth century. New forces came into play as the Christian community moved into urban areas and along the Mediterranean with its polyglot of religions and social classes. Even Constantine, who by decree had exempted clergy from paying taxes, in 326 had to forbid civil servants—among the affluent, educated, and what we today might call the middle-class—from joining the Christian priesthood as a tax shelter.

Sociologically, church-type social teachings preach inclusivity, not exclusivity, accommodation to the world, not separation from or rejection of it. They reach out to the respectable members of society and to the privileged classes. *Spiritually*, the church-type emphasis views spirituality as something related to the whole "secular" order, speaking of redemption and forgiveness rather than repentance. The world is tolerated as a good creation of God, not completely fallen as in the sect-type of spirituality, but rather having suffered a severe injury, with the church as the agent for redemptive surgery.

Theologically, the church-type understands Jesus Christ as the universal redeemer of the social order and nature rather than the law-giver for the elect. Redemption is continued through the established institutions of the church, such as the sacraments and its bishops and clerics. The state has a divine mandate for the community well-being as well, so that there is less teaching about standing apart from and confrontation with the state and more about cooperation and reconciliation. The clergy are more likely to think of themselves as chaplains and comforters to the established order than as preachers and prophets against that order. Likewise, although not articulated as such, the sacraments become important vehicles of visible unity within the established order, so that language like "being born (or baptized) into the church" becomes more indicative of Christian discipleship rather than the individual "making a decision" for Christ and the church.

The difficulty with this schema is that sect-type communities frequently become church-types and Christian communities with a church-type character also include sect-type emphasis and thinking, particularly after the original founders and first generation have been succeeded by a second generation. Certainly many current America denominations, under the influence of "Awakenings" and revivalism began as sect-type religious communities, starting with Jonathan Edwards (1745–1801) in New England and the First Great Awakening. An awakening was not only a resurgence of emotional personal religious experience and attack on the nation's corruption, sinfulness, and need of redemption; it was also a reaction to social and political events and trends at the time that led to a revival of a sect-type of thinking and preaching.

These awakenings parallel momentous periods and crises in our history when people were disoriented and acutely anxious about the unfamiliar in the rapidly changing social and political fabric of the nation. Usually charismatic religious leaders appeared, articulated these fears and anxieties, and reaffirmed the familiar and traditional. By following them or identifying with them, the people gained new confidence and felt affirmed.[9] Some say there have been three Great Awakenings in American history; others claim four. But all have been associated with economic turmoil, political unrest, and a lack of clear moral direction. The American ideology of rugged individualism and of seeing this country as God's light to the rest of the world has been rigorously appealed to as the beacon of hope amidst the morass and malaise. Thus, the idea that in the long run one's conscience is the arbiter of truth and that one should obey that arbiter only has been reinforced by the emphasis on private or individual religious experience and self-reliance. This aspect of American culture is important to note even for the Episcopal Church, which as an institution, largely went untouched by the various awakenings. Yet many of its members have appropriated the emphasis of awakenings on individual religious experience as their norm for obeying or ignoring church teachings.

Richard Niebuhr, adapting Troeltsch's classification, has shown in his book *The Social Sources of Denominationalism* that while some denominations in the United States from their inception identified themselves as church-types (such as the Episcopalians), others began as sects and changed into church-types (such as the Methodists and the Presbyterians). For example, at the height of the American Revolutionary War, a rector of Trinity Church, Wall Street in New York City, Samuel Auchmuty (1722 or 1725–77), reassured a friend in England of the Episcopal Church's displeasure with challenges to a church-type view of the state:

> I have the pleasure to assure you that all the society's missionaries without excepting one, in New Jersey, New York, Connecticut, and, so far as I learn, in the other New England colonies . . . have to the utmost of their power opposed the spirit of disaffection and rebellion which has involved this continent in the greatest calamities."[10]

Niebuhr provides another typology for understanding the complex relationship between church and world or church and state after the New Testament: (1) *Christ against culture*, described as an unwillingness to compromise or to promise loyalty to society and a rejection of that society and culture; (2) *Christ of culture*, whereby Christ is the fulfillment of all that is good in the world, the perfecter of the current values in culture; (3) *Christ above culture*, which affirms cooperation between culture and Christ while at the same time wanting to separate Christ from culture; (4) *Christ and culture in paradox*, which understands a righteous God and an unrighteous corrupt world to be in permanent conflict but is resigned to sustenance by Christ in such a world; and (5) *Christ the transformer of culture*, which believes Christ is able to redeem and transform all of human culture and movements. This latter Christ is seldom understood as judge or nay-sayer.[11]

Thus, the inclusivity and accommodation of the church-type development in the Christian tradition includes the following:

1. Patriotism or loyalty to the state (though not unbridled patriotism) such as we find in some of the early Christian intellectuals, for example, the African theologian Origen (c.185–c.254) from Alexandria in Egypt, or St. John Chrysostom (c.347–c.402), Patriarch of Constantinople;

2. Social class differences, as seen in the conflict and disagreements within the post-persecution church between the early catholic party (which consisted mostly of the educated

civil servants, the upper classes, and craftsmen of the empire) and the Donatists (whose following was largely the lower classes) and the poorer Christians said to support the martyrs and confessors of the faith in spite of the persecutions;[12]

3. The sovereignty of the state as a divine concept, illustrated in Constantine's rather flamboyant purported statement upon founding the city of Constantinople in 330 that he was "the equal of the apostles";

4. The legitimizing of "worldliness" within biblical and early Christian theological thought.

Roman Catholic Social Teachings

Since Vatican II, everything in the Catholic Church, including its social teachings, has been turned on its head, and major revision and rethinking have been set in place. Its document about the church in the modern world entitled *Gaudium et spes* (Joy and hope) builds on and adds to a tradition of social teachings begun by Pope Leo XIII (1810; Pope: 1878–1903) with his 1891 ground-breaking encyclical, *Rerum novarum* (Of new things; generally called "Of the Condition of the Working Classes"). Like Leo's encyclical, *Gaudium* aims to reassure Catholics in the midst of great economic, political, and social change. Unlike *Rerum novarum*, Vatican II seeks to engage in dialogue with other cultural and social forces in the modern world without assuming a traditional tone of superiority.

During Leo's pontificate, the Catholic Church, not fully recovered from the emergence of democracy, anti-clericalism, nationalism, and ideas of the Enlightenment spawned by the French Revolution, now had to adjust to the ascendancy of socialism and Marxism, which was capturing the imagination of many marginalized groups living on the fringes of mainstream society, such as the working classes and the poor. Such movements were viewed as threatening to Christian Europe and the church's dominance in its cultures, particularly their challenge to the Aristotelian worldview of the church that there is a natural harmony between social classes. Early in 1878 in his encyclical, *Quod apostolici muneris*, Leo attacked socialism as contrary to Christian doctrine.

At the same time anti-clericalism, a remnant of the French Revolution, was increasing in France, Germany, and Italy. Italy under King Victor Emmanuel had already confiscated the papal states and Rome in 1870 during the pontificate of Pope Pius IX, thereby depriving the papacy of a territorial power base. The disestablishment of the church itself, and the ills inflicted upon it and its clergy during the French Revolution engendered an obsession against democracy and democratic movements judged inappropriate to the Catholic Church and its tradition of natural elitism and feudalism. Such conservatism disenchanted much of the working class in European countries imbued with democratic ideas and socialism.

To counter these socialist movements, the Catholic social movement arose, which the church later baptized as its own. In France it took the form of the Society of St. Vincent de Paul for poor relief under Ozanam (1813–53) and Montalembert (1810–70), a member of the Chamber of Deputies who proposed the first labor laws in France. Yet at the same time there were the early utopian socialists who were also French Catholics: Claude Henri de Saint-Simon (1760–1825), who fought with the Americans against the British in the Revolutionary War, and Charles Fourier (1772–1837), both of whom were considered forerunners of socialism by Marx and Marxists. In Germany some of the leaders in the Catholic social movement were Bishop Emmanuel von Ketteler of Mainz (1811–77), Ludwig Windhorst (1812–91), a member of the Reichstag who sponsored the first factory laws in Germany, and the Jesuits Viktor Cathrein (1845–1931) and Heinrich Pesch (1824–1926), who were influential in reviving Thomism as a theological method for dealing with social issues and doctrines.

Finally, in some ways at the time of Pope Leo the Catholic Church was still resisting doctrines of the Enlightenment with their stress on human omniscience and autonomy being attainable.

These ideas frightened the church, especially as the intellectual basis of the new bourgeois classes tended to deny divine transcendence, to edify the supremacy of human reason, and almost to deify the inevitability of progress in human affairs without divine assistance. Revealed religion was suspect as superstition and a fetish, although *fetishism* was generally said to describe the cultures of Europe's African colonies and their traditional religion of so-called *animism*. After all, the eighteenth century Enlightenment, especially in Protestant Germany, had laid the foundations for demonstrating not only the fallibility of the church's claims about unchanging divine truth in holy scriptures through methods of higher criticism and textual exegesis, but also increased access to biblical texts and their interpretation by people other than bishops and university theologians. Pope Leo XII (1760; Pope: 1823–29) responded by condemning the new Catholic Bible societies that applied some of these methods to the study of scripture, and Pope IX (1792; Pope: 1846–78) supplemented this with his *Syllabus errorum* (Syllabus of Errors), which condemned many of the philosophical ideas about human reason and biblical scholarship he saw as eroding the faith and morals of believers.

Although Leo XIII issued some eighty-six encyclicals during his reign,[13] many of which deal with social issues, *Rerum novarum* was the first major systematic attempt of the Church to come to grips theologically and politically with the modern period and times with which it was clearly out of joint and for which it was unprepared. At the very outset, the encyclical sounds the alarm: revolutionary fervor in the air is changing the traditional relationship between master and worker, "an increased self-reliance and closer mutual solidarity amongst the working population," as well as a general deterioration in morality. To counter this historical crisis, Pope Leo rehearses the theology supporting the state's role of producing mutual happiness, private prosperity, protecting the family and the common good. At the same time the state is also to guarantee the right to private property, clearly a counterargument to the socialist teaching that all property should be owned by the community. "By the State we here understand, not the particular form of government which prevails in this or that nation," wrote Leo quite clearly, "but the State as rightly understood; that is to say, any government conformable in its institutions to right reason and natural law, and to those dictates of the divine wisdom. . . ."[14] Private property is a right from nature that the state cannot abolish but is obligated to protect.

At the same time Leo allows that strikes by working people can be morally justified because of legitimate grievances about matters such as pay and working conditions. *Rerum* advanced the idea, then only practiced in a few places like Germany and Scandinavia, that workers should have Sundays free and be given some holidays for spiritual and mental renewal and refurbishment. "Life on earth, however good and desirable in itself, is not the final purpose for which man is created; it is only the way and means to that attainment of truth, and that practice of goodness in which the full life of the soul consists."[15]

Christian social teachings must also oppose child labor because it prevents children from having a proper education during their young formative years, thereby stunting their development as full human beings. At the same time women should not be forced to work long hours because such interferes with their vocation as wives and mothers, and the man as wage-earner must be given time off and a just wage, according to the natural law: "There is a dictate of nature more imperious and more ancient than any bargain between man and man, that the remuneration must be enough to support the wage-earner in reasonable and frugal comfort."[16] To achieve such, workers need not depend solely on the good wishes of the employer, but often need their own organizations and unions advancing their own welfare.

The Pope was not particularly enthused about labor unions. He charged them with promoting social strife and violence through their socialist teachings about taking away private property, which do not conform to the church's teachings that private property is a natural right from God. But he did concede that workers should form associations as all other groups in society, since this is natural: "A brother that is helped by his brother is like a strong city" (Prov. 18:19).[17] This was intended to breathe new life in the redundant medieval concept of guilds and cooperatives where worker and factory owner joined together for a common economic goal. Such an idea also appeared at the same time in some early Anglican social teachings by F.D. Maurice.

In fact, as a counter measure, the Catholic Church in nineteenth century Europe sponsored and organized its own labor associations and financed Christian Democratic political parties, both of which were predominately Catholic, as a kind of counter-reformation to socialism and the socialist-oriented, mainly Protestant trade unions sweeping parts of Europe. When Leo was elected Pope in 1878, the large Social Democratic Party in Germany had already been established for seven years, which set off alarms among conservatives and establishments everywhere. This anxiety was intensified by the success of the Paris Commune, also in 1871, when working classes, bourgeois classes, and students joined together—not unlike what happened in Paris during the heady days of the late 1960s—to establish a socialist government in Paris, albeit briefly.

Furthermore, at the same time in Germany under Otto von Bismarck (1815–98) and Austria under Friedrich Ferdinand von Beust (1809–86), both of whom were Protestant, began what came to be called the *Kulturkampf*, a phrase created in 1873 by the famous German scientist Rudolf Virchow (1821–1902), meaning a struggle between the culture of the secular liberal state and the culture of the Catholic Church. Bismarck got laws passed which abolished church schools, thereby favoring state schools and insisting on a strict separation of church and state in education. The Jesuits were expelled from Germany in 1872, followed by the expulsion of other religious orders in 1873. Switzerland also suppressed the Jesuits in 1874. In 1873 under Bismarck the "May Laws" were enacted. These restricted church supervision of seminary training and substituted state supervision and attendance at state universities instead, after which all candidates for Catholic and Protestant ministry had to pass state examinations.

Hence, in spite of some progressive thinking about the dignity of labor and the justification of the workers' claims and grievances, the church in *Rerum novarum* states unequivocally its judgment about their political aims and parties:

> The main tenet of Socialism, the community of goods, must be utterly rejected; for it would injure those whom it is intended to benefit; it would be contrary to the rights of mankind. . . . Our first and most fundamental principle, therefore, when We undertake to alleviate the condition of the masses, must be the inviolability of private property.[18]

On the contrary, says the encyclical, it is a false idea that there is a struggle going on between classes, the rich and the poor. It is "natural" that there should be classes, the governed and the governors, the rich and the poor: "Just as the symmetry of the human body is the result of the disposition of the members of the body, so in a State it is ordained by nature that these two classes should exist in harmony and agreement. . . . Each requires the other. . . ."[19]

So significant was this encyclical for the "coming of age"

(Bonhoeffer) of the church in social teachings that subsequent Popes reaffirmed its historical significance as well as supplemented its teachings. Pius XI in May 1931, during Mussolini's fascism in Italy, issued *Quadragesimo Anno* (Reconstructing the Social Order), to mark its fortieth anniversary, even though an agreement regularizing the relationship between the state and church had been achieved in 1929 and guaranteed the sovereignty of the Vatican as a state. John XXIII in May 1961, the seventieth anniversary, issued *Mater et Magistra* (Mother and Teacher, generally referred to as Christianity and Social Progress), and Paul VI noted its eightieth anniversary with his Apostolic Letter on Social Issues, *Nuntii gratulatorii,* to the Archbishop of Quebec, Cardinal Maurice Roy, in May 1971.

What are the theological premises in this initial model of Catholic social thought? First, cooperation exists between God the Creator and humankind the created in "completing the unfinished universe" and working toward the completion of the social order in the kingdom of God.[20] Second, no area involving human beings and their relationship with each other and with their surroundings are exempt from the church's social teachings or its moral judgment. As Pius XI wrote in *Quadragesimo Anno*, ". . . there resides in US the right and duty to pronounce with supreme authority upon social and economic matters. Certainly the Church was not given the commission to guide men to an only fleeting and perishable happiness, but to that which is eternal."[21] John XXIII said furthermore in *Mater et Magistra:*

> What the Catholic Church teaches and declares regarding the social life and relationships of men is beyond question for all time valid.

> The cardinal point of this teaching is that individual men are necessarily the foundation, cause, and end of all social institutions. We are referring to human beings, insofar as they are social by nature and raised to an order of existence that transcends and subdues nature.[22]

Catholic social teachings also turn on the following theological principles, most of which were given by Leo XIII in *Rerum* and updated from time to time by his successors:

1. The dignity of each individual person warrants his or her

being treated as a subject and not as an object by civil authorities and others;

2. Labor is an act of gratitude to God to be protected as an expression of a person's dignity and personality;
3. A person is to receive just pay for his or her labor;
4. Private property and ownership are natural rights that are to be protected by civil authorities;
5. Intervention by the civil authority in a community from time to time may be justified in order to point the community to "right reason" for the preservation of the general welfare;
6. God is the foundation of all moral law;
7. Government is necessary for defining and protecting the "common good";
8. Solidarity and cooperation between all persons and classes are crucial for community;
9. The doctrine of *subsidiarity* is a key theological and political principle in Catholic social thought.

This latter principle, *subsidiarity*, derived from the Latin *subsidium*, meaning "aid" or "helpful assistance," was first enunciated by Pius XI in *Quadragesimo Anno*. Pius interpreted it to mean that although the state has a divine mandate to provide for the common good and to help all citizens within its boundaries, nevertheless things that individuals and communities can do best by themselves ought not to be taken away from them by the state. In *Pacem in Terris* (Peace on Earth), Pope John XXIII stretched this principle to include even the jurisdiction and authority of international bodies like the United Nations, saying that there are proper spheres of action for national civil authorities and proper spheres for international bodies; a world body should be expected to assist and intervene in complex problems that cannot be resolved in a just way by national states for the benefit of the entire world community.

The three most momentous postwar examples of Catholic social teachings no doubt have been John XXIII's *Pacem in Terris* and Vatican II's *Gaudium et spes* and *Dignitatis humanae* (Declaration on Religious Liberty). Significantly, the latter two were produced at a council convened by the most popular and precedent-breaking Pope of this century, John XXIII, whose brief reign captured the hearts of the world community in capitalist, socialist, and Third World nations alike. *Pacem in Terris*, released in 1963, so caught the world community's imagination that special editions appeared, including a Russian translation produced in the Soviet Union with the approval of the state. English and German publishers came out with special editions that included poetry and photography along with commentary.

Issued two months before John XXIII's death, *Pacem* was addressed not only to the bishops of the church, as is customary, but to "all men of good will." Its intention was expressed in a phrase used by John when opening Vatican II: *aggiornamento*, "openness." Since encyclicals are also widely read in Catholic countries with authoritarian regimes and anti-democratic governments,particularly in Latin America, *Pacem* defended human rights for all people on the basis of natural theology. These included not only political rights but also social rights: food, clothing, housing, leisure, adequate medical care, and necessary social services, such as health insurance, unemployment assistance, disability aid, old age assistance and subsidies. John also addressed the rights of people and duties of governments in non-Catholic countries, such as the Communist countries of Eastern Europe: the right to worship according to one's conscience, the right to establish a family without coercion from the state, the right of free association, the political right of opposition.

Furthermore, *Pacem* affirmed as divinely sanctioned the authority of the state to govern and regulate human affairs within certain limits imposed by natural and human rights:

> Since the right to command is required by the moral order and has its source in God, . . . if civil authorities legislate for or allow anything that is contrary to that order and therefore contrary to the will of God, neither the laws made nor the authorizations granted can be binding on the consciences of the citizens. . . .[23]

In addition, *Pacem* affirmed the authority of the state to govern and regulate human affairs within certain limits imposed by natural and human rights as divinely sanctioned authority: "Authority to govern is a necessary requirement of the moral order in civil society." It also affirmed that more powerful states have a duty to respect the authority and dignity of less powerful states, possibly an allusion to the Vietnam War engaged in at the time by the powerful United States against the small country of North Vietnam.

The encyclical reaffirmed the church's strong opposition to

racism and political hegemony based on assumed superior culture or history: "All men are equal in their natural dignity. Consequently, there are not political communities that are superior by nature and none that are inferior by nature."[24] Not only did many people interpret this and other passages ("the demands of justice are admirably observed by those civil authorities who promote the human welfare of those citizens belonging to a smaller ethnic group") as support for the civil rights movement in this country, but also an important rejoinder to Catholics and, indeed Western and capitalist nations that their culture and forms of government were not to be thought innately or naturally superior to those of communist countries.

At the same time there was disagreement about *Pacem's* application to the East-West conflict. Many thought its use of "mutual respect" as a theological principle for relations between nations had in mind the disarmament talks between the United States and the Soviet Union going on at the time. Also John expanded the doctrine of *subsidiarity* to include complex problems about the common good so exceeding the competence of a single religious or political authority, that a larger political authority such as the federal government or a world body is needed. On this basis the United Nations was strongly supported as a safeguard for the protection of human rights, as was the 1948 Universal Declaration of Human Rights.

Perhaps the section regarded as most radical by the media and world populace at large was John's openness to dialogue and cooperation with non-Catholics and Communist countries in mutual social and economic matters:

> Moreover, [Catholics] must never confuse error and the person who errs, not even when there is a question of error or inadequate knowledge of truth in the moral or religious field. The person who errs is always and above all a human being, and he retains in every case his dignity as a human person; and he must always be regarded and treated in accordance with that lofty dignity. [25]

The point at which such a decision is made depends on the context and the problems at hand. But, cautioned the Pope, even with works and movements that spring out of "false philosophical teachings" (obviously meaning Marxism, communism, and Marxist-oriented nationalist movements in the Third World), Catholics are not prohibited from cooperating for the sake of a common good or purpose: "Besides, who can deny that those movements, in so far as they conform to the dictates of right reason and are interpreters of the lawful aspirations of the human person, *contain elements that are positive and deserving of approval* [italics added]?"[26]

This was thought such a reversed attitude toward Eastern Europe that the Soviet foreign minister, Andre Gromyko, visited the Pope at the Vatican, the first time the Soviet government had initiated official contact with the church. This made headlines in the media throughout the world.[27] John XXIII had overnight altered the concept of truth and error, saying that even though it had a divine mandate, the Catholic Church as guardian of divine truth could cooperate with atheist states and political regimes traditionally held to be in error or violation of the truth. In *Mater et magistra* he said:

> The Church of Jesus Christ . . . makes no effort to discourage or belittle those characteristics and traits which are proper to particular nations, and which people religiously and tenaciously guard. . . . She does not seek a uniformity which is merely external in its effects and calculated to weaken the fiber of the peoples concerned.[28]

The Pastoral Constitution, *Gaudium et spes*, the product of a multicultural commission living amid a galaxy of tensions and forces in a world whose agenda it neither dominated nor shaped, moved in a very different direction. The document recognized that it was compelled to have conversation with this agenda. This was the one document of Vatican II the theologians and bureaucrats of the Curia did *not* initiate. Instead it was written "from the floor," as it were. It was not on the docket that had been drawn up by the very traditionalist civil servants of the Curia but came about because of demands from Cardinal Suenens of Belgium from the floor that the prepared document from the Curia be scrapped. Supported by other cardinals including Giovanni Montini, later Pope Paul VI (1897; Pope: 1963–78), arguments from the floor set the tone for the complete revision of the original draft.

From the beginning, the document announced that it addressed not only the Catholic Church but also "the whole people of God." It declared the church willing to be in "solidarity with the entire human family" and at the disposal of that family, a remarkable humility from a church that in *Rerum novarum* insisted on its dominance and triumphalism in the human community, at least in the Western industrial nations at that time. Its basic theological premise was the dignity of each human being and all of humanity as a reflection of the image of God: "But God did not create man as a solitary being. . . . For by his innermost nature man is a social being, and unless he relates himself to others, he can neither live nor develop his potential."[29] Conscience was defended and described as a gift from God that is sacred and not to be violated, although it can err from "invincible ignorance." But this does not diminish its dignity. Human dignity as evidence of God's image explicitly means having free choice: "Hence man's dignity demands that he act according to a knowing and free choice. Such a choice is personally motivated and prompted from within."[30]

Acknowledging its role as Christ's Body and agent of renewal and moral truth in the world, the church must be more open to new forces and worldly wisdom: "At the same time, [the church] is firmly convinced that she can be abundantly and variously helped by the world in the matter of preparing the ground for the gospel. This help she gains from the talents and industry of individuals and from human society as a whole."[31] Such an openness means that unlike the church's allegiance with capitalistic states in the nineteenth and most of the twentieth century when it thought socialism unreconcilable with the Catholic faith, now

in virtue of her mission and nature, she is bound to no particular form of human culture, nor to any political economic, or social system. . . . This Council, therefore, looks with great respect upon all the true, good, and just elements found in the very wide variety of institutions which the human race has established for itself and constantly continues to establish."[32]

Part two dealt with institutions and social issues in society: marriage, family life, culture, economic and political involvement, modern war and disarmament, and the issue of a united family of nations. These, for our purposes, can be summarized.

Marriage is not simply for the procreation of children, as traditional Catholic doctrine would have it, but is first a covenant between two partners bound by conjugal love. While such a bonding may lead to having children, nonetheless, would-be parents ought to make certain that the conditions for responsible parenthood exist. Birth control is forbidden, as would be expected, but the church appears to leave an opening for family planning, albeit an ever so small one:

> [Parents] will thoughtfully take into account both their own welfare and that of their children, those already born and those which may be foreseen. For this accounting they will reckon with both the material and the spiritual conditions of the times as well as of their state in life. Finally, they will consult the interests of the family group, of temporal society, and of the Church herself.[33]

One of the most original parts of the Constitution was its teaching about the engagement of culture and the Catholic faith. This was particularly significant for Catholics in Third World cultures wishing to incorporate their own indigenous traditions into the legacy of the (Western) church and its interpretation of the Christian faith largely under the dominant influence of Greek and Latin thought. This issue also has meaning for the Anglican Communion with its multicultural, multinational membership, but British-oriented in its theological patterns, liturgy, and traditional spirituality. For example, because of Anglicanism's distinctive British historical heritage and patterns of piety, Anglicans themselves throughout the world, even allowing for local embellishment, assume that authenticity (regardless of birthright or culture) rests on either becoming honorary English or mini-English in worship, thought, and spirituality.

Gaudium acknowledged that even the concept *culture* had undergone radical rethinking in light of modern science, the social sciences, telecommunications, and technology, not to mention such social forces as urbanization, industrialization, and computerization. But it affirmed humankind as the creator of culture, to which God speaks in his gospel and his church:

> not bound exclusively to any race or nation, nor to any particular way of life or any customary pattern of living, ancient or recent. Faithful to her own tradition and at the same time conscious of her universal mission, [the Church] can enter into

communion with various cultural modes, to her own enrichment and theirs too. [34]

At the same time, the church also conceded that Christian formation takes place in different cultures, even when there are tensions between the official church's view and the traditions of particular autonomous cultures:

> These difficulties do not necessarily harm the life of faith. Indeed they can stimulate the mind in a more accurate and penetrating grasp of the faith. . . . Furthermore, while adhering to the methods and requirements proper to theology, theologians are invited to seek continually for more suitable ways of communicating doctrine to the [people] of their times. For the deposit of faith or revealed truths are one thing; the manner in which they are formulated without violence to their meaning and significance is another. [35]

The document made gestures toward new discoveries in theological enquiry that include higher criticism in biblical and religious studies, and, a revision of the tone in the nineteenth century *Syllabus errorum* and Pius X's twentieth century attack on modernism in biblical studies. In fact, *Gaudium* insisted that such open theological enquiry and cultural sensitivity were important for priestly formation: "let it be recognized that all the faithful, clerical and lay, possess a lawful freedom of inquiry and of thought, and the freedom to express their minds humbly and courageously about those matters in which they enjoy competence."[36]

The sections on peace and economic principles were cited by American Catholic bishops in their two momentous, provocative Pastoral Letters, which signaled a new epoch for the American hierarchy. The American hierarchy's deliberate critical engagement with such controversial issues was progressive for the usually highly patriotic, uncritical Catholic Church in America. Vatican II was a primary source for such empowerment, but the bishops' critical position also indicated that the Roman Church in America had come of age as a part of mainstream religion. Generally, mainstream Christianity in America has been dominated and shaped by what Roof and McKinney call the Protestant big colonial three: the Congregationalists (now the U.C.C.), the Episcopalians, and the Presbyterians. They define *mainstream* or *mainline* as "the obvious, the normative, the taken-for granted. It is the standard of comparison against which the marginal, the fringe, the curious are all defined."[37] These churches consider themselves guardians of public or established manners and virtue and wish to be perceived as such.

Roman Catholicism since the nineteenth century has been a church mostly of working class immigrants. It not only was treated by the Vatican as a less than independent church, but also subjected to great suspicion and hatred in Protestant America. The Know-Nothing movement in the East and the Ku Klux Klan in the South, for example, directed their prejudices and virulent nativism toward Catholics, due in large part to resistance to immigration. This nativist prejudice was fanned by sermons of such national preachers as Lyman Beecher (1775–1863) at Yale (after whom its most distinguished lectureship on preaching is named):

> The Catholic Church holds now in darkness and bondage nearly half the civilized world. . . . It is the most skillful, powerful, dreadful system of corruption to those who wield it, and of slavery and debasement to those who live under it.[38]

Local journalists and the media in general conspired to be cheerleaders by publishing inflammatory anti-Catholic articles, as illustrated in the Louisville *Journal*, predecessor of the current liberal *Courier-Journal* which supported the Whig Party and its fierce anti-Catholic sentiments. In 1855, the newspaper stirred up nativist sentiments and a riot, in which more than twenty Catholics were murdered:

> Rally to put down an organization of Jesuit Bishops, Priests, and other Papists, who aim by secret oaths and horrid prejudices, and midnight plottings, to sap the foundations of all our political edifices. . . . So go ahead Know-Nothings, and raise just as big a storm as you please.[39]

For self-protection, the church evoked a kind of siege and battlement mentality against assaults of the Protestant Establishment and hate groups. Indeed, after Al Smith, governor of New York, was defeated in 1928 as a presidential candidate largely because of his faith, no Catholic was ever successful in a national election until John Fitzgerald Kennedy's election in 1960 as the first

Catholic president. His election also is thought by many to have hastened the middle-class transformation of American Catholicism.

The American bishops' strong positions in their Pastoral Letters on issues of public virtue and policy in American society were vigorously disputed among Catholics and non-Catholics alike. The Pastorals were entitled "Challenge of Peace: God's Promise and Our Response" (1981), "Economic Justice for All: Catholic Social Teaching and the U.S. Economy" (1986), and "Partners in the Mystery of Redemption: A Pastoral Response to Women's Concerns for Church and Society" (1988). In them the bishops adapted the social teachings of earlier encyclicals and Vatican II as the measure for studying the social and economic scene of the United States.

However, the Pastoral on the American economy also engaged peculiar issues and forces in the American capitalist economy. After much consultation with many economic experts, trade union leaders, sociologists, priests, professors from other churches, and theologians, and after three draft revisions, its final release provoked many of its prominent, more conservative laity to publish a rejoinder refuting the teachings of the bishops, which in itself is a sign of a church come of age as a mainstream denomination.[40] Following the urging of Vatican II "to scrutinize the signs of the times and interpret them in the light of the Gospel," the bishops' Pastoral was really a follow-up to a previous one dealing with communism. At that time a number of bishops insisted that a critical study of U.S. capitalism be undertaken with the aim of writing a Pastoral for the faithful on the U.S. economic system and its relationship to Catholic social teachings. Given the size, visibility, and power of the Catholic Church in American society, particularly in the cities, the release of the Pastoral on the economy drew much attention. As in the advertisement of a now defunct national brokerage firm, when the Catholic bishops speak, everybody or almost everybody listens.

The Pastoral was grounded on six theological principles:

1. All economic institutions and decisions are to be judged as to whether they protect or undermine human dignity.
2. Human dignity is realized and protected only in community, not in isolation.
3. Participation in the economic life of society is a right and an issue of social justice for all people.

4. All institutions of society have a special obligation to the poor and marginalized.
5. Human rights include economic and social rights.
6. Society has the obligation through its economic institutions of lifting up human dignity and protecting human rights.[41]

Under these principles, they stressed the following: (1) the unbreakable link between justice and economic issues; (2) the link between human rights and people on the margin and fringe of the American economy struggling for survival; (3) theological support for the concept of trade unions and their necessity in our capitalistic society; (4) employment as a human right for all citizens; and 5) interdependence between Third World social systems and the U.S. economy. Economic systems are fundamentally systems that also affect ethics and morality and therefore are a proper issue for the church:

> Every perspective on economic life that is human, moral and Christian must be shaped by three questions: What does the economy do *for* people? What does it do *to* people? And how do people *participate* in it? The economy is a human reality: men and women working together to develop and care for the whole of God's creation. All this work must serve the material and spiritual well-being of people."[42]

The baseline of economic issues as moral questions is human dignity. Using this criterion rather than political liberty, freedom of choice, a higher standard of living, or even the "free market ethic," the bishops looked at the U.S. economy for its equity and justice or its restriction of such. A moral litmus test suggested was the biblical measurement of justice with regard to how the poor and powerless, the widow, orphans, and strangers are treated in the society.

The economic factor that enhances human dignity and links justice to individual self-worth is human labor and having a productive job:

> The economy of this nation has been built by the labor of human hands and minds. Its future will be forged by the ways persons direct all this work toward greater justice. The economy is not a machine that operates according to its own inexorable laws, and persons are not mere objects tossed about by economic forces. . . . Thus it is primarily through their daily

labor that people make their most important contributions to economic justice.[43]

Work in an industrialized society has at least three important ethical functions: (1) a vehicle for self-expression and the realization of personal growth; (2) a means for material, spiritual, and creative self-fulfillment; and (3) a way for every able person to make a contribution to the well-being of the larger community. These criteria can be used by Christians to judge all work, whether blue collar or white collar, whether politician or professor. To abridge or deny them to those engaged in any kind of human labor is to violate the Catholic principal of *subsidiarity:*

> This principle guarantees institutional pluralism. It provides space for freedom, initiative and creativity on the part of many social agents. At the same time it insists that *all* these agents should be working in ways that express their distinctive capacities for action. . . . [44]

Furthermore, work is a basic human right that sustains other minimum human rights, such as shelter, clothing, an adequate diet, leisure, adequate health care, and proper working conditions that ensure that the workers' physical health is not endangered. Attaining them in daily life not only depends on fair wages and "other benefits sufficient to support a family in dignity," but also on workers' organizations acting in the best interests of the workers. Because of the way that power is often distributed in a free market economy such as in the United States, the church strongly affirms that it is essential for workers to sustain their own organizations and trade unions in order to negotiate with employers and managers from a position of strength, since the former harness much power through their control of the corporate means of production. "No one may deny the right to organize without attacking human dignity itself. Therefore we firmly oppose organized efforts, such as those regrettably now seen in this country, to break existing unions and prevent workers from organizing."[45] Also the bishops acknowledged that even though the labor movement has been important for much of the social progress in the United States, this movement has also been inconsistent in defending and advancing the rights of minorities and women within its own ranks.

At the same time, the church defends private ownership of companies and corporate management, urging that the freedom to be entrepreneurs and to engage in high finance is to be protected and encouraged because such a freedom enhances our capacity for creativity and initiative. Nevertheless, this freedom is not to be exercised without being accountable and responsible to the common good and norms of natural justice:

> Resources created by human industry are also held in trust. Owners and managers have not created this capital on their own. They have benefited from the work of many others and from the local communities that support their endeavors. They are accountable to these workers and communities when making decisions.[46]

The letter also devoted a good deal of attention to the poor and the marginalized in the U.S. economy, particularly with regard to unemployment. "Full employment is the foundation of a just economy. . . . Employment is a basic right, a right which protects the freedom of all to participate in the economic life of society. It is a right which flows from the principles of justice. . . ."[47] Joblessness enhances marginalization, which is destructive to human dignity and human community and therefore against the moral law of social justice for all. Justice takes place when all people in the community can participate in the economic life of the community by being productive.

Finally, the Catholic bishops examined the challenges to the church by the U.S. economy and its role in that economy. They looked at what they called *conversion* (a warning against attachment to material goods and total self-reliance for the sake of greed and a sought-after safety in material comforts); *worship and prayer* (thanksgiving for the gifts of life and goods and the awareness of sharing that life and goods with others); *holiness in the world* (directing our heart and life toward God in order to bring the Gospel to economic affairs); and *leisure* ("The Christian tradition sees in leisure time to build family and societal relationships and an opportunity for communal prayer and worship, for relaxed contemplation and enjoyment of God's creation, and for the cultivation of the arts, which help fill the human longing for wholeness.") [48] Yet as the Catholic Church itself is also an actor in the economic processes with its property, workers, schools, social welfare agencies, and investments, it also has to be an exemplar for the larger society. For example, its own personnel should get fair wages and amenities that meet the minimum conditions necessary for a secure life expected of the other economic institutions in the country. Investments must be examined not only with an eye toward getting a fair return but also as a means for promoting social justice.

Economic issues are complex and multifaceted. Still, the bishops insisted, the single most important measuring rod for a just economic system is the question of how the system affects the lives and being of all people. "No utopia is possible on this earth, but as believers in the redemptive love of God and as those who have experienced God's forgiving mercy, we know that God's providence is not and will not be lacking to us today."[49]

Notes

1. Bryan Wilson, *Religion in Sociological Perspective* (New York: Oxford University Press, 1982), pp. 61-2.

2. Gerd Theissen, *Sociology of Early Palestinian Christianity*, trans. John Bowden (Philadelphia: Fortress Press, 1978), p. 41.

3. Ibid., p. 65.

4. Hermann Dörries, *Konstantin der Grosse* (Stuttgart: W. Kohlhammer, 1985), p. 68.

5. M.A. Huttmann, *The Establishment of Christianity* (New York: Columbia University Press, 1914; reprint, New York: AMS, 1967), p. 155.

6. Karl Kautsky, *Foundations of Christianity* (New York: International Publishers, 1925).

7. See Werner Stark, *The Sociology of Religion: A Study of Christendom* (New York: Fordham University Press, 1967), vol. 3, pp. 95-6.

8. John Bunyan, *Pilgrim's Progress* (Grand Rapids, Mich.: Zondervan Publishing House, 1966), p. 13.

9. For a fuller account of the correlation between the religious development and the social issues in the awakenings, see William G. McLoughlin, *Revivals, Awakenings, and Reform* (Chicago: University of Chicago Press, 1978).

10. Quoted in H. Richard Niebuhr, *The Social Sources of Denominationalism* (New York: Meridian Books, 1957), p. 23.

11. H. Richard Niebuhr, *Christ and Culture*.

12. Full discussion of these early class differences in A.H. Jones, *Constantine and the Conversion of Europe* (Harmondsworth, England: Penguin Books, 1962), p. 124.

13. See the complete set in *The Papal Encyclicals, 1878–1903*, Claudia Carlen Ihm, ed. (Wilmington, NC: McGarth Publishing Company, 1981).

14. *Rerum novarum*, par. 25, *Seven Great Encyclicals* (Glen Rock: NJ: Paulist Press, 1963), pp. 1-30.

15. Ibid., par. 32.

16. Ibid., par. 34.

17. Ibid., par. 37.

18. Ibid., par. 12.

19. Ibid., par. 15.

20. *The New Catholic Encyclopedia* (New York: McGraw-Hill Book Co., 1967), vol. 13, p. 341.

21. *Quadragesimo Anno*, par. 41, *Seven Great Encyclicals*, pp. 125-68.

22. *Mater et Magistra*, par. 218-19, *Seven Great Encyclicals*, pp. 219-74.

23. *Pacem in terris*, par. 51, *Seven Great Encyclicals*, pp. 289-326.

24. Ibid., par. 89.

25. Ibid., par. 158.

26. Ibid., par. 159.

27. President Mikhail Gorbachev under his program of *perestroika* (structural reform) in the Soviet Union visited Pope John Paul II in December 1988, an unprecedented gesture for a Soviet head of state since the October Revolution.

28. *Mater et magistra*, par. 181.

29. *Gaudium et spes*, art. 12., *The Documents of Vatican II*, ed. Walter B. Abbott (New York: Guild Press, 1966), pp. 199-308.

30. Ibid., art. 17.

31. Ibid., art. 40.

32. Ibid., art 42.

33. Ibid., art. 50.

34. Ibid., art. 58.

35. Ibid., art. 62.

36. Ibid.

37. William McKinney and Wade C. Roof, *American Mainline Religion: The Changing Shape of the Religious Establishment* (New Brunswick, NJ: Rutgers University Press, 1987), p. 73.

38. Quoted in James Hennesey, S.J., *American Catholics: A History of the Roman Catholic Community in the United States* (New York: Oxford University Press, 1981), p. 119.

39. Ibid., p. 125.

40. See *Toward the Future: Catholic Social Thought and the U.S. Economy, A Lay Letter* (New York: Lay Commission on Catholic Social Teaching and the U.S. Economy, 1984).

41. "Economic Justice for All: Catholic Social Teaching and the U.S. Economy," introduction, par. 12-18.

42. Ibid., chap. 1, art. 1 (hereafter 1:1, 2:1, etc.).

43. Ibid., 2:96.

44. Ibid., 3:100.
45. Ibid., 2:104.
46. Ibid., 2:113.
47. Ibid., 3:136, 137.
48. Ibid., 5:338.
49. Ibid., 5:364.

Chapter 2
What Do Anglican Social Teachings Look Like?

Roots of Classical Anglican Social Thought

Although the Episcopal Church organically broke with the Church of England after the defeat of the British in the Revolutionary War, a dependency lingered. This was seen in the continued legal or quasi-legal establishment of the Episcopal Church in some mid-Atlantic and southern colonies and its use of the liturgy and spirituality in the slightly altered *Book of Common Prayer*. A peculiar congregationalist and decentralized polity developed, but no distinguishable American theology emerged in the Episcopal Church throughout its first one hundred years. So British theological imports increased its dependence and sustained a familiar air of class and privilege in a country given constitutionally to egalitarianism.

However, when Anglican social thinking came about in nineteenth century England, many Episcopalians, particularly Anglo-Catholics, felt the need to affirm this link of dependence by claiming British Anglican social thought at one with Episcopal social theology through British imports. This occurred more organizationally than theologically, even though, as we shall see, the American bishops moved at about the same time to provide social teachings more pertinent to the American context. But neither the classical social teachings of the Church of England as a theological framework nor the early efforts of the American bishops captured the consciousness of most Episcopal bishops and priests, the seminaries that trained many of them, or the mentors under whom many future clerics read for orders.

When we think of those high points that have been definitive for Anglican social thought, we begin with Frederick Denison

Maurice (1805–72) and possibly end with William Temple (1881–1944). Both wrote during momentous changes in British society. During Maurice's times, for example, England was trying to reshape itself as a religious pluralistic society. The Reform Act of 1832 forced the two ancient universities, Oxford and Cambridge, to matriculate non-Anglicans and Non-Conformists, which in turn was interpreted by many Anglicans as a serious threat to their ecclesiastical guardianship and intellectual stronghold hitherto at the universities. John Henry Newman (1801–90) and other Tracterians, in fact, were so offended by this act as well as the disestablishment of the Church of Ireland (Anglican) that Newman was inspired to preach his famous sermon at Oxford's University Church against what he called "national apostasy."

These were also times of great political anxiety as the very social and fabric of England was being critically questioned by such groups as the Chartist movement. This movement was active largely in the north of England but also in other parts of England, as well as Scotland and Wales. It was mostly led by Robert Owen (1771–1854), a factory owner who started cooperatives as a form of communal production and ownership, and free schools for the workers and poor. This popular reform movement first published a "People's Charter" in 1838, hence the name Chartist. That charter called for universal suffrage for all males over 21 years of age; abolishing property qualifications for members of Parliament so that workers could run for office; salaries for members of Parliament, thereby eliminating the unspoken requirement that only the wealthy and upper-classes could candidate for office; correcting numbers in the electoral constituencies, which favored the land owners; and parliamentary elections annually instead of quinquennially. Their goal was to open up the political process to all citizens and disenfranchised social classes. The movement attracted clergy, workers, women, pub owners, artisans, factory workers and miners, all united by a mutual outrage over the exploitation and monopoly of power by a privileged elite. There were Chartist chapels and churches (as well as hymns) where crowds would flock to hear the most famous socialist preacher of his day, Benjamin Rushton. Marx called the Chartists the first proletarian movement and used their teachings in his analysis of capitalist society.

Ironically, Maurice and his friends, John Ludlow (1821–1911) and Charles Kingsley (1819–1875) are known as Christian Socialists in the Anglican tradition. (Kingsley was called the last of the "squarsons" by Charles Raven: "someone who exercised himself in oratory on Sundays and in fly-fishing and fox-hunting during the rest of the week.")[1] But this group's engagement with social matters began in 1848 with their opposing a working class populist movement: the Chartists. The three published a tract, "To the Workmen of England," in which they said that the working classes were not yet ready for the right to vote, since this was a privilege that demanded education and superior intelligence because of the complexity of political issues. The misnomer "Christian Socialist" really came from pamphlets and tracts written mostly by Maurice in consultation with Ludlow and Kingsley. The first was published in 1850, entitled *Christian Socialism: Dialogue Between Somebody (a person of respectability) and Nobody (the writer)*. In it he wrote that Christian Socialism aimed to Christianize the unChristian Socialists and to socialize the unsocial Christians—a bit of Oxbridge rhetoric that went down well in church circles and Oxbridge senior common rooms, but had little scientific or empirical content in any kind of Marxist socialist sense, which Maurice called "secular" socialism.

In 1848, socialist and trade union groups gathered in London for an international meeting and published the *Communist Manifesto*, which was written hurriedly by Karl Marx (1818–83), an exile from his native Germany living in England, and Friedrich Engels (1820–95), the son of a German industrialist living in Manchester, England. Mini-revolutions were breaking out all over the continent, most notably in Paris where the Paris Commune had been established.

Born a Unitarian in his father's parsonage, F.D. Maurice, as he was popularly known, was admitted to Cambridge University as a Nonconformist because he resisted subscribing to the Thirty-nine Articles of Religion, a requirement both for Oxford and Cambridge until abolished in 1871 by the Liberal government's reforms. In fact, because of his refusal, the university would not give him a degree at graduation, which was a First Class (the equivalent of *summa cum laude* in American academic parlance) in law. However, even at Cambridge, his real interest was religious questions. In an article about Percy Shelley, he wrote that religion is the realization of God who permeates the whole universe and reveals himself to us in our interior, our hearts and souls. We have free will to accede or resist this revelation and knowledge.

Maurice abandoned the rationalism of Unitarianism when he was baptized March 1831 in the Church of England and decided to prepare for its priesthood. This time he chose not to return to Cambridge, but to attend Exeter College at Oxford University instead. Three years later on January 26, 1834, he was ordained and assigned his first curacy at a parish church in Bubbenhall, Warwickshire. While there, Maurice supported the Anglican Articles of Religion as a requirement for entrance at Oxford and Cambridge in a book, *Subscription No Bondage*. After a number of incumbencies and academic appointments, including posts in moral philosophy at Cambridge and divinity at Kings College, London, and the founding of his Workingmen's College in London, Maurice died in 1872. His feast day was added to the Episcopal Church's calendar of saints in its 1979 new Prayer Book and is celebrated on April 1.

Maurice's theological starting point is the doctrine of Christ, traditionally called *christology*. Through Jesus Christ all of humankind is a corporate fellowship. Christ as the head of the entire human race and the archetype of humanity revealed that neighborliness rather than individualism is the universal goal in life. Neighborliness does not rule out individuality; rather it denies all claims to exclusiveness, superiority, and competition that fuel individualism. Jesus Christ in his relationship to the rest of humanity is an analogue for neighborliness.

A second foundation is the church. As Wolf rightly pointed out, the church for F.D. Maurice is necessary as the agent for implementing the gospel. Its presence in the world witnesses to Jesus Christ as the true head and center of all humanity, as well as to the "divine order." He understood the divine order to be a mandate given by God in nature that includes what sociologists might call the *primary institutions*, such as the family, and the *secondary institutions*, such as the nation and the church. The church acts as a conscience to the nation and a support for the family, so the three have an interdependence and correlation with each other in the divine order. In *Theological Essays* (1853), which incidentally resulted in his 1854 dismissal from King's College, London, as professor of English literature, he wrote:

The Church is, therefore, human society in its normal state; the

World, that same society irregular and abnormal. The world is the Church without God; and the Church is the world restored to its relation to God, taken back by him into the state for which he created it. Deprive the Church of its Center and you make it into a world.[2]

Hence, what Maurice called the "six signs" of the church (clergy, liturgy, the Bible, sacraments, creeds, ministry), are visible marks and reminders instituted by God for the benefit of all humanity. All aspects of human life are included in the divine order as well as all people, Christians and non-Christians alike, since they are neighbors. As neighborliness also means being social, the three ideological pillars of the early Anglican Christian Socialists are (1) brotherhood, (2) cooperation, which included education, and (3) private property.

In their first tract, these utopian socialists understood *brotherhood* to mean a mutual goal for Christian Socialists and secular socialists alike. Given to us by Christ himself, it fosters cooperation and fellowship between the classes. Brotherhood is also the means for ending greed and competition, which is based on greed. The difference between the concept of brotherhood in secular socialism and Christian Socialism is that the former fails to realize that its sought-after goal, the classless society, has already taken place. The Bible and the creeds show that God has already established an order in society without classes that is based on cooperation. "The Socialists were not fighting for a new system of their own device, but for God's established order against the new competitive world which man's selfishness has created. . . ."[3]

Cooperation, the second objective, is brotherhood in action. The practical tool for doing this is education, thought to be the best way of bringing factory owners and their workers together to regard each other in mutual love as friends rather than enemies. This, of course, is a fairly middle-class idea for achieving socialization based on the belief that reconciliation of opposites is a particular Christian claim and duty. Maurice devised what he called "Associations": groups of people from the privileged and poor social classes, brought together on a regular basis for education, that were to be financed by wealthier Christians as well as taught by them. With this pattern in mind, Maurice established his Workingmen's College in London in 1853, but it failed. In fact, he and Ludlow violently disagreed about this concept and the purpose of the associations. Maurice saw them as upholding the existing social order, albeit with small reforms to reduce class differences. Ludlow, the more radical of the three, having spent his formative years in France during the turbulent aftermath of the French Revolution, expected them to be ways of challenging the existing social order.

For Maurice, social injustices and evils were irrational and came about through ignorance of God's divine order established in Jesus Christ and witnessed to by his church. Ignorance is almost the same as unbelief. Through education, the church can convert this ignorance into knowledge of the divine order "by drawing forth of the real man in each individual so that he can realize that Christ is really his Elder Brother as well as the Brother of all mankind, that everyone is wholly dependent on Him and shares His humanity and all the gifts of grace and love."[4] Ludlow understood injustices to be much more products of the social and economic systems and their inherent privileges, which disenfranchise the poor. The systems have to be changed by the workers and the poor for justice and equity to emerge.

The third pillar of Maurice's social teachings is *private property*. Maurice tended to defend the naturalness of a model with an elite (though not privileged) and followers (though treated justly). This view no doubt was influenced by with his own upbringing and education in the citadels of privilege, such as the ancient universities of Oxford and Cambridge. His primary interest is to renew the existing British society, as William Wolf notes, without revolutionary change. Unlike secular socialists, he feared revolutionary change in the social order and overthrowing of private property. Private property was not a source of injustice and class superiority in society for him, but something natural and meaningful for reminding the landed classes about their responsibility to the poor. His friend Kingsley had written in his *Letters to the Chartists* that, although the Bible showed God had taken on the "People's Cause," it did not urge revolution against the aristocracy, an essential part of British society. The Bible reminds the upper classes of their special responsibilities toward the poor because of their privileged position. Kingsley and Maurice wished reform but were unwilling to risk destabilization by overthrowing the class structure in British society.[5] The internal wrangling between Maurice and Kingsley on one side and Ludlow on the other carried over into Christian Socialist circles in the Church of England, so much so that Christian Socialism had fairly well died out as a important force in the church before Maurice's death in 1872.

H. Richard Niebuhr in *Christ and Culture* calls F.D. Maurice a representative of "Christ the transformer of culture" school in Christian social ethics, as contrasted with "Christ against culture" or "Christ above culture." Maurice and his circle are still credited with laying the basis for social thought and social action in an otherwise comfortable Victorian Church of England. As one writer put it:

> Maurice was repelled by Victorian attempts to restrict religion to a narrow moralism, to a mere anxiety for personal moral behavior and personal salvation. In Maurice's view the Kingdom must encompass nothing less than the whole of God's creation and religion cannot stand aloof; it must concern itself intimately with the fate of all mankind and with the condition of the secular world in which men are forced to live.[6]

A revival of Anglican Christian Socialism in the late 1870s stirred some clergy who also belonged to the upper and upper-middle classes of England like Maurice, Ludlow, and Kingsley: Thomas Hancock (1832–1903), who liked to annoy his parish by lauding the *Magnificat* as a hymn ushering in the expected social revolution; Brook Foss Westcott (1825–1901), Bishop of Durham and sometime Regius Professor of Divinity at Cambridge; Henry Scott Holland (1847–1918); Regius Professor of Divinity at Oxford; Stewart Duckworth Headlam (1847–1924) founder of the Guild of St. Matthew who operated from a theology that socialized even the sacraments; Henry Carey Shuttleworth (1850–1900); and Charles Gore (1853–1932), Bishop of Oxford and former Bishop of Worcester. All were under the influence of Maurice and the earlier Christian Socialists, whose philosophical method appealed to their own bent toward natural theology. However, there were both social and religious reasons for this revival.

First of all, England experienced an economic depression in 1873 that had only worsened the plight of the poor and working classes, although the so-called second industrial revolution was in full swing, thus empowering the urban middle classes. Britain was at the apex of the European imperial powers club whose entrance dues consisted of having overseas colonies. Britain's reliance on coal, iron, and cotton faltered since their markets no longer were growing. Unemployment greatly increased and large numbers of farm workers migrated to the cities due to failures in agriculture. Potato crops failed four consecutive years, which compelled the largely Irish tenant farmers to migrate to the United States in the 1870s and 1880s because they could not meet their payments to their English landlords. Second, the Liberal government under Gladstone initiated a great number of reforms aimed at creating new opportunities for the working classes in education, housing, and public health. Likewise, the right to strike by trade unions was legalized, which was exercised by the unions, thereby only furthering the impression of crisis in society at large.

Parallel events pointing to winds of change also occurred in the Church of England. A Church Congress was held in 1873 that dealt entirely with labor problems and the social tensions in British society. Various clerics already worked as teams in the slums of London and Manchester. And although the Church of England, like Queen Victoria, was not amused or bemused at these efforts, still the spirit of renewal took place in small doses. One of those doses was the Guild of St. Matthew, founded in 1877 by Stewart Duckworth Headlam, educated at Eton and Cambridge and a curate in St. Matthew's Church, Bethnal Green. This was an Anglo-Catholic organization that Headlam used as a hammer for reviving Christian Socialism, which might be called "sacramental socialism," in thought and deed in Anglican churches.

Headlam taught that the sacraments—all seven of them—are the best verification of the socialism of Christ, especially the sacraments of Holy Baptism and Holy Communion. Sacraments signify, first, that all of human life is sacred and therefore cannot be divided into sacred and profane or secular. When Headlam later became a residentiary canon at Westminster Abbey, he would infuriate the dean and other canons by announcing that the Holy Communion was open to all people "simply on the grounds of their humanity."[7] Thus, he said the holy sacrifice of Christ in the eucharist also has an important social function:

It becomes impossible for a priest, who knows what the Lord's

Supper means, not to take part to the best of his power in every work of political or social emancipation; impossible for an earnest communicant not to be an earnest politician.[8]

Second, the sacrifice of Christ demonstrates the lordship of Jesus Christ over all spheres of human endeavor. The church as an "organized brotherhood" is the agency for bringing about social justice as the Body of Christ. Even the incarnation—"the Word was made flesh and dwelt amongst us"—has a social function, for it tells us that Christ as the center of all life and civilization has abolished all class distinctions and unbrotherly monopolies. Headlam was brought up before the Royal Commission on Ecclesiastical Discipline, a ploy devised by the Archbishop of Canterbury Archibald Campbell Tait (1811–82), a former Presbyterian, and the government to deal with "ritualism," which Tait perceived as Anglo-Catholic cryptopapism. Summing up his views, Headlam declared boldly, "Ecclesiastical discipline should be directed against the real disorders in the Church; those disorders are social and industrial, not ritual."[9]

Although two other organizations promoted revived Christian Socialism, they did not make a significant theological contribution to Anglican social thought. However, they ought to be mentioned to illustrate how clerics tried to put these social teachings into praxis, their utopian character not withstanding: the Christian Social Union (CSU), founded in 1889 by a host of northern Englishmen, such as Charles Gore, Holland, and Westcott—all divinity dons who graduated or taught at Oxford and Cambridge—and the Christian Socialist League (CSL), founded in 1894 also in the North of England. Later, in the twentieth century the Church Socialist League (1906–24) was established with the motto: "Christianity is the religion of which Socialism is the practice."

Whereas the Guild of St. Matthew was flamboyant and unpredictable, the CSU was moderate. Its objectives were (1) to claim the authority of Christian law (doctrine) over all areas of social relations, (2) to apply Christian moral truths and principles to the social and economic problems of the time, and (3) to present Christ publicly as a practical master and king opposed to wrongdoing and selfishness and defender of righteousness and love between all social classes. And whereas the Guild operated through demonstrations, sit-ins, marches, and injury to private property of the upper classes, the CSU operated more cerebrally through the publication of books, articles, and pamphlets. It stressed cooperation as had Maurice, saying that the method of Christian Socialism is cooperation, while the method of individualism is competition. The influence of the CSU reached its peak in 1908 when both Lambeth and the Pan-Anglican Congress met to deal almost exclusively with social issues and problems. The bishops at Lambeth in their Encyclical Letter urged Christians not to distance themselves from economic issues, lest workers gain the impression that the church was the ally of the comfortable rather than of the poor, "and that it identifies with the interests of wealth and property; with the result that the people become indifferent to the Church [and] distrustful of its interest in their lives."[10] The work and influence of the CSU particularly impressed a cleric named William Temple (1881–1944), later to be Archbishop of Canterbury but at the time chairman of the Westminster branch of the CSU and future husband of that branch's secretary.

The most radical Christian Socialist group was the Christian Socialist League (CSL), which had three objectives: (1) equal opportunity for all social classes, (2) common ownership of the means of production, and (3) universal cooperation among all classes. In contrast to the other organizations, it had no qualms about using Marxist terminology for shock-effect. One of its major proponents, the Reverend Paul B. Bull, founder of the Church Socialist League in 1906, said that competition, which creates both material and moral poverty and inflames greed and covetousness, was started at the Protestant Reformation with its emphasis on individualism.

By the early 1920s, Christian Socialism and its allied organizations had spread to the United States, where affiliates were established as a part of the Catholic social action movement in the Church of England. Its teachings included the following:

1. The incarnation, which signifies the consecration of daily life to God, has removed the false distinction between material values and spiritual values;
2. The Holy Trinity, which is a model and metaphor for cooperation in community as well as the embodiment of universal love, is to be extended to all of humanity regardless of class;

3. The crucifixion, resurrection, and ascension have social relevance: the cross as the symbol of self-sacrifice which stands in judgment on the narrow self-interests in capitalist industrial society, the resurrection and ascension as symbols of the love that will triumph eventually over the sins of selfishness and competition;

4. The Lord's Prayer points to the social nature of the Christian faith and the concern for all classes as noted through its use of "our" instead of "my" and "us" instead of "me";

5. The Anglican catechism is the "people's charter of social reform" in society;

6. The doctrine of divine immanence demonstrates that God is not restricted to the Church but also is to be found in the home and school, in the office and the factory.[11]

Christian Socialism, however, pointed to something beyond itself. Its convictions are called *classic* because they were the first systematic, theological ideas about social renewal in Anglicanism in Victorian England. They emerged at a time when a self-confident Victorian society was breaking down and being threatened by the twentieth century. Both America and Germany were fast overtaking England as an industrial power in the world, something accomplished by the end of the nineteenth century. The growing trade union movement with its socialist orientation also was viewed as a political threat to the established order in England with its traditional attitude of *noblesse oblige* toward the poor. Frequent recessions, increasing unemployment because of a failing agricultural sector, and an overabundance of workers attracted to the cities by the factories acerbated the tensions.

Revealed religion with its indifference had lost credibility among such classes, save for the efforts of the Methodists, founded by John (1703–91) and Charles (1707–88) Wesley for work among the urban poor, and the Salvation Army (founded 1865). There were sporadic Anglo-Catholic groups and individuals within the Church of England also doing such work. For example, at a Church Congress in 1873, the Bishop of Oxford, J.F. Mackarness, in a debate on "the church's duty in regard to strikes and labor" urged the adoption of a policy of neutrality but also an admonishment to factory owners about their responsibility for charity and kindly treatment toward their workers. In 1876, the Church of England Working Men's Society was organized with the goal of training laity for work among the poor and working classes. By 1886, its membership had grown to ten thousand. In 1882, the Church Army was founded by an Anglican cleric, Wilson Carlile, who cut his eyeteeth in the slums of Walworth. Likewise, seven years later, in 1889, Charles Gore, principal of Pusey House in Oxford, started the Community of the Resurrection (the Mirfield Fathers) to work among the poor. And the religious community at Kelham, the Society of the Sacred Mission, founded by Herbert Kelly in 1891, worked with boys of poor families who were either school dropouts or could not attend university because of the high fees.

Yet on the whole, the Victorian church was rejected by the poor and the workers as their church. Nor did most of its bishops and priests understand their ministry as focusing on the poor in spite of Maurice, Ludlow, and others. The Bishop of Manchester, James Moorhouse, summed up the Victorian church's view of that society's working classes and the poor at the time: "Christianity seeks to make men prosperous and wise and good, not by the force of laws or bayonets, but by the change of individual hearts, and the introduction of a new brotherhood in Christ."[12] Maurice himself said the task of the church was to extend "eternal life." But eternal life did not mean life unending or life in heaven; it is life with a certain quality. "Eternal life is to know God, to seek the truth, and to practice righteousness in one's daily life."[13]

William Temple was the last great personality who can be counted as influencing classical Anglican thought. Born in 1881 with the ecclesiastical equivalent of a silver spoon (the second son of an Archbishop of Canterbury, Frederick Temple, whom he succeeded as archbishop in 1942), Temple was educated at that Oxford college breeding high intelligence, Balliol. His father also had been educated there. Young Temple took a first in Greats (classics) and was promptly hired as a lecturer in philosophy and fellow at Queen's College, Oxford. Plato and Graeco-Roman classical philosophy captured Temple as possibly no other literature with the exception of the Gospel of St. John.

He left Oxford in 1910 to be headmaster of a fairly respectable fee-paying school, Repton. One of his successors, Geoffrey Fisher (1887–1972) also would be appointed to the archiepiscopal see of Canterbury in 1945. At Repton, Temple worked to expand the number of working class pupils in the school but failed to win over his staff and other headmasters. He was offered a canonry at Westminster Abbey and the vicariate at St. Margaret's, Westminster, commonly called the church of Parliament because of its proximity to the Houses of Parliament. But the proposal was withdrawn when it was embarrassingly discovered that he was ineligible because of insufficient years in the ministry. It was offered again in 1919, which he was able to accept. In 1914, fashionable St. James's Piccadilly, known for its grand weddings and music programs as well as its beauty, called him to be its rector, which Temple accepted. This was Temple's only parish experience. But unlike the American Episcopal Church, this is not held to be an insurmountable impediment in England for a call to higher office.

In 1921 he was made Bishop of Manchester, an industrial city in the north with compounded social problems. (Engels had written *The Condition of the Working Class in England in 1844* while living in Manchester.) It was obvious that Temple was on what American corporations call the "fast track." He remained in Manchester only eight years when in 1929 he was appointed by the Prime Minister to be Archbishop of York in 1929. As his public ministry began during the First World War, so it ended during war. Soon after his appointment as Archbishop of Canterbury in April 1942, he died in October 1944. And with his death, says E.R. Norman, Victorian Christianity came to an end, with its belief that society was really redeemable and that the established church was the appointed agent for the task. "The whole orthodoxy of social radicalism, which had so permeated Church leadership in the first half of the twentieth century, was moving to the periphery; and there it stayed until the revival in the 1960s."[14]

During his lifetime, Temple visited the United States. He lectured at Harvard University and the College of Preachers in Washington, D.C. He authored over twenty-five books, the most celebrated being his *Mens Creatrix* (1917), *Christus Veritas* (1924), his 1932–34 Gifford Lectures, *Nature, Man and God, Readings in St. John's Gospel* (1939), and *Christianity and Social Order* (1942). William Temple is considered one of the most able minds produced in the Church of England this century, although not one of its most original. The American theologian Reinhold Niebuhr (1892–1971) intrigued Temple so much that he called him "the troubler of my peace,"[15] particularly Niebuhr's emphasis on the relationship between sin as self-centeredness and justice as other-directed. Central to Temple was the incarnation, a doctrine that traditional Anglicanism has preferred in explicating God's redemption for humanity rather than a doctrine of the cross. Thus, a fully developed doctrine of sin and sinfulness within the Anglican tradition often appears to be slighted (except for the evangelical school in Anglicanism) compared with classical Protestant thought. The incarnation within Anglicanism also often is used as a catch-all for a kind of unfocused divination of humanity and nature. Hence, even under the influence of Niebuhr, Temple reflected:

> In Jesus Christ we shall find the one adequate presentation of God. . . . But in Jesus Christ we shall find also the one adequate presentation of Man. . . . Man as he is in his truest nature, which is only made actual when man becomes the means to the self-expression of God.[16]

At the same time the incarnation allowed him to affirm the sacramental principle of the Christian Socialists, coining his well-known phrase: "Christianity is the most materialist of all the world's great religions."

Temple acknowledged that while the cross reveals the evil of human sin, it also reveals that it has been forgiven and overtaken:

> Our hearts and wills are drawn to God, so that we take His Purpose as our own, as we do so, we vindicate the claim made for Christ that His Personality is representative and inclusive. . . . When we call His Personality representative we mean that in it we see what all men shall become. . . .[17]

Thus, Christ is a prototype for the best in humankind rather than the revelation of what true humankind is.

Temple's most remembered contribution to social ethics and Anglican social thought was *Christianity and the Social Order* (1942). Written at the height of World War II when he was chairman of the Malvern Conference on the Social Order, this small book immediately sold over 140,000 copies. Its purpose was "to make the Christian church's voice heard in matters of politics and economics." The small book seized the climate of crisis in Britain, just as Maurice had done in 1853, to raise critical questions about the church's engagement in social and political matters, in this case, the enormous unemployment in Britain. Although its context was that of Britain, it was not simply a provincial or national document; rather it was read throughout the Anglican world and the Christian world in general. "What right does the Church have to interfere?" asked Temple at the very beginning of the book, an appropriate question since many Christians in England assumed that the Christian faith was only another cultural department of state like the arts and sciences or trade and business. Temple said this question arises particularly in modern industrialized nations because they assume that civil life consists of autonomous areas, each of which is presided over by a mutually exclusive institution such as the state or the church. Yet the church has always interfered in political matters when there was the need to be a voice for and a defender of the poor and the marginalized in society, he retorted. Temple cited the fairly unbending seventeenth century Archbishop Laud as exemplary for using the authority and visibility of the archiepiscopal office to be "a friend of the poor with a genuine passion for justice."[18] He maintained the Church of England had abandoned any concern for economic and social justice until the Methodists began to combat the evils of slavery and urban conditions for the poor and, later on, the early Christian Socialists such as Maurice, Ludlow, and Kingsley.

Interference and critique by the church in public policy is justified on four counts: (1) people suffering due to injustices and evils in public welfare, such as bad housing, unemployment, malnutrition, and social conditions that deny or injure human dignity; (2) secular morality that permits excessive individualism, aggressive competition, self-interest and greed at any cost for the sake of profits as normative; (3) class injustices that reward privileged classes and ignore benefits for workers and the poor; and (4) negation of the "natural order," the place where the purpose of God is revealed. By natural order, Temple meant things that can be verified by "observing the generally accepted standards of judgment," such as love (the primary impulse for Christian interference) and justice (the social organization of love).

As already mentioned, Temple in his later years was greatly under the influence of Niebuhr's ideas about the relationship of love and justice in an immoral or imperfect society. Love transcends justice, but it cannot ignore justice. Justice is a necessary factor in a society with various groups making claims and counterclaims. When love is truly established, such will not occur. Suggate says that Temple was really assimilating Niebuhr's theology. But unlike Niebuhr, Temple made no sharp distinction between love as self-sacrifice and love as mutuality:

> Behind this language lies the central though unobtrusive motif of the complete mutuality of self-giving among the Persons of the Trinity, which for Temple must be a model for the relations of men to God and men to men. The painful sacrifice of Christ . . . is the means by which God brings men back to a right relationship with Himself, and is made effective in the Eucharist, where we continue to receive Christ's offered life, so that we can give ourselves more completely to God.[19]

Temple was really repeating Maurice's rather conservative paradigm of Christian brotherhood as reconciliation of opposite sides after reasoned discourse without paying serious attention to social circumstances, conflicts, and existing injustices in the social order between sides. Such an idea reflected a liberal concern for reform in the social fabric with as little displacement as possible. (Third World liberation theologians, however, ask whether it is possible to reconcile such opposites and generate love of enemy when the enemy is the privileged classes that maintain the very institutions that in turn support a have and a have-not disparity.) Temple based his claim on what he called Christian *primary* social principles and *derivative* social principles.

Under primary social principles he included the inherent dignity of human beings as children of God, capable of communion with God:

> All his life should be conducted and ordered with this dignity in view. The State must not treat him as having value only so far as he serves its ends, as Totalitarian States do; the State exists for its citizens, not the citizens for the State. But neither must a man treat himself, or conduct his life, as if he were himself the center of his own value; he is not his own end. . . .[20]

Under derivative social principles, Temple meant (1) freedom, which takes place when the state provides the greatest opportunity and most favorable conditions for making choices, especially the possibility of education in order to exercise this opportunity: "Freedom . . . must be freedom *for* something as well as freedom *from* something. . . . Freedom is self-control, self-determination, self-direction"[21]; (2) fellowship, which includes affirmation of a person as a self by engagement with one's neighbors, since "no man is fitted for an isolated life," and what he called "intermediate groupings," meaning trade unions, parish churches, universities, mutual help or improvement associations; and (3) service, which includes (a) the state providing favorable working conditions so that labor is self-enhancing and leisure is self-affirming, and (b) using our narrow loyalties to serve the wider community: "A man is a member of his family, of his nation, and of mankind. It is seldom that anyone can render a service directly to mankind as a whole. We serve mankind by serving those parts of it with which we are closely connected."[22]

Thus very much in the spirit of Maurice, Temple aimed for stability and inclusiveness in the existing social order by tinkering with it under the rubric of reform. He did not question the foundations of the social order itself, although he had some misgivings about the central ethic of private ownership and private property in capitalist society. Insisting that the Bible says all land belongs to God, he noted humanity only enjoys the use of it as stewards. This means that land and private ownership of land can be regulated according to the common good benefit of the larger community:

> It is thus evident that it is part of the common Christian tradition from primitive times to the fullest development of medieval thought that Christian faith should find expression in relation to economic questions. It is further evident that in this tradition the rights of property, while perfectly legitimate, are always an accommodation to human sin, are subordinate to the general interest, and are a form of stewardship rather than of ultimate ownership.[23]

William Temple was one of the most radical of modern Anglican archbishops when it came to advancing the cause of the poor and the working classes in the entrenched class system of Great Britain, although, as one of his biographers admits, "except for the butler at Fulham [residence of the Bishop of London] and Lambeth [London residence of the Archbishop of Canterbury] and his scouts [college servants] at Balliol and Queen's, he had hardly spoken to an adult handworker till he joined the W.E.A. [Workers' Educational Association], whose president he became (in 1908)."[24] Consequently, Iremonger labeled Temple "a Conservative with a bad conscience."[25]

Lambeth Conferences and Social Teachings

While not carrying canonical or binding authority in the various national (provincial) churches making up the eclectic international network called the Anglican Communion, Lambeth Conferences increasingly have acquired authority as a source of collective Anglican social thought and teachings. Several national churches, including the Episcopal Church, sometimes have adapted statements from Lambeth as part of their own social postures on particular subjects.

This body has not long been a part of the Anglican tradition or the Anglican vocabulary. In fact, the name comes from the site at which the first such conference was held in 1867, Lambeth Palace, the London residence of the Archbishop of Canterbury since the thirteenth century and located across from the Houses of Parliament on the Thames River. Lambeth Conferences were inaugurated at the request of the Canadians to the archbishop in 1865. They wished a conference of all Anglican bishops to deal with the controversy over the publication of a collection of articles by liberal theologians entitled *Essays and Reviews* (1860) and the writings of a South African bishop, John Coleman Colenso (1814–83), Bishop of Natal. Both publications were roundly denounced by many Anglican bishops in England and outside England. In fact over 10,000 Church of England members in reaction against the *Essays and Reviews* signed a petition proclaiming their belief in the divine inspiration of scriptures and the existence of hell as a place of eternal punishment. Colenso's writings challenged conventional ways of understanding some New Testament teachings and urged tolerance for and even allowance of the indigenization of some African traditions into Christian worship, including polygamy. This also evoked the wrath and dismay of many church members, high and low alike, and Anglican missionaries.

The Archbishop of Canterbury, Archibald Campbell Tait, who had publicly criticized *Essays*, after some delay in acquiescing to the Canadian appeal, finally in 1867 invited all Anglican bishops to Lambeth Palace. Some seventy-six bishops attended (although it does not appear that the first African bishop, Samuel Ajayi Crowther, bishop in Nigeria, was invited; certainly he was not in attendance). From that first Lambeth Conference to the latest one in 1988 (attended by over five hundred bishops from a polyglot of cultures, languages, and traditions) its influence as an authority in the international Anglican Communion has grown.

At the very first Lambeth bishops did not want to be an Anglican model of Roman *magisterium*. In his address to the 1875 Convocation of Canterbury meeting shortly before the second Lambeth, Archbishop Tait, said:

> There is no intention whatever on the part of anybody to gather together the Bishops of the Anglican Church for the sake of defining any matter of doctrine. Our doctrines are contained in our formularies, and our formularies are interpreted by the proper judicial authorities, and there is no intention whatever at any such gathering that questions of doctrine should be submitted for interpretation in any future Lambeth Conference any more than they were at the previous Lambeth Conference.[26]

Although the first Lambeth was summoned to deal with doctrinal issues of biblical scholarship and authority, the bishops in their "Address to the Faithful" were very much aware of the growing multiracial, multicultural character of Anglicanism. Yet, either due to the insularity of the dominating British episcopate, or diplomatic silence by American bishops, no reference was made to the racial turmoil and Jim Crow segregation against blacks occurring principally in the southern United States at the time. The first Lambeth Conference to deal deliberately with social issues was in July 1888, which debated the issue of socialism. Under the Bishop of Manchester, James Moorhouse, the report of the committee "Appointed to Consider the Subject of the Church's Practical Work in Relation to Socialism" defined socialism as "any scheme of social reconstruction . . . which aims at uniting labor and the instruments of labor (land and capital), whether by means of the State, or the help of the rich, or of the voluntary cooperation of the poor."[27] This was really an adaptation of the Maurice/Kingsley concept of brotherhood and divine harmony between social classes under the auspices of Christianity, what Marxists call utopian socialism because a scientific, systematic analysis of actual social and economic conditions failed. Considering the countries of the attending bishops (Britain including Ireland, the United States, Canada, India, the Caribbean, Australia, South Africa, and miscellaneous lands in Africa, South America, and Asia), socialism would not likely have been a burning issue except in Great Britain and the United States. Yet although Eugene Debs was roaring as a lion in the United States, a viable socialist political party did not come into its own until the Socialist Party was organized in 1901 in Indianapolis (also the headquarters of the largest Ku Klux Klan in the 1920s).

The report saw no contradiction between socialism and Christianity. If there appeared to be such, this was due to a misunderstanding or an accident. Even though some socialists were atheists and anarchists, "at the same time with what they profess to be their central aim, the improvement of the material and moral condition of the poor, [the church] must have the deepest sympathy. Spoliation or injustice in any form is abhorrent alike to her sentiment and belief."[28]

Private property was defended and what they called "state socialism" was rejected. They cited utilitarian rather than theological arguments, urging workers to use their wages either to purchase land privately or to form cooperatives for land purchase and they doubted that the state could operate industries with the same efficiency and economy as private owners. Also socialistic schemes for nationalizing private lands restrained freedom, parental responsibility, and individuality. "The best help is self-help. More even than increase of income, and security of deposit, thrift and self-restraint are the necessary elements of material prosperity."[29]

The 1897 Lambeth reaffirmed brotherhood and cooperation as "natural" Christian principles, since the cooperation "helped spread and strengthen the feeling of mutual fellowship or brotherhood, and to conciliate interests of the capitalist, the workman, and the purchaser."[30] In their Encyclical Letter, the bishops praised the brotherhood of humanity as the principle that could reconcile labor and capital: "Obedience to this law of brotherhood would ultimately, in all probability, prevent many of the mischiefs which attend our present system."[31]

This concept of brotherhood sacralized Victorian middle-class morality that stressed self-help and self-reliance within the current social fabric over against counterclaims that the very structure of the social fabric might be a contributing factor to class differences and hostilities. Theologically, the bishops also held to embryonic natural theology: since all people are assumed "naturally" reasonable, issues about mutual cooperation and reconciliation can be resolved through rational discussion by all classes regardless of existing economic forces and power structures in the existing society. (Such a teaching obviously appealed to an established church that also had much to lose in a changed situation, where God might be looked at from "down under" from the perspective of the workers instead of "above down.") The bishops acknowledged that as poverty itself was a force shaping the destiny of workers and the poor, from which "the rich are comparatively free," the church should provide them with hope and inspiration, motivating them to live according to "higher principles."[32]

In the report of the committee on "the Office of the Church with Respect to Industrial Problems," the bishops named four moral principles for building community: (1) brotherhood or fellowship in Christ; (2) labor or service to God and humanity, rather than idleness; (3) justice to eliminate inequalities in the social order, although recognizing that such are woven into the "whole providential order of human life and are recognized emphatically in our Lord's words"; and (4) public responsibility, whereby Christians are to work for a wholesome economic and social order of the nation.[33]

The Christian Socialist lingering in Anglican social teachings really came into its own at the 1908 Lambeth Conference, described by some as a "socialist field-day."[34] Many English bishops belonged to the Christian Social Union, including the wife of the Archbishop of Canterbury, Randall Thomas Davidson (1848–1930; Archbishop: 1903), who himself was a close confidant of the Queen. Christian Socialism had become radically chic with the British upper classes. "Practical principles of morality, which are already recognized by the people as true" were identified: social justice, brotherhood, racial justice, honesty, purity, peaceableness, self-education, cleanliness, good health, the sin of idleness, responsibility for the upkeep of private property, doing public service, the incompatibility of "selfish luxury" and the Christian faith, and applying Christian morality when considering investments and their likely effect on the workers.[35] This latter principle was a forerunner of the later movement urging social responsibility in corporate investments as a part of the church's ministry.

The 1908 Lambeth Conference also spoke out sharply on racism and racial discrimination:

> All races and peoples, whatever their language or conditions, must be welded into one Body, and the organization of different races living side by side into separate or independent Churches, on the basis of race or color, is inconsistent with the vital and essential principle of the unity of Christ's Church."[36]

The state of affairs in some African colonies no doubt was in mind, particularly South Africa and East Africa. Standing acts of violence were also happening in the Southern states, where whites were lynching blacks and legalized segregation between the races existed. Furthermore, for the American bishops to have concurred with the resolution's text deriding separate, independent racial churches was a sign of their own limited knowledge of the history of Christian churches in the American context. Most American blacks at that time belonged (and still belong) to separate black denominations (such as the AME, AMEZ, CME and National Baptist churches) that began as freedom movements among blacks because of separation and racism in white churches. Also the American bishops must have known that race historically divided other white Protestant denominations across sectional and regional lines, such as the Methodist Church, the Southern Baptists, and the Presbyterian Church, not to mention the sectional split within the Episcopal Church itself during the Civil War. The Confederate church even produced a separate *Book of Common Prayer* for the soul of that region.

This largely baptized middle-class idea of brotherhood as the operative metaphor for ending injustices and class differences was reaffirmed in succeeding Lambeth Conferences. The word was changed to *fellowship* at the 1920 Lambeth Conference but continued to avoid any analysis of economic structures they wanted to change. In one of the resolutions, the bishops agreed that the church should teach the principle of cooperation in industrial relations as the agent for systematic economic change:

> An outstanding and pressing duty of the Church is to convince its members of the necessity of nothing less than a fundamental change in the spirit and working of our economic life. This change can only be effected by accepting . . . the principle of

cooperation in service for the common good in place of un-restricted competition for private or sectional advantage . . . by which alone we can hope to remove class dissensions and resolve industrial discords.[37]

One of the reasons for this well-sounding principle lacking in concreteness lay with division among the bishops about the degree of the church's critical engagement in the existing social and economic order. One Englishman summed up well the opposition to church interference in economic affairs: "Our Lord Himself did not regard it as part of His mission to try and set the industrial and social injustices of His own day aright."[38] This division no doubt also accounted for the compromise that the church can be neither an advocate nor a partisan in political and social disputes when it is not clear that moral issues are involved. How strange this sounds to twentieth century ears when many Christians are saying that the church must be not only a voice with and alongside the poor in society, but also a voice in discourse about public policy.

Lambeth of 1930 attended to issues of the pending war as well as racial issues. Fascism in Europe and fascistlike events in South Africa were emerging. In 1926, for example, the South African government enacted the Color Bar Act, which reserved skilled jobs for whites and assigned unskilled jobs to blacks. This simply continued a pattern of racial separation already established in public policy in that country when the British recast it as the Union of South Africa in 1910 and made it a self-governing territory. The influx of blacks into its cities had been regulated already and restricted through the 1923 Native (Urban Areas) Act, which required blacks to carry the hated passbooks.

The bishops cautioned against any group, particularly Anglo-Saxons, claiming racial superiority, which they called "an infec-tion." "The ruling of one race by another can only be justified from the Christian standpoint when the highest welfare of the subject race is the constant aim of government, and when admis-sion to an increasing share in the government of the country is an objective steadfastly pursued."[39] They also insisted that the Holy Communion in all churches be available to all members regard-less of race or color, the foreshadowing of a conflict some thirty years later in many Southern white Episcopal churches that refused civil rights workers and other blacks communion at their altars during the civil rights movement of the 1960s.

Lambeth's rejection of war as a method for settling disputes between nations, being incompatible with biblical teachings (Resolution 25), was reaffirmed at subsequent Conferences: 1948, 1968, 1978, and 1988. At the same time the bishops did not support pacifism as a Christian alternative, noting rather ambivalently that "peace will never be achieved till international relations are controlled by religious and ethical standards," without detailing these standards. Again, they curiously avoided mentioning the American context, where the churches and theological circles were vigorously debating issues of war and peace led by Reinhold Niebuhr and pacifists. Given the numerical strength of the Episcopal bishops at the 1930 Lambeth, it might be thought that some reference to the American scene would have been made. Of course, it is entirely possible also that the theological debates in America about war were not priorities for the American bishops themselves.

Not much was said about birth control, although the Conference condemned abortion undertaken for convenience and selfish purposes. It also approved contraception in family planning under certain exceptional medical and social conditions, which it did not specify: "[I]n those cases where there is a clearly-felt moral obligation to limit or avoid parenthood, and where there is a morally sound reason for avoiding complete abstinence [from sexual intercourse], the Conference agrees that other methods may be used, provided that this is done in the light of the same Christian principles."[40]

Just as the First World War interrupted Lambeth's ten-year cycle of meetings, so also the Second World War delayed the 1940 Lambeth Conference until 1948, which resolved to return to a decennial pattern of meetings. At the 1948 Lambeth the bishops, reacting to Stalinism in Communist Russia, a defeated Germany, as well as the social legislation taking place in Britain in 1945, said the state exists to serve its citizens, not to enslave and claim their total being. Treating citizens as means and not ends is a Christian aim in political and social affairs of state that does not rest entirely upon "any concession by an earthly state, but upon a divine endowment and prerogative which no human agency gave, or can take away."[41] Nevertheless, the social democratic state with its expressed welfare programs and compassion for the poor and workers was mentioned as carrying out a ministry of God:

> We believe that the State is under the moral law of God, and is intended by him to be an instrument for human welfare. We therefore welcome the growing concern and care of the modern State for its citizens, and call upon Church members to accept their own political responsibility and to cooperate with the State and its officers in their work.[42]

The church's role is to act decisively to protect personal freedom and provide a counterculture to the "natural bias" of the state toward authoritarianism.

Although the totalitarian practices of Stalinism in the Soviet Union and elsewhere were condemned and Marxism called "a heresy of Christianity," the bishops also underscored the attractiveness of Communism to some as a protest against social injustices: "Communism inherited a concern for the depressed and downtrodden which is—wherever it is true to its vocation—a glory of the Church."[43] Archbishop Cyril Garbett of York later wrote a protest against characterizing Communism a "heresy of Christianity." He found Communism's materialism, morality, lack of any hope, and methods of terror and revolution fully incompatible with the Christian faith.[44] One must also recall that this was at the height of the cold war between West and East. In 1948, Russia's attempt to isolate West Berlin by blockading the roads resulted in the United States and allies initiating the Berlin airlift, which ended in 1949. George Kennan and John Foster Dulles were advancing the doctrine of containment of Communism in our foreign policy and military strategy, which led to the creation of the North Atlantic Treaty Organization (NATO), also in 1949.

Nuclear arms were also discussed at the 1948 Lambeth. At that time the United States had a monopoly on nuclear arms, since the Soviet and European economies was still recovering from the war. No other nation ever had developed and dropped the atom bomb on a nation or possessed the hydrogen bomb except America. Lambeth said nuclear armaments were repugnant to the Christian conscience, although there were different opinions as to when they might or might not be used. One group said it was morally justifiable to use the atom bomb if it meant avoiding "political enslavement."[45] However, interesting enough, although the South African Nationalist Party with its known ideology of apartheid had come to power in 1948, the bishops only condemned racial discrimination as a whole without addressing the actual disenfranchising of blacks and coloreds in that country by the white minority government. Nor did they speak to the Jim Crow laws and racial segregation in the Southern United States.

At the 1958 Lambeth, largely due to the influence of the American bishops, who brought the largest number of bishops, a new social teaching about birth control and contraception appeared that broke with previous Lambeth teachings. Marriage has three purposes: (1) procreation, (2) the need of husband and wife to complement and "fulfill" each other, and (3) the establishment of a stable environment for a family. Hence, unlike the Catholics, procreation is not the primary purpose of marriage. Furthermore, the Conference spoke of "planned parenthood" as an option for couples wanting children:

> Those who carelessly and improvidently bring children into the world trusting in an unknown future or a generous society to care for them, need to make a vigorous examination of their lack of concern for their children and for the society of which they are a part.[46]

Sexual intimacy is entirely proper to marriage without needing to produce children; indeed, it has a "sacramental" quality about it. Hence, contraception is permitted for Anglicans as is family planning, provided the latter is "secure from the corruptions of sensuality and selfishness." Abortion is again disapproved.

Human rights and human dignity were the notable emphases of the social teachings coming out of the 1978 Lambeth Conference. This conference met in Kent near Canterbury for the first time rather than in London at Lambeth Palace because London facilities were too limited for the great number of bishops, especially from the Third World. That Lambeth testified to the change in the color complexion in the Anglican Communion, even if Anglicanism still retained much of British culture and institutions in its worship and theology. All people are made in the image of God, the 1978 Lambeth affirmed, with fundamental human rights, including "the right to be housed, the freedom to work, the right to eat, the right to be educated."[47]

The 1988 Lambeth was again held outside London at the University of Kent because of the swelled numbers. Many of the discussions, formal and informal, dealt with women in the priesthood allowed by some national churches and the likelihood of the Episcopal Church electing and consecrating the first woman to the historic episcopate. Many Third World bishops, most notably the African bishops, protested that more urgent social issues and teachings, though on the agenda, were not to be given as much time as the ordination of women, which they felt was largely a preoccupation of North American and British bishops. Soon, more time was found for the social agenda and evangelism.

The report, "Christianity and the Social Order" in its prologue spoke of the interaction between Christian formation and social forces within society:

> The mission of the Church is twofold: to seek the renewal of society by the spiritual renewal of the individual, and to seek the renewal of the individual by the spiritual renewal of society. . . . Therefore, as we strive to be loyal citizens, we are also aware of an obedience which transcends and sometimes challenges judgments which depend upon an unquestioning acceptance of the prevailing assumptions of society.[48]

All of human life and society is under God's care and concern. Human rights, based on the uniqueness of humankind created by God in his image at creation, were affirmed for all people regardless of culture as were those named in the United Nations Declaration of Rights: moral rights, civil rights, legal rights, social and economic rights, and self-determination:

> Christians are called to be faithful to Christ and to the Word of God where he always and unconditionally stands alongside the poor, the disadvantaged, and the oppressed. The people of God ought, therefore, to be the voice of those whose voice has been silenced and suppressed, speaking and acting not necessarily on a political party platform but out of Christian conviction about the God who demands justice and whose will is peace and reconciliation.[49]

Anglicans can be guided by the classic Anglican triad of the Bible ("It is the great themes of creation—redemption, sin, judgment, glory and hope, human dignity and worth, the need for human community, and other central truths of our faith—which need to inform and guide us.");[50] tradition ("a long-term aspect . . . [that] point us to a long tradition of Christian ethical and social thinking which is often overlooked in the search for answers to new problems [and] . . . a short-term aspect, perhaps better described as 'experience'. . . . It is in this context that the voices of the poor, the oppressed and the marginalized gain their special authority.")[51]; and reason ("The poet, the artist, the psychologist, the economist, the philosopher and the scientist can contribute to this discernment, and especially at our time, through the scientific approach. . . . [S]cience can claim to provide rational knowledge about important aspects of our world . . .).[52] It is the latter, according to Lambeth, which allows Christians and the church to pass moral judgments on the conditions of society and in individual lives.

On issues of peace and war, the 1988 Lambeth reaffirmed the teaching about war being unacceptable to Christians as a method for settling international conflicts, and commended non-violence, civil disobedience, and conscientious objection as ways of countering militarism. At the same time it gave indirect support for those "who, after exhausting all other ways, choose the way of armed struggle as the only way to justice," yet at the same time pointing to the dangers in such a posture.[53] The anti-apartheid struggle in South Africa by blacks and others was what the report had in mind, but Irish bishops complained that the text could be misunderstood in Ireland as supportive of the IRA forces fighting the British in Northern Ireland in the war between Catholics and Protestants. The final amended text addressed the different reasons for armed opposition: "It is not our purpose to condemn or condone those who in conscience can see no other way to defend themselves and their communities from the violence done to them except by acts of violence and war. . . . Christian leaders have particular responsibilities to promote negotiations between parties caught in the midst of conflict."[54]

The issue of affluent nations and citizens sharing their resources with poorer nations, or the haves and the have-nots, allowed the bishops to address the global economic complex and the racial complex under the issue of power:

> To the powerful—be they in the structures of government, of academia, of science and technology, of the military, of finance or of the media—the Church is called to be a disturber of

conscience. To the poor, to the oppressed, to the homeless, to the unemployed and to those on the margins of society, the Church is to be voice and servant.[55]

At the same time, the disparity of power also creates conditions for racism and elitism, not to mention sexism and conflicts between social classes. Apartheid was called particularly evil and repugnant to Christians because it claims to be a Christian-based system.

In discussions about marriage, family, and sexuality, enflamed by many American bishops wanting a positive decision on homosexuality and extra-marital life-styles, Lambeth reaffirmed sexual intercourse as "an act of total commitment which belongs properly within a permanent married relationship" and the family "in its various forms, as the fundamental institution of human condition."[56] Homosexuality was not endorsed as a proper interpretation of Christian sexuality or Christian life-styles. They affirmed that homosexuals are a part of the church's pastoral and human rights ministry. They also admitted the complexity of the concept of "sexual orientation" and that it has not yet been resolved within the church. Still the church should "give active encouragement to biological, genetic, and psychological research, and consider these scientific studies as they contribute to our understanding of the subject in the light of Scripture."[57]

Notes

1. Charles Raven, *Christian Socialism, 1848–1854* (London: Macmillan, 1920), p. 94.

2. F.D. Maurice, *Theological Essays* (New York: Harper, 1957), pp. 276-7.

3. Cited in Tǿrben Christensen, *Origin and History of Christian Socialism, 1848–54* (Aarhaus, Denmark: Universitetsforlaget, 1962), p. 137.

4. Ibid., p. 25.

5. Ibid., p. 217.

6. Peter D'Arcy Jones, *The Christian Socialist Revival, 1877–1914* (Princeton, NJ: Princeton University Press, 1968), pp. 11-12.

7. Ibid., p. 160.

8. Ibid.

9. Ibid., p. 162.

10. Randall T. Davidson, *The Five Lambeth Conferences (1867–1908)* (London: SPCK, 1920), p. 410.

11. Ibid., pp. 233-5.

12. E.R. Norman, *Church and Society in England, 1770–1970: A Historical Study* (Oxford: Clarendon Press, 1976), p. 178.

13. Cited in Jones, *Christian Socialist Revival*, p. 9.

14. Norman, *Church and Society in England.* p. 371.

15. Alan M. Suggate, *William Temple and Christian Social Ethics Today* (Edinburgh: T. & T. Clark, 1987), p. 187.

16. William Temple, *Christus Veritas* (London: Macmillan, 1924), pp. 234, 124-5. Cited in Suggate, William Temple, p. 57.

17. Quoted in Suggate, *William Temple*, p. 58.

18. Temple, *Christianity and Social Order* (London: SPCK, 1976), p. 30.

19. Suggate, *William Temple*, p. 199.

20. Temple, *Christianity and Social Order*, p. 63.

21. Ibid., p. 68.

22. Ibid., p. 75.

23. Ibid., p. 51.

24. F.A. Iremonger, *William Temple, Archbishop of Canterbury: His Life and Letters* (London: Oxford University Press, 1984), p. 87.

25. Cited in Norman, *Church and Society in England*, p. 283.

26. Quoted in *The Lambeth Conferences* (1867–1948) (London: SPCK, 1948), p. 9.

27. Davidson, *The Five Lambeth Conferences*, p. 137.

28. Ibid., p. 137.

29. Ibid., p. 140.

30. Cited in Norman, *Church and Society in England*, p. 131.

31. Davidson, *Five Lambeth Conferences*, p. 184.

32. Ibid., p. 185.

33. Ibid., pp. 266-67.

34. Jones, *Christian Socialist Revival*, p. 216.

35. Norman, *Church and Society in England*, p. 239.

36. Resolution 20, Davidson, *Five Lambeth Conferences*, p. 321.

37. Ibid., Resolution 74, Davidson, pp. 51-2.

38. William Cunningham, *Personal Ideals and Social Principles* (London, 1919), p. 5. Cited in Norman, *Church and Society in England*, p. 243.

39. Resolution 21, *Lambeth Conferences* (1867–1948), p. 167.

40. *Ibid.*, p. 166.

41. *The Lambeth Conference, 1948* (London: SPCK, 1948), p. 10. Cited in Norman, *Church and Society in England*, p. 375.

42. Ibid., p. 377.

43. Ibid., p. 385.

44. Ibid., p. 386.

45. Ibid., p. 406.

46. "The Family in Contemporary Society," *The Lambeth Conference, 1958*, p. 146.

47. James B. Simpson and Edward M. Story, *Discerning God's Will: The Complete Eyewitness Report of the Eleventh Lambeth Conference* (Nashville, Tenn.: Thomas Nelson Publishers, 1979), p. 300.

48. *The Truth Shall Make You Free, The Lambeth Conference 1988*, par. 7, 9 (London: The Anglican Consultative Council, 1988), p. 157.

49. Ibid., par. 49, p. 167.

50. Ibid., p. 161.

51. Ibid., par. 26-27.

52. Ibid., par. 28.

53. Ibid., p. 221.

54. Ibid., p. 177.

55. Ibid., par. 64, p. 169.

56. Ibid., resolution 34, p. 224. The report said family may be "a unit of one parent and children, an adult child and an elderly par-

ent, adult relatives, a husband, wife and children, or whatever other shape." (par. 48)
57. Ibid., par. 154, p. 187.

Chapter 3
Beginnings of Episcopal Church Social Teachings

The Episcopal Church is quite untidy, undisciplined, unsystematic, and episodic when it deals theologically with social issues for a church that claims as its norm a theologically educated ministry. The first social issue looked at theologically was the South's secession from the union in the nineteenth century. The first vehicle for official Episcopal teachings, as far as I can discover, was the bishops' Pastoral Letter of 1862 (as distinct from social policy or positions).[1] Indeed, the Pastoral Letters are a primary source for social teachings in the church.

The Civil War and the First Social Teachings

The 1862 Pastoral spoke, for the first time, to a national crisis. The bishops noted very carefully that they were speaking to the church as "official expositors of the Word of God."[2] That is, the bishops intended this Pastoral to be authoritative as a teaching of the church and listened to seriously because it was based on "the Word of God," i.e., the Bible.

The Prayer Book and Scripture were used for their thinking that the secession of the Confederate states was a seditious and rebellious act that violated the divine mandate given the state by God:

> Ever since our Church has had her Litany, we have been praying for deliverance 'from sedition, privy conspiracy, and rebellion.' And now that all three are upon us, and in a depth of scheme, a force of action . . . shall we refuse to tell you in what light we regard that gigantic evil?[3]

Citing Romans 13, the traditional text for the state's mandate, they said unmistakably, albeit too triumphantly, that the concrete manifestation of this mandate was the Constitution and government of the United States of America:

Under them, the people of all the States, now resisting them, were just as much bound to render obedience, when such resistance began, as we, whose allegiance is still unbroken. According to the Scriptures, that resistance, so far from making null and void those powers, is a resistance to ordinances of God still in force; and, therefore, brings, His condemnation to those so engaged.[4]

This was a very powerful accusation, considering that some Southern bishops owned slaves and that others were related to Northern bishops through marriage and family and personal ties. The ideology of slavery was not addressed directly in the Pastoral, but the bishops did insist that a solidarity clearly existed between all citizens, black and white, based on a natural defense of the duly constituted government of the United States:

We have now, brethren, . . . ascertained a basis of principle and duty on which we may heartily rejoice in all the active and energetic loyalty with which the members of our Churches, in union with their fellow-citizens, *of all classes and conditions,* [italics added] are sustaining the Government in its vast efforts to reinstate the rightful control of its laws.[5]

This first instance of a social teaching exhibited four pillars that shape an Episcopal *official exposition* of the Word of God: (1) the context or situation of the issues; (2) Holy Scriptures as the norm and point of reference; (3) the *Book of Common Prayer*; and (4) a "church-type" understanding of the relationship between church and government. H. Richard Niebuhr would describe this approach as a "Christ of culture" theology. That is, Episcopal bishops understood their church to be a guardian of established mainstream public morality for the nation and its own constituency, in spite of ideological differences about race within that constituency.

Industrialism and the Second Social Teachings

The second major national occasion for Episcopal social teachings was the monumental industrial, urban, and religious shifts taking place in nineteenth century America. An authority on nineteenth century Christian social thought, Charles Hopkins, claims that the Episcopal Church was the first major Protestant body to address the economic and social issues at the time. In 1877, for example, the House of Bishops approved a report that said property owners, people of privilege, and society as a whole have obligations for providing equal rights to the working classes and the poor.

With the peace at Appomattox ending the Civil War, America was free to restore its tattered economy. Its great leap into industrial capitalism provided a means and a national will for reestablishing stability and economic expansion. Between 1865 and 1894 the United States moved from fourth place as an industrial power to first place, thereby giving it world political clout. The discovery of iron-ore fields in Michigan and Minnesota near water, the canal system, and the invention of the Bessemer process, which converted the iron ore into steel, allowed a railroad network to be put into place. Commerce and trade expanded frontiers beyond the settled East Coast. Now able to manufacture and transport steel cheaply to places like Chicago, Cleveland, Milwaukee, and Pittsburgh, American capitalism grew with a vengeance. For example, in 1869 there were 2 million wage earners in factories and small industries producing goods worth approximately $3.4 million. Thirty years later 4.7 million wage earners in factories alone turning out goods worth $11.4 million.

In fact, it was during the late nineteenth century that the national vocabulary was enlarged by such terms as *robber baron* and *multimillionaire*, the latter created after the death of Cornelius Vanderbilt (Episcopalian) to describe his wealth of more than $100 million dollars. John D. Rockefeller (1839–1937) began as a bookkeeper near Cleveland, Ohio; Vanderbilt (1794–1877) began as a ferry boat operator in New York City; Andrew Carnegie (1835–1919), a telegraphist near Pittsburgh; Edward Henry Harriman (1848–1909), a stockbroker in New York City; and Philip Danforth Armour (1832–1901), a farmer and butcher during the Civil War. Industrial giants such as these, many of whom were Episcopalians, became the nineteenth century equivalent of twentieth century film star celebrities and European royalty all in one. To every thing there is a season, and this was the season of uncontrolled, unlimited *laissez-faire* capitalism and private ownership. Indeed, not until 1887 did the United States government try to regulate the vast industrial enterprises and monopolies by passing the first Interstate Commerce Act, an act aimed at breaking existing price-fixing agreements and industry-wide monopolies.

Industrialism in the nineteenth century, however, not only brought economic benefits for some; it also brought military, economic, and social turmoil. Militarily, the United States asserted its newly acquired economic strength in world affairs for the benefit of its domestic business interests, which were steadily in search of new markets, raw materials, and natural resources. Many businessmen had long eyed the Spanish colonies of Cuba and the Philippines as future markets. Many militarists had also long coveted Cuba as a possession of the United States. Both were accommodated in 1898 when the United States government, alarmed at the heavy losses inflicted on American investments in Cuba after Spain retaliated against an uprising led by José Marti, used the alleged sinking of its battleship *Maine* to wage war against Spain. America not only successfully occupied Cuba, but also confiscated the Philippines and Puerto Rico as well, ending in less than a year the brief Spanish-American War, described by Secretary of State John Hay (Episcopalian) at the time as "that splendid little war."[6]

Moreover, during this time, economic aggression increased against the original "Americans," the Indians, as a kind of patriotic rite of passage among an American public imbued with rugged individualism and Manifest Destiny. Writers like Ned Buntline (1823–86), author of *Buffalo Bill, King of the Border Men* and *The Scouts of the Prairies*; Bret Harte (1836-1902), author of *The Luck of Roaring Camp*; and Mark Twain (1835-1910), who authored the American classic *The Adventures of Huckleberry Finn*, romanticized the West and the white pioneers. With the exception of Helen Hunt Jackson's *Century of Dishonor* (1881), few wrote favorably about the Indians and their plight.

In 1875, after the discovery of gold in Black Hills, South Dakota, and later in Idaho, this aggression reached new heights. The Black Hills were the traditional sacred grounds of the Sioux, who themselves in 1876 established a kind of western Appomattox by totally defeating Colonel George Armstrong Custer and the Seventh Calvary at Little Big Horn, Montana. Between 1869 and 1876 there were at least 200 fiercely fought wars between American troops and Indians, who wanted to protect their traditional territory and burial grounds of their ancestors. (Indian territory had first been invaded when British Anglicans landed in Jamestown, Virginia, in 1607, and British Puritans in Massachusetts in 1620.)

Railroad thugs hired by industrialists and protected by the U.S. Cavalry destroyed much of their land, while settlers and mindless miners occupied most of the rest. It was reported, for example, that one railroad magnate swindled the Cherokee out of 800,000 acres of land in southern Kansas, while another tried to manipulate another tribe to sell him eight million acres for a mere 20 cents an acre. Between 1887 and 1917 Indian lands decreased from 140,000,000 to 48,000,000 acres. Two million acres were confiscated and given free to settlers as homesteads in Oklahoma, which in 1907 became a state dominated by whites.

Finally, during this industrial period, another force that shaped the American context was the growth of cities and the enormous social and economic upheavals caused by what we call *urbanization.* Cities underwent a fourfold population explosion largely for two reasons: (1) the migration of rural inhabitants to the cities in search of new jobs created by the rapid industrial expansion and new factories, and (2) a second wave of largely European immigrants in vast numbers coming to the cities for economic opportunity. From 1860 to 1890—thirty years—New York City's population grew from 1,080,330 to 3,437,202; Philadelphia (at the time still the second largest city) from 565,529 to 1,294,000; Boston, from 177,840 to 561,000. During the first immigration wave in the mid-1800s, some 5 million people came to America. During the second wave, more than 10.3 million immigrated. This hugh influx meant cheap labor, cheap tenement housing, enormous health problems, and excessive exploitation by the industrialists and business people. In 1885, the weekly wages for men averaged $6 to $7 and considerably less for women in the sweatshops. A report from the New York Bureau of Labor Statistics estimated that at the time even if all members of a family of six worked fourteen hours a day, which was not unusual, at best that family could clear $12 to $15 a week. Nor was it infrequent that as many as eight people lived in two rooms without indoor toilets, plumbing, or ventilation.

One consequence of this heavy immigration was an eventual dethroning of the Protestant establishment in cities, since most immigrants were Catholic. Many Protestant churches fled sections of cities as immigrants and the poor moved in. But such a threat failed to deter other organizations and parish churches that were alarmed at the growing problems of poverty, social upheaval, and lack of services for the urban poor. The Young Men's Christian Association (YMCA) and the Young Women's Christian Association (YWCA), set up in 1855 in Boston and later in New York by wealthy Christians to deal with some of these problems, also sprang up in other cities. Several Episcopal parishes, such as St. Mark's Church, Philadelphia, as early as 1870 organized associations just for the working classes and the poor. The association at St. Mark's, the Workingmen's Club and Institute, provided educational, recreational, and temporary financial relief. Available to any man eighteen years of age and over, the club was open six days a week from 7:30 to 10:00 P.M. Programs included evening classes in basic literary skills, bookkeeping, and accounting, a building and loan association, a Coal Club cooperative that sold coal to its members at wholesale prices, a job placement bureau, a library, and a recreation room. Monthly dues were twenty-five cents. Eventually, other parishes organized similar clubs attracting more than ten thousand members.

This was only one example of Episcopal churches and other Protestant churches exemplifying a different kind of social teaching in the midst of much industrial and social strife. Arising from such came "social Christianity," understood by many in the Episcopal Church as a summons to be a catalyst for some rapprochement between the two opposing forces of capital and labor, whose battles against each other in many ways resembled those of the Armagnacs and the Burgundians in fifteenth century France.

Social Christianity programs paralleled what has come to be called in the twentieth century the Social Gospel movement in mainstream churches and seminaries. Fueled by such leaders as Washington Gladden (1836–1918), Congregationalist pastor in Brooklyn, New York, and later in Columbus, Ohio, and considered by many to be the "father" of the Social Gospel; Stephen Colwell (1800–1871), Presbyterian layman, iron merchant, and trustee of Princeton Theological Seminary: Richard Ely (1854–1943), an Episcopal layman and university economist whose widely read book *The Social Aspects of Christianity* (1889) made him one of the most influential figures at the time (he was also secretary of the more radical Christian Social Union); and Walter Rauschenbusch (1861–1918), pastor of the Second German Baptist Church in New York City, later professor of church history at the Rochester Theological Seminary (now a part of the fused Colgate-Rochester-Crozier-Bexley Hall theological complex), and author of the famous *Christianity and the Social Crisis* (1907), the Social Gospel thrived on outrage at the existing social injustices and inequities, particularly in the cities. It died out shortly before the First World War.

Its leaders felt that competition, profit-taking, individual greed and selfishness lay at the root of the social malaise suffered by the poor and the workers. Gladden wrote: "the state of the industrial world is a state of war. . . .' While the conflict is in progress, labor has the same right that capital has to prosecute the warfare. . . ." Instead, they taught cooperation, profit-sharing, communal responsibility, brotherhood among all classes, and social justice. As God was also at work in the social order, the Kingdom of God could be established on earth. Rauschenbusch said, "[the Social Gospel] is the religious reaction to the historic advent of democracy. It seeks to put the democratic spirit, which the Church inherited from Jesus and the prophets, once more in control of the institutions and teachings of the Church."[8]

Other experiments focusing on ministry to workers and the poor in the Episcopal Church in addition to St. Mark's program were also taking place. In 1874, the first Episcopal Church Congress with bishops, clergy, and laity assembled in New York to discuss issues related to capital, labor, and private property. In 1887, under the leadership of the Reverend William Reed Huntington (1838–1918), the Church Association for the Advancement of Interests of Labor (CAIL) was organized in New York. Its principles included (1) recognizing God as the Father of all and the brotherhood of all classes; (2) accepting labor as the exercise of body, mind, and spirit and a sacred duty for everyone; (3) upholding the social worth of labor and its importance for enhancing and affirming the laborer; (4) fair wages for the laborer's work. Among its members were thirty-eight American bishops, four Canadian bishops, and Frederick Huntington, father of William and the Bishop of Central New York, who was its first president.

Episcopal Social Teachings in the Late Nineteenth Century

Theological reflection about social problems and issues in the Episcopal Church largely took place through the Pastoral Letters in the late nineteenth century, although there were theological fragments in statements about social policy and programs at that time as well. Curiously, even though the Episcopal Church had worked among the Indians for a long period of time—the Chippewa in Minnesota and the Oneida in Wisconsin, for example—not to mention Bishop Henry Whipple's untiring ministry in Minnesota, none of the Pastorals during this time addressed their plight, the government's wars against them, or the injustices inflicted upon them by settlers and businessmen. Lacking information could hardly be claimed, since Custer's defeat and the discovery of gold on Indian lands commanded national attention.

Pastorals, however did address the capital-labor strife, saying that in such conflicts the church sympathized with the "weaker and suffering classes; victims of social wrong, of unequal laws, of intemperance in drinks . . . and sometimes of merciless wealth."[9] Their theological teachings focused on a model of the church as the "organic Body" of Christ from which faith flows, with Christians acting as exemplars of God's love so that "the outcast and alien and captive, the overtasked and underpaid, would learn to love and bless the Ministry which they have cursed . . . ; capital and labor might worship side by side."[10] But in the 1886 Pastoral the bishops shifted from a theological model of the church as advocate for the weaker classes to a model of the church as mediator between opposing forces, labor and capital. The Letter reminded the wealthy of their responsibility toward the poor and workers as their brother's keeper, but added:

> These are not days to preach platitudes about doctrine, or to philosophize about religion. The Church must, in the spirit of Christ, be the *mediator* [italics added] to reunite these sundered bonds. The rights of labor are primary rights, with which neither the tyranny of mobs nor the oppression of capital may interfere. The rights of capital are not less sacred, to enjoy the reward of honest labor and wise forethought, and use for the benefit of others.[11]

Immigrants' problems were also briefly addressed in the 1883

Pastoral, noting that, as Jesus provided for the bodily hunger of the crowds in his day as well as their souls, so Christians must imitate his ministry. But it neglected to address the growing Protestant nativist movements that were anti-Catholic and violent. Most of the immigrants were Catholic. Nativism was so rampant in many of the cities that in the 1884 presidential election, supporters of the Republican party felt free to publish advertisements denouncing the Democratic party as a party of "rum, Romanism, and rebellion." On the whole, Pastoral Letters during this period focused on in-house spiritual and moral matters.

Episcopal Social Teachings in the Early Twentieth Century

The problems of the nineteenth century inaugurated the twentieth century and led to a second source of Episcopal social teachings: General Convention joint commissions and committees and their reports. In 1901, a Joint Commission on Relations of Capital and Labor was established to give guidance to the church and to announce to the public that the Episcopal Church stood ready to act as a broker in the social conflicts of the times. The resolution setting up the joint commission commented that the church as "friend and counsellor of all sorts and conditions of men, rich and poor alike" would violate its divine mandate from Christ "if she were not the friend of the laboring man and did not hold his welfare dear to her heart as that of the employer."[12]

The joint commission's first report was strange. Rather than setting out theological guidelines for Christian involvement and concern, it gave a hurried philosophical overview of the cause of strikes and labor disputes, which it based on trust and distrust existing between labor and capital. This may have been due to both its mandate from the Convention and its own internal understanding of *commission* as a formal board of enquiry used in governmental and political parlance. The commission said it was to (1) study the purposes of labor organizations; (2) investigate the reasons for industrial strife currently taking place; and (3) be available as mediators and arbitrators "with a view to bring about mutual conciliation and harmony in the spirit of the Prince of Peace."[13] The first report, however, neither analyzed the economic structures that caused the suspicion and mistrust nor examined the separate agendas which each party pursued.

Now, the model of the church was that of reconciler of opposites regardless of their respective economic and social circumstances or their hold on power and political influence in society at the time. The church did rebuke those who depreciated and blamed the embryonic labor movement for causing social strife: "The lockout and the strike are of the same nature, and there is no great difference between such endeavors." The report supported the principle of trade unions, and noted that "without organization the standard cannot be maintained in the midst of our present commercial conditions."[14]

In the commission's 1907 report, the church moved toward a theological understanding of labor for Christians. Adapting a statement from the Presbyterians, it agreed: "The labor question is fundamentally a moral and a religious question, and that it will never be settled upon any other basis." The church was to uphold the moral aspect of labor over against a mere economic emphasis.

> Capital should be taught its duty of treating labor fairly, listening to its complaints patiently, and redressing its grievances wherever possible. . . . Labor, on the other hand, must be taught respects for the rights of capital, reliance upon reason and persuasion, and a knowledge that violence and lawlessness are unworthy of a cause which claims to be the cause of humanity.[15]

The church reaffirmed its approval of the theological model in the commission's earlier 1904 report: Episcopal clergy and bishops were to referee disputes and conflicts between labor and capital. As preparation, they were urged to read a list of books then attached to the report. It also criticized both the clergy for their hitherto indifference about assuming such a role and the church for failing officially to coordinate any such efforts. Several unofficial, voluntary Episcopal groups working with trade unions, such as CAIL, CSU, the Companions of the Holy Cross, and the Eight Hour League, were mentioned. But it noted that there was not official body in the church to do the same. As a corrective, the commission proposed that it be made the permanent body responsible for promoting the church's model of reconciliation as well as education within and outside the church, even though the labor movement and workers justifiably were suspicious of the church.

The twentieth century also saw greater use of General Convention resolutions and memorials for the formation of social teachings in the Episcopal Church, though lacking the considered theological substance frequently found in Pastorals and joint commission reports. And with the addition of canons providing for a National (now Executive) Council that was authorized to speak for the church between General Conventions, by the 1920s all structures were in place shape church teachings dealing with social, political, and economic problems.

Notes

1. See Appendix B.

2. *Pastoral Letter of the Bishops of the Protestant Episcopal Church,* October 17, 1862, Archives of the Episcopal Church, Austin, Texas, p. 9.

3. Ibid., p. 8.

4. Ibid., p. 9.

5. Ibid., p. 11.

6. Samuel Eliot Morison, *The Oxford History of the American People,* Vol. 3 (New York: New American Library, 1972), p. 118.

7. Washington Gladden, *Working People and Their Employers* (Boston: Lockwood, Brooks and Co., 1876), p. 3.

8. Charles Hopkins, *The Rise of the Social Gospel in American Protestantism: 1865–1915* (New Haven: Yale University Press, 1940), p. 20.

9. *Pastoral Letter of the House of Bishops, 1883,* Archives of the Episcopal Church, Austin, Texas, p. 8.

10. Ibid., p. 9. Their reference to cursing the ministry has to do with the popularity of socialist movements among the workers that mistrusted the churches as a part of the Establishment's fear of Marxist doctrines about change at the time.

11. *Pastoral Letter of the House of Bishops, 1886,* Archives of the Episcopal Church, Austin, Texas, p. 10.

12. *Journal of the General Convention, 1901,* pp. 125-6.

13. *Journal of the General Convention, 1904,* p. 95.

14. Ibid., p. 97.

15. *Journal of the General Convention, 1907,* p. 527.

Chapter 4
Pictures of an Exhibition:
Episcopal Social Teachings I

War and Peace

The church's concern about war and peace has appeared ambiguous at times, as during the Indian wars in the nineteenth century, and forthright at other times, as during World War I and World War II. Apart from the 1817 Pastoral praising the 1776 war against the British as an act of "divine providence" and the 1832 Pastoral, written during the Black Hawk Indian War, in which the bishops said it is a Christian duty to obey civil authority if that authority acts within the guidelines of "Christian behavior," the Episcopal Church was strangely silent about issues of war and peace until the Civil War. This conduct may have been due to the church's perception of itself as guardian of or at one with the young nation's stability and patriotism. It also may have been a tactic to win approval as a suspect former British institution, many of whose clergy were pro-British.

The silence generated an uncritical and unreflective posture about war, even when the United States engaged in war against Tripoli (1801–5), England (War of 1812: 1812–15), the Sac and Fox Indians (Black Hawk War: 1832), Mexico (the Alamo: 1836, 1845–48), and especially during the brutal Indian wars. (The 1877 report of the board of missions praised the church's Indian work, but said nothing about the wars and injustices, past or present.)[1] And except for a plea at its 1886 General Convention urging the church to meet the spiritual needs of the soldiers fighting the Indians, again the silence.

Yet after the Civil War, the 1892 General Convention called war between Christian nations "a blot upon the fair name of Christians." And the 1898 Convention, meeting during the United States' war with Spain, said that war was un-Christian and changed the name of its War Cross to "Cross of Peace." But these were no more than pronouncements rather than theological teachings. And, curiously enough, the church continued to append to General Convention journals, which are the official and permanent record of the church, the 1865 canon prohibiting its clergy from bearing arms in the military. This canon was published continuously in the journals until 1910. The result has been that Episcopal social teachings about war and peace often reflect an ambivalence and the public mood at the time without giving careful attention to previous doctrines about war in the Christian tradition.

The ambivalence was noticeable in the 1913 Pastoral Letter. In 1912, the U.S. Marines invaded Nicaragua—the first of several invasions in that Latin American country—and occupied it until 1933. The 1913 Pastoral appropriately referred to the church as an "organized army" but otherwise ignored this act of military intervention in Latin America. Again, just prior to the United States joining the allies of World War I against the Germans, it invaded Mexico a second time (1913–16) and Haiti a first time (1915–34). The U.S. military occupation of small countries within the Western Hemisphere continued, such as the 1916 occupation of the Dominican Republic, which lasted eight years. But the church maintained a discreet patriotic silence about such aggression, possibly not wanting to distract from the greater national objective of preparation for war in Europe a year later.

World War I (called the Great War in Europe because of its enormous atrocities) lasted from 1914 to 1918, although the United States only fought the final 18 months. It was the occasion for unbridled patriotism and nationalism in the United States. Suspicions and accusations were heaved about with a fierceness comparable to that of the Ku Klux Klan and the White Citizens Councils when they accused Southern whites of being sympathizers to Negro causes in the 1930s through the 1960s. That fierceness was reminiscent of McCarthyism in the 1950s with its virulent abuse of civil liberties and constitutional rights under the umbrella of anticommunism. People suspected of being German sympathizers were often attacked physically, especially immigrants, be they German or non-German. One of the patriotic legacies of World War I that became a national ritual was the Pledge of Allegiance to the flag. Many states and cities required this ceremony in public schools after the war. (This peculiar American ritual of allegiance and loyalty to a flag—which does not occur in any other major democracy in the world—started in the late nineteenth century after the pledge was published in a magazine to mark the four hundredth anniversary of Columbus's landing in America.)

Some 3,000,000 men were conscripted into the military during that war. More than 360,000 died, 4000 were classified as conscientious objectors, of whom 450 were imprisoned, 1300 assigned to noncombatant jobs, and 1200 to jobs in industry and agriculture. The main peace churches opposing the war, the Quakers, the Mennonites, and the Jehovah's Witnesses, were abused by the public and frequently imprisoned for disloyalty. However, these churches supported conscientious objectors financially and morally. The American Friends Service Committee was organized in 1917 and recognized publicly for such assistance.

In his opening sermon at the 1916 General Convention, Daniel Tuttle, Bishop of Missouri and Presiding Bishop, preached about the "American flavor" of the Episcopal Church, possibly knowingly using it as *double entendre* in such highly patriotic times:

Anglican precedents we will study and respect and even admire, but in our respect and admiration we will leave them alone, unpracticed, if American spirit and American taste and American habit do not take to them. . . . We have a Church penetrating into all parts of the United States and its possessions. . . . Is that not American?

We are a united Church. We have no North, no South, no East, no West. There is no cleavage of separation on sectional lines of latitude or longitude, or for differences of race or color or class or taste. Is that not American?[2]

The bishops' Pastoral, however, the same year attacked what they saw as a relationship between social disorder in the United States and the aggressive and ugly nature of nationalism at the time. They called American nationalism "false patriotism" built on "unconsecrated prosperity which is bound to cause manhood to decay." They described war as "a *discipline* [italics added] which man has imposed upon himself." And even though the

United States was not yet at war, such a peace was shallow and not firm. "God hates a godless and empty peace as much as He hates unrighteous war." They linked nationalism and racism, on the one hand, and nationalism and greed, on the other. However, they also supported patriotism for the national cause against the Germans:

> [America] must expect of every one of her citizens some true form of national service, rendered according to the capacity of each. No one can commute or delegate it; no one can be absolved from it. National preparedness is a clear duty. . . . The only thorough preparedness is that exemplified and taught by Christ, the preparedness of character based upon life with God.[3]

The church's ambivalence was tested by the case of the Bishop of Utah, Paul Jones, who opposed the war. In 1917, his diocesan Council of Advice (then called a missionary district), the supreme judicatory in the diocese after the bishop, asked the House of Bishops to remove him for disloyalty and pacifist views toward the government's war efforts. During the debates, the bishops in 1918 resolved that participating in the war was a "moral necessity," without explaining why either theologically or in terms of Christian tradition. They defended a bishop's constitutional right to free speech, but said he should be mindful of the office he holds and therefore use some caution before rushing to exercise this right. In another resolution calling the demand for the bishop's resignation "an excited state of public opinion," they declined to accept Jones' resignation, which he had in fact submitted, and blamed agitated public opinion for the controversy. Jones resubmitted his resignation, which then was accepted by the bishops, who justified this reversal by saying that Jones' usefulness as a diocesan bishop was now impaired.

This was a church whose Anglican tradition abides by the model of a "bridge church," moving resolutely between Catholic and Protestant traditions as a reformed catholic church. This was also the church that began the modern ecumenical movement toward church unity in 1910 by proposing the first Faith and Order conference. So it was most peculiar that before and during the First World War, its bishops were silent or shy about drawing either on the Catholic tradition with its doctrine of just war or the

Protestant tradition with its Lutheran and Calvinist doctrines of war. The Episcopal bishops' attitude and statements about dissent hankered between suggesting, on the one hand, that critiques, whether social or theological, were letting the side down and therefore betraying the national cause and, on the other hand, thinking them peculiar as a loyal opposition within a democracy during such times. They also said nothing about the issues of pacifism and conscientious objection as viable ethical Christian alternatives, even though the canons of the church displayed a definite theological teaching about the mandate of the state and its use of force.

Pastoral Letters were issued each of the years that the United States fought the Great War, 1917–18. Yet apart from homiletical phrases and resolutions more suitable to sermons than to a corpus of considered Christian social teachings about war and peace, neither the bishops as guardians of the faith and public morality nor the General Convention produced substantial theological guidelines for the benefit of clergy, laity, and the general public that awaited some guidance from the mainstream churches. As World War II approached, the bishops in their Letters furthered truisms about peace, such as "everyone wants peace," rather than theology. However, an exception was their 1933 Pastoral that reminded the church that loyalty to the cross as Christians preceded loyalty to the state:

> Love of country must be qualified by love of all mankind; patriotism is subordinate to religion. The Cross is above the flag. In any issue between country and God, the clear duty of the Christian is to put obedience to God above every other loyalty.[4]

General Convention in 1933, the year the Reichstag elected Hitler Chancellor in Germany, reaffirmed the 1930 Lambeth's condemnation of war as a method for settling international disputes.

In 1931, the church moved to resolve its ambivalence about dissent and opposition to war. General Convention resolved to petition the government for a change in current immigration laws, so that immigrants who objected to war because of conscience could become U.S. citizens, something forbidden them at the time. In 1934, it created the Joint Commission on Non-

Combatant Service with the mandate to support congressional legislation for all "Christian men who, though prepared to risk their lives in non-combatant service, are prevented from their conscience from serving in the combatant forces of the United States of America."[5] An effort to abolish this joint commission in 1937 failed. In 1940, support of conscientious objectors became a program at the national church headquarters, and the head of the department of Christian Social Service was mandated to be the official registrar in the Episcopal Church. But the church rejected giving financial assistance to those interned in federal work camps, and whose families received no allowances during their internment. In 1939 the unofficial Episcopal Pacifist Fellowship (now renamed the Episcopal Peace Fellowship) was founded on Armistice Day, November 11th.

In the religious world, perhaps the most momentous event was the formation of the German Confessing Church (*Bekenntniskirche*) and its issuance of the now famous 1934 Barmen Declaration, written largely by Karl Barth (1886-1968) but approved by mainly the Reformed Church pastors at Barmen in the Rhineland. This declaration insisted on the uncompromising independence of God's revelation in Jesus Christ and his word from all national and cultural powers. The Word of God is the primary source of obedience for Christians, and Jesus Christ is their only Lord, contrary to the claims made in Nazi Germany by the pro-Hitler "German-Christian" groups. Likewise, the church is inclusive of all cultures and races rather than exclusive. The church, said Barmen (with considerable courage, given the massive displays of German patriotism and nationalism), acknowledges the state, but not as a divine or natural order given by God that can demand the same kind of ultimate obedience as the Word of God. Rather the state is a human creation with an assignment by God to fashion our temporal existence. Jesus Christ continues to be lord over the state and its authorities just as he is lord over the church and all of creation. Barmen was really a theological protest against natural theology, a theological position the Nazis used knowingly to their advantage both with Catholics and Lutheran Christians.

The 1934 General Convention in Atlantic City reaffirmed the 1930 Lambeth statement about war and the Pastoral resoundingly denounced war also in stirring phrases:

War is murder on a colossal scale. The only armed force, whether on land or sea, which is justifiable, is a constabulary designed to regulate and safeguard those interests that have to do with the prosecution of an orderly social and economic life. . . . The Christian Church cannot and will not deny loyalty and fealty to its Lord by being partner in any scheme, national or international, that contemplates the wholesale destruction of human life. It refuses to respond to that form of cheap patriotism that has as its slogan, 'In times of peace prepare for war.' It regards as wicked the waste of the nations' wealth in the building of vast armament and the maintenance of greatly augmented forces on land and sea.[6]

Two years later in violation of the Versailles Treaty, Hitler resurrected the Reichswehr (the German army), and remilitarized the Rhineland. Benito Mussolini's troops invaded and occupied the ancient, poor nation of Ethiopia during 1935–36. In Spain General Francisco Franco led insurgents in civil war against the republican government in 1936. Thus, in less than 20 years all of Europe, still healing from the first war, quivered yet again over rumors of war. The infamous appeasement pact between Hitler, England, and France in Munich in 1938, thought to be the balm in Gilead all were hoping for, instead licensed Germany to seize the Sudentenland in Czechoslovakia and Poland in 1939.

In 1937, General Convention resolved that the Episcopal Church should cooperate with and support existing peace movements. In their Pastoral, the bishops said modern war could no longer be justified, as it can no longer be limited to battalions of armed men. (They might have possibly been thinking of the air power, chemical weapons, and the mechanized canons of the first war that were used against defenseless cities and civilians.) Again, war was linked to social injustices: "It is highly important that nations renounce war, but first there must be the abandonment of that group selfishness which is satisfied at the expense of the weak and ignorant."[7]

The 1939 Pastoral, coming after England and France had declared war on Germany, was devoted entirely to the subject of war. Entitled "In Days of War," it was the most deliberate and theologically considerate teaching on war since the 1862 Pastoral. Reasserting the foundations for social teachings outlined in 1865:

Scripture, the context or situation, the Prayer Book, and a "church-type" (Troeltsch) concept of the church, the bishops denied that the Christian God is abstract or tribal. "He has no favorites among races of tongues or peoples." But he is a just and freedom-giving deity, described as "the terrible gift." War is not willed by God, but is an instrument of national policy chosen and molded by humanity in its freedom, even though it is a "hideous denial of God." They admitted that at times when all else fails, nations go to war, but God does not will war. Nor is it the case that any one nation is guilty or guiltless; all of humanity share in the evil conditions which cause war. Jesus Christ is both the judgment of our straying from God's will and the only sure foundation for finding peace. "How do you know what God wills," asked the bishops rhetorically, "how can you tell when you are on God's side? Our answer is certain and sure. It is not in a book but in a Person, not in a law but in a Life . . . the divine Person and Life and Spirit of Jesus Christ." One must love country as a dutiful Christian, but "the Cross comes before the flag."[8]

Peace and War

After the Second World War, the bishops emphasized peace as a concrete possibility and objective for Christians, rather than preparation for war. Their 1945 Pastoral, however, continued to connect peace with the social context and moral character of America:

> These evil spirits (!) do not confine their operations to the nations with which we are at war. They are here in America, infiltrating our political, industrial, social, and domestic life. They fill our penitentiaries, jails, and mental hospitals with their victims. They set race against race, class against class. They poison, distort, and destroy the souls of men. Always deadly, they find added opportunity in war and in the aftermath of war.[9]

A relationship exists between the external control of such spirits and the internal authority of Christ and his gospel for the Christian; therefore, a renewal of Christian allegiance and duty to Christ and the church was called for. "So the warfare of the Prince of Peace against sin and degradation is won by men and women who offer their lives for Christ's service at home and abroad."

In 1962 and 1979, the church moved more aggressively toward teaching peace as a central objective. The bishops' 1962 Pastoral dealt theologically with contemporary Pentagon terms often seen in the media (such as *preventive war, nuclear deterrent, obligation bombing*) under the light of Christian doctrines about war. The year 1979 saw (1) the creation of a Joint Commission on Peace, forerunner of the Standing Commission on Peace organized in 1985; (2) a reiteration of and reception into the Episcopal corpus of social teachings of the 1978 Lambeth Conference resolution on "War and Violence," which basically reaffirmed the 1930 Lambeth teaching that was is unacceptable to Christians as a means for settling international problems; (3) rejection of a peace-time draft and compulsory national service, except in the case of a national emergency declared by Congress.

The 1962 Pastoral was the most determined effort this century to provide theological and ethical guidance for the church and the public. Previous Episcopal statements on peace had been published: (1) the 1931 General Convention resolution urging the United States to join the League of Nations and World Court "as evidence of our desire for world peace and as the contribution of a great and powerful nation to the stabilization of the world"; (2) the 1934 General Convention's rejection of war as a means for settling international disputes between nations and its incompatibility with the teachings of Christ; (3) the bishops' special message on peace at the 1937 General Convention; and (4) reports of the Joint Commission on Non-Combatant Service to the 1937 and 1940 General Conventions.

But the impetus for a more thorough analysis of the issue of peace no doubt was the absolutely unimaginable human and ecological waste envisioned from a nuclear war that was riveted into the consciousness of the church and indeed America after the atomic bombing of Hiroshima and Nagasaki in 1945 by the United States, and the continuing cold war between America and the Soviet Union. In 1962, the bishops issued four Statements about social issues instead of a Pastoral Letter. They acknowledged that the increase of nuclear weapons and missiles and changed ideological and economic conditions impelled new theological appraisals of peace. Describing their approach as *Christian realism*, a theological concept made popular by the ethicist Reinhold Niebuhr, the Episcopal bishops spoke against total war, saying it lacked any moral merit and made no positive contribution toward peace. They did agree on the concept of limited wars, provided there are clearly defined objectives. Furthermore, reflecting an Augustinian view of sin in society, they said the legacy of corporate sin in the world obliges the United States to remain "strong militarily as long as the threat of military attack from without remains."

The bishops defended the idea of a nuclear deterrent, a position diametrically opposed to that of the Methodist bishops' Pastoral Letter *In Defense of Creation: The Nuclear Crisis and a Just Peace*. They linked it to corporate sin, without spelling out what they meant by deterrent. They also repudiated the concept of massive retaliation in the event of nuclear warfare. They supported the position that the production, ownership, and threatened deployment of nuclear weapons necessitated a kind of strategy for an international police permitted under the umbrella of the just war doctrine. That doctrine includes stating a just intent to restore peace and justice after a war, discriminating between populations to be attacked, and having a just cause for starting a war, such as "an aggressor nation intent upon military conflict," which the bishops cited.[10] Niebuhr's concept of *Christian realism* was particularly apparent in the bishops' teaching about what a Christians can do personally: "Encouragement of Christians for thorough study of the problems of disarmament . . . balancing wisely the requirements of national security and the Christian obligation to seek to settle conflicts by means other than war."[11] Interestingly enough, no sections were devoted to a theological understanding of aggression or cooperation in the midst of a sin-infected social order.

The most recent definitive document about war and peace was the 1982 report of the Joint Commission on Peace entitled *To Make Peace*, which was adopted as the official statement of the church at the 1985 General Convention. The document gave a systematic analysis of the issues based on Scripture, Christian tradition, and the social context. The Catholic bishops had already issued drafts of their Pastoral Letter on peace, the final draft of which would later be published in 1983. The Methodist bishops were also completing their Pastoral that was published in 1986. Additionally, the World Council of Churches, meeting in Vancouver, Canada, in the summer of 1983, had rejected the concept of a nuclear deterrent:

Nuclear deterrence is unacceptable because it relies on the credibility of the *intention to use* nuclear weapons: we believe that any intention to use weapons in mass destruction is an utterly inhuman violation of the mind and spirit of Christ which should be in us. We know [however] that many Christians and others sincerely believe that deterrence provides an interim assurance of peace and stability. . . .[12]

Furthermore, in their 1982 Pastoral Letter the bishops rather self-consciously admitted that they were echoing more secular fears about war than relying on a theological rationale or tradition. They again affirmed the need for a "dedicated military," but observed that many Christians would disagree. Also they rejected the idea that Christians can have "dual citizenship," thereby compelling them to obey one set of moral criteria in the secular world and another in a Christian world. They stressed a "heavenly citizenship," meaning that the claims of the kingdom of God as the first allegiance and obedience for the Christian transcend all political systems; indeed for the Christian the kingdom of God is a "corrective clarity" for all earthly political systems.

However, in a shift from their 1962 Statement that morally justified a nuclear deterrent, the bishops charged that the United States arms strategy was based on fear of the Soviet Union. This fear in effect imprisons both peoples and governments: "From whence shall come the moral freedom to break the spiraling thrall of seeking security in instruments that only purchase a diminished safety for both countries and a mounting insecurity for the whole world?"[13] Instead they pointed to the unannounced United States policy of deterrence based on a massive first-strike against urban populations and rural areas as a policy based on evil intention. They also called for the cessation of unlimited production and deployment of nuclear weapons.

American fever to match the Soviet Union weapon for weapon appears to be damaging the personality structure of a whole generation . . . [and] distorts the spiritual and moral formation of children. Salvation lies with Christ, not with nuclear weapons or even disarmament, as important as the latter is toward peace. And to show their determination to bring the benefits of prayer to efforts toward peace and nuclear disarmament, the bishops obliged "to weekly fasting and daily prayer for peace."[14]

The document *To Make Peace* also gave the pros, cons, and mixtures of prevailing arguments, and spelled out the tensions and ambiguities for the church and Christians when they give allegiance to the state and allegiance to the Christian faith, which it called the "dual citizenship". It noted the tension between the need for national defense and security in the modern state against a perceived enemy and the dangers of total devastation in a nuclear war that destroys not only the enemy but also non-enemies as well. A nuclear deterrent was "at best a necessary evil for the short term. . . . [I]ts primary purpose [is] the buying of a little more time to work for other, more peaceful, less apocalyptic alternatives."[15] At the same time Christians also could hold honorable anti-war positions: the pacifist position, the limited use of weapons, having nuclear weapons as a brake or deterrent in the international order. Resolutions at the 1982 General Convention reflected how far the church lacked a consensus about the Christian and culture in military matters. Even though a clear theological corpus and a definitive social ethic were not evident, still the resolutions had some substance that can be discerned as social teachings. First, the 1930 Lambeth teaching about war was reendorsed. Second, Christians engaged in nonviolent civil disobedience against military and defence policies of the state are to be supported and encouraged:

> That this General Convention urges all members of this church to support by prayer and by such other means as they deem appropriate, those who engage in such non-violent action, and particularly those who suffer for conscience sake as a result . . . [and] to consider the implications for their own lives of this call to resist war and work for peace. . . .[16]

That is, members are to support even those who disobey laws related to war, much like the peace churches. Third, a nuclear "freeze" on the production of further weapons is morally permissible, provided that the freeze is bilateral and not unilateral, as a first step in nuclear arms reduction. The United States and the Soviet Union would have to agree to a 50 percent reduction in all arms with safeguards to see that neither side cheated.[17] The church also endorses the idea of the United States making "no first strike" with its nuclear weapons in the event of war. [18]

In the long run, Episcopal social teachings that allow Christians to dissent from obeying and respecting the laws of the state through civil disobedience also challenge the doctrine of the just war. That doctrine calls for Christians consenting to war, if the war advances the cause of a duly constituted state, which the United States certainly is, and which always announces national interest or security or protection of American citizens as reasons for going to war. And the duly constituted state practices its legitimacy through its laws. But not obeying the laws, such as objecting to statutes and laws supporting war, negates the legitimacy and the just cause of the war, as well as the state, in this case the United States, for that Christian.

Certainly, this was the case with the resolution on refusal to participate in war. It linked war resistance and "selective" pacifism to the fact that the nuclear technology of modern warfare means war no longer can be limited and discriminating, therefore falling outside the just war doctrine: "non-violent refusal to participate in or prepare for war can be a faithful response of a member of this Church and a decision to participate in war should be made only after careful and prayerful consideration."[19]

This text was reaffirmed at the 1988 General Convention, indicating that the Episcopal Church had distanced itself from the 1862 Pastoral, which taught that Christians ought not resist the Constitution and government of the United States since both are vested with a mandate and ordinances ordained by God in Scripture. Similarly, during the 1980s when many male college students and others refused to register with the Selective Services as required by law, the Episcopal Church taught conscience as a legitimate basis for supporting such people, particularly those in minority groups and poor communities.

In resolutions passed at both the 1982 and the 1985 General Conventions, the church also called for a nuclear freeze and a lowering of defense costs in order to have an "economic conversion of our national resources, especially our labor." Furthermore it opposed the Strategic Defense Initiative (or "Star Wars") and authorized a letter to Congress stating its opposition to funding such research.

Finally, with an increasing U.S. military budget and a

resurgence of Cold War ideology (whereby the Soviet Union was denounced as an eternal mortal enemy by a U.S. President, who publicly marked it as an "evil empire"), the church cautioned against the moral danger to Christian ethics when citizens of America and Russia always view each other as the permanent enemy. To counterbalance such negativity, it directed its national education staff to develop educational materials on Soviet culture, values, politics, and religion for distribution to parish Christian Education programs. (Oddly enough, the reason given for such a mandate was celebrating the 1000th anniversary of the Russian Orthodox Church rather than any kind of Christian ethic of love for one's enemies.)

Commentary

Tensions and uneasiness frequently have been a part of the relationship between the Christian faith and war beginning with the New Testament, particularly St. Paul, and the early patristic fathers of the church. Even in modern Christianity, military images are evoked, for example, in the very name of the Salvation Army. The Episcopal Church has a Church Army. Jesus himself sounded militaristic when he said, "I have not come to bring peace, but a sword." At the same time, he seemed antiwar when he scolded Peter: "He who lives by the sword shall die by the sword." Such language is not unique to the early Christian tradition. It is now known that in daily life in the Roman Empire during the time of Christ and the early church the language and culture were full of military terminology.[20]

One of the earliest Christian opponents to war was Marcion of the second century. Marcion and his followers contended that the Christian gospel is a gospel of love, which led them to reject the God of the Old Testament for being a warrior-god, warlike, wrathful and vengeful. Jesus Christ of the New Testament is compassionate and full of love. (By contrast, the apocryphal gospels, which were also popular in the early Christian communities, depict a very different Jesus than the loving person in our four Gospels. There he exercises vengeance and great power.)[21]

Tertullian (c.160–225), an early Latin father (in contrast to the patristics who wrote in Greek), wrote in *On Idolatry* that a Christian cannot serve in the military and remain a good Christian nor can anyone who has fought in war join the Christian faith: "There is no agreement between the divine and the sacrament,[22] the standard of Christ and the standard of the devil, the camp of light and the camp of darkness. One soul cannot be due to two masters—God and Caesar."[23] Some scholars think Tertullian banned Christians from the military because the oath of allegiance (*sacramentum!*) required worshipping Caesar as a god and sacrificing meat to idols. However, others dispute this interpretation. Certainly in another Christian commentary from the third century, the *Canons of Hippolytus* (ca. 170–256), Christians and candidates for baptism were forbidden to serve in the military. Those who became Christians during their military service or were compelled to join the military were forbidden to kill.

The very first official recognition of the Christian faith as the established religion of the empire happened during war. Emperor Constantine hoisted a Roman military standard embroidered with the first two letters of the Greek word for Christ, X and P, because of his vision that said: "In this sign you shall conquer." Shortly after that war, attributed to the Christian god, he exempted Christians from their military oath: "we leave them perfect liberty of choice, either to occupy their former stations . . . or after an honorable discharge, to live in undisturbed tranquillity."[24]

The just war doctrine, advanced by Augustine, Aquinas, and others, insisted that for Christians to support a war, it must meet several conditions: First, war must be declared by a legitimate government (*auctoritas principis*). Second, it must have a just intent (*justa intentio*) of restoring peace when complete. Third, it must have a just cause (*justa causa*). That is, it is a vindication of justice in response to a serious evil or attack. Fourth, it must be the last resort after trying everything else (*jus ad bellum*). Fifth, a reasonable hope of victory must be presumed. During the conduct of war (*jus in bello*), certain conditions intended to promote justice are to be met: *discrimination*, meaning respect for the rights of the enemy and no wanton violence and uncalled-for atrocities, and *proportionality*, meaning that the damage inflicted upon an enemy people must be in proportion to the ends sought. War for the sake of war is forbidden.

In the Anglican tradition, war is dealt with in article 37 of the Articles of Religion (1571), which are found in every edition of the

American Prayer Book, though assent to the articles is not obligatory in the Episcopal Church as it is in the Church of England: "It is lawful for Christian men at the commandment of the Magistrate to wear weapons and serve in the wars." The historical context for this pronouncement was the medieval view that as the state and church are one in God's creation, the sovereign of England is head of state and the *temporal* "supreme head in earth" of the Church of England. Consequently, every Anglican subject (and indeed dissenters as well) in England owed obedience to the state through the sovereign. Furthermore, the Supremacy Act of 1534 obliged bishops and clergy to assent to the sovereign. The Crown had "full power and authority . . . to redress, reform, order, correct, restrain and amend all such errors, heresies, abuses, offenses . . . which by any manner, spiritual authority or jurisdiction ought or may lawfully be reformed. . . ."[25] Therefore the article, no doubt including both of these ideas, permits Christians to engage in war when ordered to do so by the state, in this case, the Crown, as the legitimate, duly constituted political authority.

In the West, the first "peace" church was the Mennonites, followers of the teachings of the German Menno Simons (1496–1561). Simons taught nonviolence and nonparticipation in war. The Mennonites migrated to Pennsylvania at the invitation of William Penn, who gave them 18,000 acres of land, which included present-day Germantown. The Quakers (Society of Friends), another peace church founded by George Fox (1624–91) as a Christian peace group in England, settled first in New Jersey and later in Pennsylvania. They became forerunners in tolerating religious diversity and pluralism. Still another peace church was the Church of the Brethren, founded by Alexander Mack (1619–1735), also a radical German pietist like Simons, who migrated to Pennsylvania in 1719. The Brethren are strong in the Midwest.

In the Church's Teaching Series, an explicit theological appraisal of peace and war is lacking. The pacifist position is summarized, supplemented by general thoughts about the nuclear arms race. This absence of a definitive theological analysis of this issue and others has frequently been used as a shield by Episcopal clerics and bishops to defend the unclarity in much of the church's social thought and ethics; hence the wide tolerance of issues in the church. The question is whether this is responsible conduct when clarity from religious bodies is wanted in public discourse.

The eminent Swiss theologian, Karl Barth, reminds us that modern warfare and preparation for war in a nuclear age no longer means simply neutralizing the enemy. Rather "no more and no less than killing, with neither glory, dignity nor chivalry, with neither restraint nor consideration in any respect" is at stake. Barth contends that the issue of preparing for a just war within the context of nuclear weapons carries the assumption that war is a normal function of the state.[26] But Christians must rethink the just war doctrine under such conditions because (1) war as an action or as a policy engages all citizens, whether directly in combat or indirectly at home preparing for and supporting future warfare, or psychologically behaving and living in society without questioning such an assumption; (2) war necessitates an enemy and the killing of people, who fight for the other side and are enemies only because they believe in the truth of their cause just as we believe in the truth of our cause; (3) war means not only killing, but also committing other sins as well: stealing, burglary, arson, lying, deceit, slandering, even fornication.[27] For all these reasons, Barth says, in light of the commandment against killing, "[It] is no part of the normal task of the state to wage war; [the state's] normal task is to fashion peace in such a way that life is served and war is kept at bay."[28]

Episcopal social teachings that first focused on war and peace and then on peace and war reflect the groanings of a church that has not deliberated theologically the role of the state since the Civil War shattered the body politic of the United States. The Episcopal Church as a child of the British Establishment embraced what Ernst Troeltsch called the church-type of social teachings (as contrasted with the sect-type of social teachings). But as the church's role as a chaplain to mainstream Protestant establishment morality has shifted to that of a church on the margins of a more culturally diverse country with its different constituencies, so too have its teachings about war and peace moved from a "Christ of culture" position that baptized the best of American values, toward a more eclectic position: sometimes "Christ against culture," sometimes "Christ transformer of culture."

For instance, as we have seen, in spite of America's several attacks on other peoples and nations militarily throughout its young history, the Episcopal Church generally ignored them or neglected to provide a discernible authoritative, developed biblical and theological corpus about the nature of war and aggression. World War I failed to shake its basic theological concept about the legitimacy of the state's military ordinances and policy under the divine mandate of Romans 13. Loyalty was due it, therefore, during war, since as the bishops said in their 1862 Pastoral, resistance to legitimate political authority is resistance to God's ordinances, thereby meriting God's condemnation and the use of the state's police powers. Yet, even at that time and throughout the nineteenth century, as we saw, the church exempted its clergy from the military chaplaincy of the state with few exceptions.

At the same time until recently, this church with its claim as a reformed Catholic church drew neither from its Catholic tradition nor its Protestant tradition for theological guidance on the issue of the state and war. Ironically, such neglect of the Christian tradition about war occurred when the Episcopal Church as a reformed Catholic church in both traditions was preparing its innovative proposals for ecumenical discussions about issues dividing Catholics and Protestants. The first Faith and Order Commission grew out of these proposals. So at this time the Episcopal Church moved on two parallel tracks of tradition without linking the two. One track had to do with theological issues of church unity, proposed by a church shaped both by Catholic and Protestant doctrines and traditions. The other had to do with this church's episcopate and a national synod obliged to provide normative social teachings and ethics in times of national and international crises, but choosing to ignore Christian doctrines and positions about war.

Since World War I, it *has* supported public dissent and civil disobedience toward ordinances and laws of the United States supporting war. Although the stance of opposition to war based on conscience was approved as proper and legitimate conduct for Christians in a 1934 resolution on conscientious objectors, again the Episcopal Church and its bishops were silent about events within other branches of the Christian church sorting out issues of war and the authority of the state. This was most noticeable in its lack of reference to the Barmen Declaration and the Confessing Church in Germany, an event so outstanding that some churches have accorded Barmen the same significance as the Augsburg and other classical confessions of faith.

The atomic bomb, the subsequent arms race, and the concept of a nuclear deterrent have jarred not only the Episcopal Church, but other churches as well toward reexamining Christian doctrine about war. The current teaching is that war is un-Christian. But given the mistrust and suspicion between the two superpowers, the United States and the Soviet Union, the concept of a deterrent preventing war between them is preferred from a moral point of view: "a necessary evil for the short term . . . the buying of a little more time to work for other, more peaceful, less apocalyptic alternatives."[29] The church supports a "nuclear freeze", but has not provided a theological basis for such support, nor clarity about how the non-production of nuclear arms under a "freeze" can be reconciled with the concept of a deterrent, when the improvement and power of a superior deterrent necessitates continued research and production. The Catholic bishops in their Pastoral Letter on peace also upheld the concept of a deterrent in a contemporary world of ambiguities and evils, while continuing disarmament talks.[30] By contrast, the Methodist bishops' Pastoral called the concept of deterrent an idolatry, since it presumes the power of ultimate judgment and decision to destroy other nations and civilizations.[31]

The Episcopal Church does not support pacifism—the traditional morality found in the early church and the peace churches, as a social teaching—as an ethical position for all Christians. But it does hold to the right of dissent for reasons of belief and conscience and, indeed, maintains programs for dissidents and opponents to war. It has no clear teaching about "selective conscientious objection," a concept that arose during the Vietnam War, that is, those who may not be opposed to war as a concept, but may be opposed to particular wars.[32]

The Episcopal Church addressed an ethical issue about the impact of preparation for nuclear warfare on values and personal formation in American society. This impact has been acerbated by the enormous economic imbalance between outlays for nuclear and military armaments and those spent on social programs. Many ethicists have called the result *nuclearism*. That is, our formation and ethics are significantly influenced by the concept of a mortal enemy, i.e., the Soviet Union and Communism, as the justification for the continuous production of armaments for war and military technology. Whether considered a deterrent, or simply a part of the market ethic of supply and demand (when purchased by other countries), or *realpolitik*, arms are produced primarily to kill and pollute the ecological environment of other human beings. Nuclearism engages the entire population willingly or unwillingly both through the way we are educated and our value systems and morality. It also shapes the cultural context in which Christians and the church must ask critical questions about whether a love ethic can be normative for Christians. Ethicists say nuclear weapons have blurred the moral limits traditionally associated with conventional warfare because (1) of the possibility of unlimited, indiscriminate annihilation of the enemy and final contamination of his environment, and (2) the general acceptance of such a defense policy as a necessary part of modern statecraft.

In its document *To Make Peace* the Episcopal Church asked about the dehabilitating effect of nuclearism and its ethical values, such as the we/they dichotomy, unlimited arms competition, and a necessary nuclear superiority. The moral consequences are:

> Instead of a sense of security and comfort in the knowledge that we can kill each other many times over, there seems to be a growing sense on the part of many that we are more insecure and vulnerable than ever. . . . When our society becomes accustomed to the idea that, in its name, its representatives are prepared to launch weapons of mass destruction . . . it can become more easily become inured to and accepting of other dehumanizing social trends—e.g., the merchandizing of violence in the media; the irresponsible use of abortion as a means of birth control; easy resort to euthanasia. . . .[33]

But the deeper theological question is Barth's question: whether the state, having to cope with all the complex power structures, economic, industrial, and international forces and relationships, be they state capitalist, communist, socialist, or non-aligned, should be prodded by the church to pursue a national policy of *pacem in terra* instead of *bellum in terra*.

Pacifists and militarists are usually agreed in the fact that for them the fashioning of peace as the fashioning of the state for democracy . . . is a secondary concern as compared with re-armament or disarmament. It is for this order that Christian ethics must be opposed to both. Neither rearmament or dis-armament can be a first concern, but the restoration of an order of life which is meaningful and just.[34]

Notes

1. *Journal of the General Convention, 1877*, pp. 490-1.
2. *Journal of the General Convention, 1916*, p. 399.
3. Pastoral Letter in *Journal of the General Convention, 1916*, pp. 401-3 *passim*.
4. *Pastoral Letter Adopted by the House of Bishops*, Davenport, Iowa, November 9, 1933, pp. 6-7.
5. *Journal of the General Convention, 1934*, p. 329.
6. *Pastoral Letter by the House of Bishops*, Atlantic City, NJ., October 23, 1934, p. 6.
7. *Pastoral Letter, Adapted by the House of Bishops*, Cincinnati, Ohio, October 19, 1937, p. 5.
8. "In Days of War," *House of Bishops Pastoral Letter*, November 9, 1939, *passim*.
9. *Pastoral Letter*, Birmingham, Alabama, February 1945, p. 4.
10. Ironically, the United States called its invasion of Panama in January 1989 "Operation Just Cause."
11. *Statements of the House of Bishop—Fall 1962*, Archives of the Episcopal Church, Austin, Texas, *passim*.
12. *Gathered for Life*, Official Report, 6th Assembly World Council of Churches, Vancouver, Canada, 24 July -10 August, 1983 (Geneva: World Council of Churches and Grand Rapids, Mich.: Wm. B. Eerdmans, 1983), p. 75.
13. *The Pastoral, A Letter to the Church, 1982*, (No place given), p. 3.
14. Ibid., p. 4.
15. *The Blue Book: Reports of the Committees, Commissions, Boards, and Agencies of the General Convention of the Episcopal Church*, September 1982, p. 262.
16. *Journal of the General Convention, 1982*, p. C-122.
17. Ibid., p. C-125.
18. Ibid., p. C-127.
19. Ibid., p. C-123.
20. See Roland Bainton, *Christian Attitudes to War and Peace* (Nashville, Tenn.: Abingdon, 1960).
21. Adolf Harnack, *Militia Christi: The Christian Religion and the*

Military in the First Three Centuries, trans. David McInnes Gracie (Philadelphia: Fortress Press, 1981), pp. 46-7.

22. *Sacramentum* has two meanings in Latin: a visible sign or symbol of a spiritual reality and a military oath of allegiance.

23. Ibid., pp. 54-5.

24. Eusebius, *Life of Constantine*, vol. 2, p. 33. Quoted in Harnack, *Militia Christi*, p. 101.

25. Henry Betterson, ed., *Documents of the Christian Church* (New York: Oxford University Press, 1957), p. 322.

26. Karl Barth, *Church Dogmatics (Doctrine of Creation)*, III/4, trans. A.T. Mackay, et. al. (Edinburgh: T. & T. Clark, 1961), p. 453.

27. Ibid., p. 454.

28. Ibid., p. 458.

29. *The Blue Book*, September 1982, p. 262.

30. *The New York Times*, May 4, 1983, p. B16.

31. *In Defence of Creation: The Nuclear Crisis and a Just Peace*, The United Methodist Council of Bishops (Nashville, Tenn.: Grades Press, 1986), pp. 46-9.

32. See Paul Ramsey's essay in his *The Just War: Force and Political Responsibility* (New York: University Press of America, 1983), pp. 91-137.

33. *The Blue Book*, p. 265.

34. Barth, *Church Dogmatics*, III/4, p. 459.

Chapter 5
Pictures of an Exhibition:
Episcopal Social Teachings II

Race and Racial Affairs

A seventeenth century French physician, François Bernier (1620–88), is thought to have been the first European to use the category of *race* for classifying as well as "declassifying" human beings. He claimed four races: European, African, Oriental, and the Lapps. The Swedish botanist Carolus Linnaeus (1707–78), fostered the idea that a relationship existed between outward appearance, intelligence, and disposition. Thus, fair-haired, white-skinned Europeans were gentle, inventive, and incisive, while black, wooly-haired Africans were crafty, indolent, and governed by caprice and intrigue.

The modern medical science of comparative anatomy and the social science of anthropology left the legacy of racial categories still in popular use today. Comparative anatomy was introduced to the West largely by Johann Friedrich Blumenbach (1752–1840), a German physician who collected and wrote about human skulls. Blumenbach was enamored with classical Greek antiquity and ancient Greek civilization, a throw-back no doubt to the Renaissance period in Europe. Hence, he said that since the ancient Greek face with its symmetry and anatomy was the most perfect face and ancient Greek culture the highest expression of human intellect, the comparative study of different cultures through anatomy could tell us much about human history and development. He originated five races as a grid for comparative anatomy: Caucasian, Mongolian, Malayan, Ethiopian, and American.

Social anthropology, particularly under French influence, treated black culture as a culture beneath Greek and European cultures, thereby conveying a negative concept of Africa prevalent at the time. The French, particularly after Napoleon's return from Egypt at the end of the eighteenth century, believed that Egyptian culture was not of African origins, but of Mediterranean or Oriental origin and thus more akin to Greek-derived European culture. French painting in this period also conveyed this belief, convinced that black Africa could not produce Egypt's "high" culture. Another Frenchman, Comte Joseph Arthur de Gobineau (1816–82), author of a four-volume work about racial differences, *Essai sur l'inégalité des races humaines* (English: *The Moral and Intellectual Diversity of Races* in 1856 and *The Inequality of Human Races* in 1915), popularized the idea of the superiority of European (Nordic) races over Semitic and nonwhite races.

The Episcopal Church has struggled with the issue of race since blacks were first baptized at Jamestown, Virginia, in 1626. The fact that many of the patrician owners of plantations and their slaves resided in slave states like Virginia, North Carolina, and South Carolina, where the Episcopal Church was really the established church, only heightened the struggle. Bishops and many plantation owners in those states and other Southern states felt it both their Christian duty and a good protection of an investment to encourage religious instruction for the slaves, which indeed was undertaken. Hence, blacks are not newcomers to the Episcopal Church, nor is concern about matters of face a modern issue in the church.

Blackness as a phenomenon intrigued Christian writers as early as the second century, when Origen wrote his commentary on the Song of Songs. Its fascination for European thought and culture was especially apparent in Christian art, when a black Wise Man was represented for the first time in a fourteenth century Cistercian manuscript in Lilienfeld, Germany. By the fifteenth century this association of blackness and the Magi had become a convention in religious art, particularly in altarpieces and paintings. One of the best known artists who popularized this convention was the German painter, Hans Memling (1430–94).

Race and religion were joined in Virginia, where the Episcopal Church was first established in the United States, with the passage of its Fugitive Slave Law in 1661, the first law institionalizing slavery. This law allowed slaves to be baptized Christian, provided that "the conferring of baptisme doth not alter the condition of the person as to his bondage or freedom." In 1670, Virginia modified this clause by creating what I call "layers of privileged and underprivileged slaves." The law exempted from life-long bondage those whites who were baptized Christians when they first entered the colony. It called them "servants" instead of slaves. Nonbaptized slaves imported by land had limited bondage of 12 years if adults and 30 years if children at the time of entry—the privileged slaves. Nonbaptized Africans imported by sea were to be slaves for life—the underprivileged slaves.

The Bishop of London, Edmund Gibson (1669–1748; consecrated 1716; London: 1723), penned his infamous 1727 commentary about the link between Christian sacraments and slavery. He wrote that the gospel was indifferent to existing social conditions:

> The freedom which Christianity gives is a freedom from the bondage of sin and Satan, and from the dominion of men's lusts and passions and inordinate desires; but as to their *outward* condition, whatever it was before, whether bond or free, their being baptized and becoming Christians make no manner of change in it. . . . And so far is Christianity from discharging men from the duties of the station and condition in which it found them, that it lays them under stronger obligations to perform those duties with the greatest diligence and fidelity. [1]

Still, the Episcopal Church was the first white church to undertake work among the slaves through the Society for the Propagation of the Gospel (SPG) in 1701. By the end of the 1776 war with England, in the South, where the Anglican Church was particularly strong, slaves were a sizable portion of the population: 41 percent in Virginia, 44 percent in South Carolina, 27 percent in North Carolina, and 36 percent in Georgia. In contrast, in the North by the start of the eighteenth century, and certainly by the outbreak of the Civil War, most of the New England and Middle Atlantic states had dismantled their slave economy in favor of industrialization.

Although separate black congregations existed in the North, such as St. Thomas African Episcopal Church, Philadelphia (1794), St. Philip's Church, New York City (1810), Church of the Crucifixion, Philadelphia (1852), and the now defunct St. Philip's Church, Newark, New Jersey (1856), the strength of the Episcopal Church's work with blacks was in the South. Four-fifths of slave-owning Episcopalians lived in South Carolina, North Carolina, Virginia, Georgia, and the river delta country of Mississippi and Louisiana. In 1810 in South Carolina, the Society for the Advancement of Christianity in South Carolina was founded, which had special responsibility for mission work among the slaves. In 1834, the Bishop of Virginia in a Pastoral Letter entitled "The Duty Affording Religious Instruction to Those in Bondage," exhorted churches and priests to provide religious instruction for slaves in their environs. The first Bishop of Georgia, Stephen Elliott, also a South Carolinian, in his first Episcopal Address to the diocese in 1841 asked that religious schools be established for the slaves, and entreated his clergy "to consider them an integral part of [their] flock, watching over them as [they] do over the white children of their congregation," and present them for confirmation and admit them eventually to Holy Communion.

At the same time, many Southern clergy disagreed or were ambivalent about this "Christian" duty. The Reverend Frederick Dalcho, M.D., assistant minister at St. Michael's Church, Charleston, South Carolina, (whose memorial plaque hangs in the church's interior) preached a Fourth of July sermon that the holiday was only for whites. (An irony because St. Michael's and St. Philip's Church, the other oldest church in Charleston, had the largest colored work in the diocese.)

> The Declaration of the *Fourth of July* belongs exclusively to the white population of the United States. The American Revolution was a *family quarrel among whites*. In this the Negroes had no concern, their condition remained, and must remain, unchanged. They have no more to do with the celebration of that day, than with the landing of the Pilgrims on the Rock of Plymouth.[2]

As we have already seen, the issue of race and slavery divided the Episcopal Church geographically, politically, theologically, and liturgically during the Civil War. The nation's political division was also the occasion for the first social teachings of the Episcopal Church. Oddly enough, the 1865 Pastoral, written the same year Lincoln issued the Emancipation Proclamation liberating the slaves as an Executive Order, made no mention either of slavery or blacks. There are several reasons for this.

First of all, a great deal of tension existed as to whether the

Episcopal Church would reunite with the Confederate Episcopal Church, which claimed that it never left the church. The latter had its own canons and Prayer Book and, therefore, according to precedent established when the Protestant Episcopal Church itself became a self-governing church after the Revolutionary War with its own *Book of Common Prayer* in 1789, the confederate church was thus separate from the Protestant Episcopal Church. The *Episcopal Recorder* of the Diocese of Pennsylvania in its May 6 1865, issue called for the expulsion of Southern bishops who supported the South, declaring them rebels and felons who "should not be the last to suffer the penalties of treason" like military leaders in the Southern rebellion. Later, the same newspaper wrote disparagingly of a statement in an Episcopal newspaper called *The Southern Churchman* in which a Southern bishop lamented the defeat of the South. "In our judgment," editorialized the paper, "a more simple document, confessing the sins of slavery and rebellion . . . would have been more to the purpose."[3]

A second possible reason is that the Presiding Bishop, the Bishop of Vermont, John Henry Hopkins, was not only keen on the return of Southern bishops, but also was a known sympathizer of slavery. In 1861, he had published a book, *Bible View of Slavery*, in which he defended slavery as grounded in Scripture. During the 1865 General Convention that only two Southern bishops attended, Hopkins successfully prevented the passage of any resolutions condemning slavery or the South for seceding, even though the bishops in 1862 had denounced the South's rebellion and secession as a violation of the Word of God.

Even the 1868 Pastoral Letter failed to address slavery, although that year the Fifteenth Amendment to the Constitution was ratified, which gave the former slaves the right to vote and other civil rights. The Pastoral did speak of the family as a divine institution that is the foundation of the church's internal life. It addressed women and their role in society and commented negatively about "women who live at ease," obviously meaning women of leisure and what old-fashioned language might call "riotous living." Women in their daily life and habits were admonished to be role models "of whatsoever things are pure and lovely and of good report." Whether the bishops had in mind the militant women's movement, which was very visible and outspoken at the time, is not clear, particularly since that movement was incensed over blacks but not women being given the right to vote in the Fifteenth Amendment. In fact, because of this amendment, a period of virulent racism against blacks was initiated by some leaders in the feminist movement—a historical event that continues to make many blacks suspicious of the modern-day feminist movement under middle and upper-middle class domination and auspices.[4] Generally, however, the Pastoral dealt with the interior life and spirituality.

Nonetheless, while the Episcopal Church did not see fit to enunciate distinct social teachings about slavery and the marginalized in society, it did program nationally a new ministry to blacks through its Freedman's Commission. This commission, established at the Philadelphia General Convention in October 1865, linked mission to education. It was mandated to establish schools and orphanages for former slaves as a tool for converting them to the Christian faith and to the Episcopal Church. The commission also provided clothing, bedding, books, and other items needed for relief.

This linking of education and education as a strategy for the conversion of blacks was confirmed in the 1865 report of the church's African Mission, written by Bishop John Payne, after whom the all-black theological seminary in Petersburg, Virginia, was named in the 1870s:

> Africa is still a *heathen* country, and doubtless it was chiefly with reference to the heathen that our mission was undertaken by the Church [in 1835]. . . . The Episcopal Church, acting on the Scripture principle, 'While we have time, let us do good to all men, and especially unto them that are of the household of faith,' essayed to establish her services in the very infancy of the [Liberian] colony.[5]

During slavery, the Episcopal Church, like other Protestant churches, published special catechisms and collections of sermons written just for the slaves, usually reminding them of their duty to obey, to be industrious, and not to be rebellious. Favorite texts were Eph. 6:5-6, Col. 3:22-25, 1 Tim. 6:1-4, Titus 2:9-14, and 1 Pet. 2:18-25 among others. Although it was the established church in Virginia and South Carolina and the church of the planter class in other places, the Episcopal Church was still a small church of the elite, and its black membership was also small compared to that of other denominations in the South. Yet many Southern bishops and white clergy devoted much attention to work among the slaves. Some Southerners remained skeptical about the effectiveness of church's work in that region. W.J. Cash said the Episcopal Church could never grow in the South because its preachers could not preach with passion and its God was "without body, parts, or passion":

> The God demanded [in the South] was a God who might be seen, a God who *had* been seen. A passionate, whimsical tyrant, to be trembled before, but whose favor was the sweeter for that. A personal God, a God for the individualist, a God whose representatives were not silken priests but preachers risen from the people themselves. . . . Fully nine-tenths of the new planters—of the men who were to be masters of the great South—were, and despite some tendency to fall sway to Anglicanism as more high-toned, continued to be numbered among their adherents.[6]

The Freedman's Commission, however, continued the church's strategy for blacks. At the 1868 General Convention it reported:

> What has been done by us in this field must be regarded as an evidence of our good wishes toward these emancipated millions of the South than as a work commensurate with our responsibility or with the demands of the hour. We can claim no more than we have tried to educate a race suddenly elevated to political power and inequality in the midst of their ignorance and inexperience. . . . The Church has no proper call to engage in the work of school teaching at all, except as she can make it subserve her dominant purpose, viz: the gathering into her fold for religious instruction and discipline of those whom she teaches in her schools.[7]

That this commission was created by the Episcopal Church after the war is all the more remarkable when we recall that most blacks attending white churches, including the Episcopal Church, abandoned them for black churches after emancipation. At their own churches, they heard black preachers, created indigenous patterns of worship with their synthesis of African survivals and evangelical Christianity that spoke to their community and spirituality, and were leaders in charge rather than servants under the charge of whites.[8]

Before the Civil War, for example, four-fifths of slave-owning

Episcopalians lived in South Carolina, North Carolina, Virginia, and Georgia, where the bulk of the slave population lived as well. Of the total black Episcopal membership in the South estimated at about 6400, over 5000 lived in Virginia and South Carolina, while another 900 were in North Carolina.[9] In South Carolina, for example, the slave population outnumbered the white slave-owning population: in 1830, 55.6 percent of the entire population were slaves; in 1830, they were 58.6 percent.

At the 1869 General Convention meeting in New York, the Diocese of Georgia reported that there was such a drastic decline in black membership since 1866 that it had closed its best work among the slaves on the Ogeechee River along with other black missions along the Georgia coast, which made up 25 percent of the entire Episcopal population in Georgia. The 1877 General Convention heard a report lamenting that in South Carolina alone there were 2500 black communicants before the Civil War; yet after the war the black Episcopal population in the entire United States was less than half this number. The Diocese of South Carolina consoled itself that those remaining in the church were "of the better class of the colored population," meaning free blacks with education, property, and social status.[10]

But blacks in the South were jeopardized by more sinister events during the Reconstruction period after the Civil War, namely, the terrorist Ku Klux Klan, created in 1865, and Jim Crow laws, first enacted in 1867. The Ku Klux Klan originated as a male social club in Pulaski, Tennessee. The rash of Jim Crow laws succeeded in legalizing racial apartheid and legitimizing white supremacy throughout the South until the 1970s.

While the Klan also attacked Catholics and Jews, its primary target was blacks and black sympathizers, who were beaten, sexually mutilated, and lynched.[11] Its nightly acts of terrorism in black communities were even reported in national as well as local newspapers. By 1871 its membership was estimated to be 550,000. Its influence declined after that, but grew again with the influx of European immigrants in 1878–97 and 1898–1914, most of whom were Catholics and Jews. Black "crimes" ranged from a black threatening to take a white to court to registering to vote to being "disrespectful" to a white man to "watching" a white woman. Between 1882 and 1888 an estimated 600 whites were beaten or killed and about 450 blacks. By 1892, however, within one year

162 blacks were lynched over against some form of violence against 69 whites. This statistic continued to climb as lynching became the weapon for keeping blacks "in their place."[12]

Jim Crow laws were used to restrict black voting and to disenfranchise them from voting. Access to public accommodations by blacks was limited or segregated as was education. Some states like South Carolina, where the Episcopal Church was very much a part of the Establishment, passed laws excluding blacks even from learning marketable skills and trades in much the same way that South Africa's apartheid laws reserve certain jobs and professions for whites only. These laws, based on "black codes" the South passed in reaction to Reconstruction, were not opposed by a federal government headed by a friendly Southern president, Andrew Johnson from Tennessee, nor by Congress, even though Congress intended the original 1867 Reconstruction Acts to erode the sovereignty and authority of the former Confederate states and to advance blacks in all phases of civil life in those states.

Mississippi was the first Southern state to disenfranchise blacks. It amended its constitution in the 1890s. South Carolina followed soon behind and was joined by Louisiana, North Carolina, Ala-bama, Virginia, Texas, Oklahoma, and other states in the Deep South. Literacy tests for blacks but not for whites were required for voting. Blacks had to prove that they owned property to vote, and had to pay a voting poll tax. So-called *grandfather clauses* restricted the right to vote (in spite of the Fifteenth Amendment) to those whose ancestors had voted in 1860 or before.

By 1878, all the Southern states had separate systems of education for whites and blacks backed by law. These systems were supported by the historic *Plessy v. Ferguson* case in 1896 in which the Supreme Court ruled that the Constitution permitted racially segregated public facilities as long as they were "separate but equal." Hence, just as the Supreme Court was primarily responsible for attacking racial segregation in the 1950s and 1960s, so it was largely responsible for upholding racial segregation in the 1880s and 1890s. For example, in 1883 it invalidated the Civil Rights Act of 1875, which prohibited discrimination and in 1898 upheld literacy tests and poll-taxes for blacks.

Amid such violations, again as with the wars against the Indians, the Episcopal Church was silent in its social teachings about the subject of race and racism. The bishops in their 1886

Pastoral spoke of missionary work among blacks, calling them "our brethren, the children of God, the redeemed of our Saviour," but failed to address how the brutalities unleashed against these black "children of God" related to a Christian ethic or morality. It spoke of blacks as superstitious subjects for conversion rather than a marginalized people deprived of social justice:

> We bid you realize that their ignorance is dense, that their helplessness is absolute. While we rejoice to believe that God has given them many teachers . . . yet it is still true of the larger number that they are blind followers of blind guides and are, alas! satisfied wanderers in a wilderness of superstitious folly, believing themselves in the way of righteousness. . . . [T]hey need to be taught the simple Gospel of Jesus Christ, and to be trained as little children in the habits of Christian living.[13]

That the bishops could make this statement about black religion in spite of the fact that such black churches like the AMEs, the AMEZs, and the Baptists were quite active and vibrant among blacks in the postbellum period, particularly in the South, revealed the isolation between the races and white churches' woeful lack of knowledge of black religion.[14]

The only other mention of blacks during these violent years was the Pastoral Letter of 1895. It again regarded blacks primarily as subjects for conversion and assimilation into the national life: "[We] regret that their still imperfect ethical standard is so little aided by the ideas of religion most prevalent among them. . . . To redeem and elevate these people is a demand which the American Church cannot safely or reasonably decline."[15]

Black migration out of the South in large numbers began in the twentieth century. Whereas in the first U.S. census in 1790, the Negro population stood at about 757,000 after 180 years of slavery, by the end of the nineteenth century blacks numbered 7.5 million, 90 percent of whom lived in the South. At the time of World War I, blacks began their great migration North. Between 1900 and 1910, 170,000 blacks left the South, 50 percent of whom settled in the Northeast and the rest in the Midwest and West.

The percentage of blacks living in Northern urban areas between 1890 and 1910 increased from 20 percent to 27 percent. Some of the reasons for this migration, which lasted through the war years, were (1) the worn-out lands of the rural South where many blacks worked as sharecroppers; (2) severe damage to the cotton crops by the boll weevil from Mexico; (3) natural disasters that ruined the land in many parts of the South; (4) the industrial expansion of Northern industries; and (5) the reign of Jim Crow laws, lynchings, and mob violence, which also continued in the North.

This migration to areas already crowded with the European immigrants, who were also seeking jobs and economic betterment, led to the rise of the urban "ghetto," although the term itself is an export from medieval Europe. Conflict between largely rural blacks and immigrant unskilled workers competing for the same jobs, plus Northern racism led to rampant urban riots in the North. A resolution condemning violence and lynching was introduced at the 1904 General Convention, but was tabled because the committee reporting said, "it does not devolve upon this Convention to pass specific resolutions touching particular forms of crime or violence."[16]

Mob violence by whites against blacks, which caused many deaths, became increasingly characteristic of the American urban scene: Philadelphia; Chester, Pennsylvania; New York City; and especially East St. Louis, Missouri, and Houston. In the summer of 1919, more than twenty race riots flared up. White middle-class Americans were startled by the violence and the deaths, although they seldom dealt with the causes. Finally, the church at its 1919 General Convention stopped ignoring this social problem and passed a statement condemning mob violence and lynching. Understandably, the church was preoccupied with the war during the early twentieth century. However, when the war ended in 1918, the church, provoked by the urban riots, shifted from thinking of blacks only as subjects for education and conversion to addressing them as victims of injustices.

Preparing for a "Christ against culture" position, the first Pastoral Letter after the war, in 1919, sampled boldness:

> If the Church's mission threatens to carry us into unpopularity or contempt, let us remember that the Church's Master was the most unpopular and despised man of His day. . . . A Church afraid of the cross of unpopularity could never retain Christ in its life. If we distrust minorities let us remember that all the world was against Christ when he died.[17]

Lynching and mob violence were condemned. "The problem is one of our own creation. We must meet it by the same sure principles of brotherhood and common citizenship which the Church is never afraid to apply freely to every human problem." While such a statement just as easily could have been made by humanists or non-Christians without compromising their position at all, still it was a sign that the church was moving into unchartered waters in its social pronouncements.

The 1919 Convention set up a joint commission "to study the conditions under which the race is living in this country" as well as the state of the church's welfare programs for blacks. However, this apparently was only a "paper" commission, since there is no record of a report being submitted at the next General Convention, even though this was a part of its mandate. The church continued to wrestle with the issue of race. So once again, in 1931, General Convention set up a commission to report on the status of the Negro in the Episcopal Church at the next convention.

The commission's report to the 1934 Convention insisted that the Negro in the Episcopal Church be regarded without distinction in the church's liturgical and spiritual life. From a commission survey of diocesan bishops, it reported that the needs of blacks were adequately looked after in the dioceses by their bishops, who were important for interpreting blacks' concerns to whites and whites' concerns to blacks. The document said little about including blacks in the church's political offices and social institutions, no doubt due to segregation practiced in most dioceses in the North and the South. (Early on in the century two black bishops had been consecrated to look after blacks in their respective dioceses: Edward Thomas Demby [1869-1957; consecrated 1918], Suffragan Bishop of Arkansas, and Henry Beard Delaney [1858-1928; consecrated 1918], Suffragan Bishop of North Carolina.) Furthermore, the commission treated the issue of race as a leadership problem for the church rather than a theological and ethical issue for church teachings: "The opportunities and capacities for leadership can be determined only by experience. Leadership is a matter of personality."[18]

At the 1934 Convention, the Bishop of Mississippi led a successful fight for approval of an anti-lynching resolution, but failed to persuade the church to support an anti-lynching bill then before Congress. In 1937, a joint commission to study the causes of lynching was created, but again no record can be found in the official journal of this commission's report. In fact, at the next convention the joint commission was discharged without having made any study available. Throughout this time, black congregations in Southern dioceses were not permitted seats at diocesan conventions and had to meet separately usually under an Archdeacon for Colored Work. (Indeed, the Diocese of South Carolina did not end its policy of racial segregation in the councils of the church until the 1950s.)

Resisting or acting cautiously about providing considered social teachings about racial affairs, the church relied more on policy and programs to exhibit in its institutional life at the national level what failed in the life of its clergy, parishes, and dioceses at the local level. Yet, as noted previously, social policy in the Episcopal Church often models unarticulated social teachings. In a report from the Joint Commission on Strategy and Policy in 1943, it was agreed that the "first responsibility of the Church is to demonstrate within its own fellowship the reality of community as God intends it. It is commissioned to call men into the Church, into a divine society that transcends our national and racial lines and divisions . . . especially in its own life and worship. . . ."[19] Consequently, in 1943 on its National Council staff, the office of Executive Secretary for Negro Work was created. The first occupant was Bravid Washington Harris (1896–1965; consecrated Bishop of Liberia: 1945), then Archdeacon for Colored Work in the Diocese of Southern Virginia. This office was merged and resurrected many times subsequently during the tenure of his successor, Tollie Caution (1902–87), who for many years was responsible for all ethnic ministries at the national level. His office was the precursor of the other ethnic staff officers at the church's headquarters in New York.

The church as an exemplary model for society also was the focus of a resolution at the Convention called "The Christian Approach to the New World Order," a New Testament motif. Paul and the Book of Revelation especially speak of Christ and the church having ushered in a new order in the midst of the old order. Adapting such a motif hinted that the Episcopal Church was prepared to move critically against the existing order, including places in its own life afflicted by racial segregation and discrimination. However, the report did not elaborate theologically on this theme, despite this glimpse of a church daring to reform or even break free of its "establishmentarian" or "church-type" of thinking.

Teachings and modeling moved an additional step when a report of the committee on social reconstruction was accepted. For the first time, an unmistakable reference to the dignity of every person was mentioned. "Recognition of the intrinsic worth of every person," read the report, which also taught the right every citizen "to equality of opportunity" and the doctrine that "the Negro must be treated as a man and citizen, and not as a Negro."[20] The 1946 General Convention created the Bi-Racial Commission, a joint commission with membership from bishops, clergy, and the laity. The difference this time, however, was the inclusion of a new principle that specified that the commission's structure should be at least 50 percent black.

In 1949 the canons were tested as vehicles for social teachings. Clifford Morehouse (1904–77), later president of the House of Deputies (1961–67), proposed that

> every communicant or baptized member of this Church shall be entitled to equal rights and status in any parish or mission church thereof. He shall not be excluded from the worship of the sacraments of the Church, nor from the parochial member-ship, because of race, color, or nationality.[21]

The resolution did not pass; the committee reporting called it unnecessary. Such sentiments, however, were adopted as a canon some fifteen years later under the pressure of progressives and the 1960s civil rights movement in the South, after a number of Southern Episcopal churches refused blacks and civil rights workers admittance to the Holy Communion.

Social teachings about race simmered during the rest of the forties but took a decisive turn in the 1950s in a dispute at the University of the South and its seminary. This Episcopal college was governed by a board of trustees that included most of the bishops in the Deep South grouped together as the Fourth Province. Conflicting opinions about racial equality on campus came to the forefront when the provincial synod (which, like the General Convention, includes bishops, clergy, and laity) agreed by vote to request the trustees of the university's school of theology to rescind its admissions policy rejecting blacks. This resolution had been aggravated by the closing in 1949 of the church's all-black seminary, the Bishop Payne Divinity School (named after a Virginia seminary graduate and first Bishop of Liberia), founded in 1878 by Virginia Theological Seminary in Petersburg, Virginia. Subsidies to this school in the national church's budget were ministered through an agency called the American Church Institute for Negroes, which also financed the other black Episcopal schools and colleges.

When Bishop Payne Divinity School closed, most of the other Episcopal seminaries, which were predominately white, admitted Payne's students. One seminary, the Philadelphia Divinity School (whose later merger with the Episcopal Theological School in Cambridge, Massachusetts, led to the new merger being named the Episcopal Divinity School), even hired one of its black faculty. The theological seminary at the University of the South in Sewanee, Tennessee, however, steadfastly refused to admit either Payne's students (or any black students full time) or to appoint any black faculty. The university board of trustees in June 1952 reconfirmed its admissions policy of racial exclusion, in spite of a petition from its own seminary faculty. Soon thereafter, the seminary's dean and several of its faculty resigned along with thirty-five of its fifty-five students. Furthermore, in February 1953 the university's racial policy became a national embarrassment when James Pike, then dean of the Cathedral of St. John the Divine in New York City, refused to preach there and to accept an honorary degree in what Pike called "white divinity." The trustees changed the admissions policy later that same year at its June meeting.

In September 1952, General Convention met in Boston, three months after the Sewanee trustees initially had resisted changing the university racial admissions policy. But the bishops gave neither leadership nor clarity about racial inclusiveness within the church and its institutions in light of Sewanee. In their Pastoral Letter they spoke of accountability to God, "Who gave us at the beginning a society where there was 'neither Greek nor Jew, circumcision nor uncircumcision, barbarian, Scythian, bond nor free,' Who gave us unity, that we might give it to the world."[22] The House of Deputies, however, was unhappy with the Sewanee trustees. A number of resolutions were proposed opposing the trustees' action as being incompatible with the Christian faith, until finally one won the bishops' concurrence:

> It is the clear duty of Christians to lead, in seeking the justice
> and equality of opportunity for all men, regardless of color or
> racial origin. . . . This Convention confirms its conviction that
> no branch of the Christian Church should rest content while
> any injustices in racial relations obtained in parishes, schools,
> and agencies, under their control or in association with her; and
> it urges every member of the Church to labor unceasingly for
> the elimination of such injustices. [23]

The 1952 Convention also mandated a racially inclusive deployment policy in parishes and agencies, saying the Christian teachings were "incompatible with every form of discrimination based
on color or race." The church pledged itself to "oppose and combat
discrimination . . . in every form both within our Church and
without, in this country and internationally."[24]

The United States Supreme in 1954 Court voted unanimously
in its historic *Brown v. Board of Education of Topeka* decision that
racial segregation in schools was inherently unconstitutional. And
in 1955 Rosa Parks, a weary black tailor's assistant at a Montgomery, Alabama department store going home from her labors,
climbed into the city's segregated buses, as usual. But that day
she refused to surrender her seat to whites and stand in the aisle,
as she was expected to do by tradition and statute. She described
later this mild protest: "I was thinking that the only way to let
them know I felt I was being mistreated was to do just what I
did—resist the order."[25] Her refusal and subsequent arrest not
only sparked the Montgomery bus boycott and birthed the civil
rights movement; it also transformed the vocation of a disciple of
nonviolence, Martin Luther King, Jr., the young pastor of Dexter
Avenue Baptist Church in Montgomery.[26]

Two other memorable events in race relations stood out in 1955:
the lynching of a fourteen-year-old black youngster from Chicago,
Emmett Louis Till (1941–55), in Mississippi, and the removal of
the General Convention from its original site, Houston, Texas, to
Hawaii because of racial segregation. Till, who was visiting
relatives in Mississippi in August 1955, was accused of whistling
at a white woman. He disappeared and his decomposed body
was fished out of the Tallahatchie River three days later. The
lynching of a teenager aggrieved the soul of the nation and the
media as had no other lynching of blacks at the time. The second

event was Presiding Bishop Henry Knox Sherrill (1890–1980) taking General Convention from Houston, Texas, to Honolulu, Hawaii, because the Bishop of Texas, Clinton S. Quin, could not ensure integrated hotels for all the church's delegates. This was the first time that the actual site was changed as far as anyone could recall in the church's history.

Discerning an impatience for change in the visible life of the church as a model advancing social justice and reform in society, the church's national staff issued "Guiding Principles for Negro Work" in 1956. Full integration of races in worship, church administration, institutions, and agencies were announced as goals for the entire church. Other Episcopalians, inflamed by the civil rights movement and scenes of mob violence against blacks in the media, and displeased with a church hesitant or unable to rid itself of racial discrimination with the same "deliberate speed" mandated of secular institutions by the courts, organized themselves. Hence, clergy and laity, mostly from the South but also from the North, gathered under the leadership of two Southern white priests in 1959 to establish a civil rights group within the church: the Episcopal Society for Cultural and Racial Unity (ESCRU). Cornelius Tarplee was from the national office of Christian Social Relations, and John B. Morris was a parish priest in South Carolina At a black Episcopal college, St. Augustine's (Raleigh, North Carolina), in December 1959, ESCRU's founding body pledged "to promote increased acceptance and demonstration of the church's policies of racial inclusiveness in its own life, as well as its role of providing leadership in the community and nation. . . ."[27] Its goals and programs struck a chord, for within one year membership totaled over 1000, 25 percent of which lived in the South. Its voluntary contributions exceeded budgeted income by $5000. It shared the infamy of many progressive organizations at the time: the accusation of being a Communist organization by many Southern clergy and bishops.

The bishops' posture during these turbulent years was support for the existing rule of law without asking critical questions about its implementation and enforcement by white authorities in the racially segregated society of the South. The law is a minister of God for the good, wrote the bishops meeting in 1958 at Miami Beach (itself a segregated city at the time), and like government makes civilization possible and unity thinkable. The opposite of law and order is anarchy, "a greater evil than tyranny, and leads to tyranny." But they allowed that when both law and government are thought to be unjust, resistance by Christians and others through civil disobedience was sanctioned:

> It is only for the gravest and clearest principle of conscience relating to a serious moral issue that one may contemplate civil disobedience. And, because all order is at stake, such disobedience can only be justified when it is based on a higher ethical principle than the law represents. . . . We call upon you, therefore, at this time to honor and obey the laws of this land.[28]

They acknowledged also that the Pastoral was motivated by an ethnocentric fear for whites coupled with the biblical mandate of "love for all men":

> We must remember that the majority of mankind belong to the colored races, and that the American racial problem is discussed the world over. Much of the good will which early missionaries gained has been lost. Much of the good will which our nation has enjoyed has been lost. . . . If Africa and Asia should turn finally against us, it could well be because the colored races became convinced they must look elsewhere for justice.[29]

Resolution of these tensions and problems, continued the Pastoral, lay with "the clear light of reason." Such recalled the Enlightenment model of reason and the earlier Episcopal model of "reasonable" people sitting down together to reach consensus without considering the depth of grievances, social and societal conditions, and power structures also at stake in such a discussion. Reason was made synonymous with intelligence, calmness, and reform in contrast to intelligence, conflict, and militancy by aggrieved parties and races:

> There is only one way for free men to overcome conflict, and that is by talking together in reasonable self-control, and thus find a third way which will lead to peace. Christians who believe in the God who is the source of all truth ought to be the first ones to claim this privilege of reason.[30]

On February 1, 1960, four students at black North Carolina A&T College in Greensboro sat down at the lunch counter reserved for whites in the local downtown Woolworth's, which, of course, was against the law. They were not served, and returned to their dormitories when the store announced closing hours. But the word was out, and soon student demonstrations, now called "sit-ins," became a tactic of empowerment for black college students throughout the South protesting segregated public accommodations. Later, at Easter 1960, over two hundred students gathered at Shaw University, Raleigh, North Carolina, under the leadership of Ella Baker, herself a graduate of Shaw and member of the staff at Martin Luther King's Southern Christian Leadership Conference (SCLC) in Atlanta. The students organized the Student Nonviolent Coordinating Committee (SNCC) to coordinate demonstrations, sit-ins, and civil rights activities.

Mainstream churches, forced to address these escalating events, found the task difficult and perplexing because neither they nor the usual Establishment had charge of events. In 1961, the Congress for Racial Equality (CORE) and college students organized a mission into the South that captured both the media's and international sympathy: the Freedom Rides. White mob violence against Freedom Rides that challenged segregation laws forbidding whites and blacks to sit together on interstate bus travel, stirred up international disfavor. Local law officials did nothing until the media paid more attention to them. Race in America's South was suddenly internationalized. Presiding Bishop Arthur Lichtenberger (1900–68) and the national church staff issued a study document on the student protest movement that gave a theological rationale for civil disobedience against unjust laws, despite protests by many Southern bishops, who said the church was condoning lawlessness.

ESCRU adapted the direct-action strategy of the Freedom Rides movement by making a Prayer Pilgrimage to segregated church institutions in the South and North. Organized by ESCRU'S executive director, John Morris (1930–), the Pilgrimage began in September 1961. Its itinerary included New Orleans, a stop at the segregated All Saints Junior College, Vicksburg, Mississippi, whose rector was John M. Allin (Bishop of Mississippi [1966–74] and Presiding Bishop [1975–85]), and stops by separate groups thereafter. General Convention in Detroit was the final stop. Martin Luther King praised the prayer pilgrims: "The Episcopal clergymen who will ride on this pilgrimage, using terminal facilities at the bus stations en route, will implement the spirit of the Freedom Rides fully. . . ."[31] After Vicksburg, one group journeyed on to the University of the South in Sewanee, Tennessee, and a second to Jackson, Mississippi.

The university, owned by twenty-one Southern dioceses, that year at commencement gave an honorary degree to Thomas R. Waring, editor of the *News and Courier* in Charleston, South Carolina, and known as a segregationist. ESCRU's pilgrims held a public service of worship on the campus that was attended by students and faculty. In Jackson, a group of fifteen priests and a layman went into the bus terminal and were arrested as they tried to enter its whites-only restaurant. Among themselves they agreed that thirteen would plea *nolo contendere* and two would remain in jail. Those released went on to Michigan, where they were reunited with the Sewanee group, which then journeyed to Dearborn, Michigan, to pray for an end of segregated housing there. Afterwards, they reached Detroit, where General Convention was already in session. Presiding Bishop Lichtenberger issued a statement supporting the civil disobedience action of the pilgrims, saying they were bearing witness "to their Christian convictions about justice for all people in this land. . . . They are doing the right as they see the right. Whether they have chosen the right way to bear witness to their convictions, time alone will tell."[32]

The House of Bishops itself again refused to address the issues of civil disobedience and segregation in their Pastoral Letter that year. The Convention, however, did. It passed several strong resolutions condemning racial segregation, saying prejudice is inconsistent with the gospel of Jesus Christ, and pledging the church to "conform herself to the reconciling comprehensiveness of the Body of Christ, specifically by recognizing ability wherever it may be found, for example in considering persons at national, diocesan, and parochial levels here and abroad. . . ."[33]

The war to rid both the social fabric and the church of racial apartheid escalated in the summer 1964 when SNCC students called for nationwide help in voter registration and education mostly in Mississippi under the auspices of COFO (Council of Federated Organizations). COFO was an umbrella organization in Mississippi created by SNCC, CORE, the NAACP (National Association for the Advancement of Colored People, founded 1909), and King's SCLC. Originally, its purpose was to coordinate the negotiations with Mississippi's Governor Ross Barnett about violence against the Freedom Riders. Bishops, clergy, and laity along with Christians from many mainstream, predominately white churches and black and white college students responded quickly to the summons. It was, of course, June of that year in the rural town of Philadelphia, Mississippi, in Nashoba County that one of the most dastardly acts of mob violence occurred: the Klan's lynching of three civil rights workers—a black and two Jews (James Chaney from Mississippi, Andrew Goodman and Michael Schwerner from New York City). They were led by the local sheriff and his deputy. Their bodies were discovered some forty-four days later after their disappearance in a fifteen-foot red-clay grave, which shocked most Americans and foreign countries as well.[34]

Many Southern Episcopal parish churches excluded even white Episcopal civil rights volunteers, not to mention blacks, from Holy Communion, a first experience of exclusion for many whites. Congress passed the Civil Rights Act in 1964, removing all forms of racial and gender segregation in employment and public accommodations. Meanwhile, ESCRU assaulted the exclusion of black Episcopalians from communion and the taboo that forbad interracial marriage in the church in the South by lobbying for a canon permitting both. The 1964 Convention with the urging of ESCRU and other progressives did deal with the issue of race and its sacraments. This was the first time this issue was directly addressed since the two were joined by the slave state of Virginia in 1661 and the Bishop of London in his commentary in 1727. The canons were amended, the completion of a task undertaken by Clifford Morehouse in 1949:

> Every communicant or baptized member of this Church shall be entitled to equal rights and status in any Parish or Mission thereof. He shall not be excluded from the worship or the Sacraments of the Church, nor from parochial membership because of race, color, or ethnic origin.[35]

The summer of 1967 was labeled "the long hot summer" by the media. Over one hundred rebellions and riots in black ghettos scourged urban landscapes: Watts in Los Angeles, the West Side in Chicago, Detroit, Minneapolis, Newark. Widespread anxiety and fears of being under siege disrupted the middle class model of racial integration that was King's vision, which dominated the civil rights movement. Mainstream churches also supported the model largely because of King. But the black urban poor and underclass in the North and West, seldom touched by mainstream black or white churches or persuaded by the claims of non-violence, took to the streets in rebellion against inequities and injustices. Indeed, the urban protests continued even during the lifetime of King and his movement, which was polarized by the time of his assassination in Memphis, Tennessee, in 1968.

The urban riots together with the student-led Black Power movement that joined both poor black ghettos and black middle class university students, terrified liberals and mainstream churches. The Black Power movement grew from an outburst by Stokely Carmichael, chairman of SNCC, at a rally in Greenwood, Mississippi, in June 1966, after a local sheriff arrested him on a triviality. "This is the twenty-seventh time I have been arrested," he shouted to the audience. "I ain't going to jail no more. . . . What we are going start saying now is 'black power'!"[36] In December 1966 SNCC voted out whites, thereby ending King's model of integration and, according to many, a bourgeois vision of power in an integrated society.

Black Power, which signaled an increasing disaffection of blacks with King's dream of society, was an indigenous liberation movement by blacks wanting to define their own identity and goals without imported methods (non-violence from India) or imposed racial labels by whites ("colored," "Negro"). Black Power as a liberation movement conjured up militancy and empowerment. Its impreciseness succeeded in joining the bottled-up anger and experiences of the black lower class with the pent-up, explosive frustrations of black middle class college students growing out of discrimination and rejection in the majority society. Black Power also inspired creative black religious scholars like James C. Cone, who pioneered black theology in his writings: *Black Theology and Black Power* (1969); *A Black Theology of Liberation* (1970), followed by other black theologians. An early sign of support for Black Power's claims in the black community was the rapid disfavor of the term "Negro" and the equally rapid rise of the term "black" as an expression of racial identity.

Presiding Bishop John Hines (1910–), successor to Lichtenberger, and disoriented like many about Black Power, echoed a cliché voiced by others in mainstream churches when he said whites were as much a part of the problem as the structures and prejudices that oppressed and marginalized people living in urban ghettos. Although not particularly profound or impressive as a confession, it set the agenda for one of the most controversial, radical social programs in the Episcopal Church's life: the General Convention Special Program (GCSP).

GCSP was created in 1967 after black power had captured many adherents in black communities. In April 1969, the Executive Council voted support for the Black Economic Development Conference (BEDC) that James Foreman, formerly of SNCC, had initiated through the "Black Manifesto." The council encouraged BEDC to apply to GCSP for funding, since the 1967 General Convention "affirm[ed] its commitment to the principle of self-determination for minority groups as they attempt to organize the community which they represent."[37]

Leon Modeste, a black layman, was appointed staff officer of GCSP with an initial $3 million budget. The program with its objectives and its funding criteria modelled church social teachings engaging blacks and other minorities in a far-reaching direction bound to be contested. The teaching at stake in the model was that outreach toward blacks and the marginalized by a predominately white church was based on (1) a reinforcement of self-esteem and culture of the marginalized as children of God by giving them authority in the decision-making affecting their community and control over funds for programming this authority; (2) the bonding in Jesus Christ between the humanity of a white affluent church and the humanity and struggles of the poor and marginalized; (3) possible inhumanity and injustice in structures shaped and dominated by the majority community for the benefit of minority communities. Hence, GCSP held the task of the church to be further self-determination and authority among blacks and the marginalized through direct funding, which went directly to the sponsoring body rather than through the controlling mechanism of the diocese, i.e., the bishop. Recipients were to consult the diocesan bishop in their location. But he could not veto their funding. This was to prevent Southern bishops who opposed funding groups in their area not under their Episcopal control from hampering black-initiated programs. At the same time it was an expression of what the Presiding Bishop in his address proposing GCSP, described as a way by which the church can take its place humbly and boldly alongside of, and in support of, the dispossessed and oppressed peoples of this country. . . . It will encourage the use of political and economic power to support justice and self-determination for all men.[38]

The funding criteria also modelled social teachings about the engagement of power for social justice by Christians that revealed a final shift in the church's thinking about all forces being able to be reconciled regardless of various power structures and economic circumstances: (1) power is real and is to be engaged by commu-nities trying to gain political, social, and economic change; (2) power-sharing structures and programs have integrity for the poor, when they are designed and controlled by the poor, with the church acting like a servant of the Lord empowering them through funding, training, and political influence; and (3) attainment of power and self-determination by the poor and the marginalized is best achieved by nonviolent means. The church cannot fund "any individual or group which advocates violence."[39]

In 1970, General Convention met in Houston—the same city from which Presiding Bishop Henry Knox Sherrill had removed General Convention in 1955 because of segregated accommo-dations—and effectively crippled GCSP. Its budget was severely reduced and bishops were given restored veto power over its grants to local organizations in their diocese (although these vetoes could be appealed). In 1973, General Convention abolished GCSP's funding committee, and replaced it with a new creation intended to weaken its independence: the Community Action and Human Development (CAHA).[40] Outreach was restricted to work and mission under direct Episcopal auspices. Also in 1973, the staff officer for black ministries was resurrected at the national headquarters (after having been abolished in the 1960s) along other ethnic staffs: Hispanics, Indians (Native Americans), and Asians. In December 1973 the Executive Council under Presiding Bishop John E. Hines officially killed GCSP and expressed its gratitude to Leon Modeste who "effectively and fearlessly moved the Church onto the scene of desperate human need among the powerless and the poor."[41]

During the 1970s, the Vietnam War consumed the nation's energy and attention. However, the church voiced a new policy that got little attention, but modelled yet another level in its social teachings about race: its minority empowerment policy. At its February 1972 meeting, the Executive Council approved empowerment as the major objective in mission and ministry: a "liberating process for oppressed and oppressor, for powerful and powerless, whereby God's Spirit breaks the walls of separation that dehumanize people."[42] The council was clear that this mission objective of the church was especially addressed to the poor and the marginalized:

> Our 'empowerment' goal is to bring the presently disadvant-
> aged to a position of self-determining equals, not to a position
> where they will impose their will on all other people. . . . There
> is nothing in the Gospel that says this will be either popular or
> easy, and some may have to pay a price, judging by secular
> standards for this certain kind of integrity and rationality and
> honesty. . . .[43]

In the 1980s, most of the major issues raised by the civil rights movement either had been adjudicated in the federal courts or legislated in Congress. The shift was to politics of gender and sexuality. The general populace felt that racial issues had largely been resolved to the benefit of blacks (and women) and to the disadvantage of whites via such reforms as affirmative action. In 1978, a black sociologist published a controversial book, *The Declining Significance of Race*, which said that class was more pivotal in explaining race relations and conflict than race itself because of the gap between the new black middle class and the poor black underclass.[44] A 1981 Executive Council resolution set out the teaching that church assist "the victims of discrimination" in its own life and personnel by modelling its staff at national head-quarters to be "as representative as possible" racially and sexually. "Victim" clearly meant groups traditionally discriminated against: American Indians, Alaska Natives, Blacks, Hispanics, women, aged, handicapped, and Vietnam veterans.[45]

The 1982 General Convention commended to the churches and dioceses the concept of affirmative action, which had become government policy in the employment of minorities and women. A link between evangelism and education among blacks, which was first established in the nineteenth century, was reaffirmed in another resolution to raise capital funds for the three black colleges, all located in the South: St. Augustine's College in Raleigh, North Carolina (founded 1867 by the church's Freedman's Commission), St. Paul's College in Virginia (1888), and Voorhees College in South Carolina (1897). Finally, the 1982 Convention focused on racial inclusiveness in the church's liturgy by endorsing the creation of a national holiday observing the birthday of Martin Luther King, Jr., commending his birthday as an addition in the church calendar.

The concept of racism was enlarged in 1988 to include American Indians and Native Hawaiians, both of whom were also historical victims of racism in the church and in the United States: the Indians through racial stereotypes about their drinking, education, and groups urging abrogation of the Indian treaties and the Hawaiians as victims of white supremacist violence (and resistance to electing a native Hawaiian to the episcopate).[46]

Commentary

The Episcopal Church in its social teachings about race has until recently been of a divided mind. On the one hand, it has understood its mission to maintain order and consensus in matters of race; on the other hand, it has frequently insisted on separate black congregations without full membership in regular diocesan conventions and structures. In the antebellum South, congregations of freed blacks sometimes existed in the cities and towns under the supervision and control of white clergy; slave chapels existed on the plantations along with Sunday schools, also under the supervision of white clergy and the control of the plantation owner. Legislation upholding slavery and its penal systems was generally not opposed by the Episcopal Church in the South. And since some Southern bishops and Episcopal planters owned slaves, the church in the South supported and enjoyed the benefits of slavery and slaves.

Apart from the 1727 letter from the Bishop of London, the Episcopal Church neglected to provide any Christian teachings about slaves as the children of God or the issue of slavery until the crisis of the Civil War. But the moral issue of slavery was not dealt with; rather the political issue of secession was the occasion for the first social teachings in the Episcopal Church. Although the church had a divided mind, each region had its own Prayer Book with appropriate alterations of prayers and services supporting its understanding of civil authority.

The church was disposed to adopt what Richard Niebuhr calls a "Christ as transformer of culture" position in its first social teaching, which can also be called a *conversionist* stance. This position strongly affirms culture and the social fabric based on the belief that (1) culture as a part of creation has been redeemed by Christ and is steadily being renewed through new creations in our world; (2) God uses cultural institutions for renewal and transformation even in a fallen world; and (3) culture is under the sign of God's grace, the divine "Yes," rather than God's wrath, the divine "No."

At the time of World War I, when mob violence, race riots, and the lynching of blacks abounded, the motif in the church's position on race moved from "melting pot" and "candidates for conversion" to "reconciliation." That is, its position changed from a "Christ as transformer of culture" to "church as transformer of culture." At first the church's teaching paid little attention to the evil in the violence inflicted upon blacks except as to link it to the violence of war, which obviously had much to do with the federation character of the Episcopal Church and its sensitivity to each bishop's sovereignty in his diocese. With regard to race, episcopal sovereignty was an ecclesiastical version of states' rights—the doctrine invoked by Southern politicians in the 1950s and 1960s to resist federal court decisions against racial discrimination.

Hence, because of its weak episcopal system, the Episcopal Church delayed until the 1930s any judgment on mob violence against blacks in dioceses. Also, with its church-type theology with regard to the state, many in the church no doubt thought the laws as written were just until changed. Even after the civil rights campaigns of civil disobedience against an unjust legal system, the bishops continued to say that the law was a mandate from God advancing and preserving civilization for the good of all.

Even during the period of violence against blacks and civil rights workers in the South in the 1950s and 1960s, the church at first resorted to programs rather than theological guidelines. This changed after ESCRU and groups like SNCC and CORE used nonviolent means to show up the violence inflicted upon blacks and those working with them in the South.[47] Also what became increasingly clear to all was that what Auschwitz was to Jews in the 1940s, the South was to blacks in the 1950s and 1960s.

Small lights in the maze appeared, however, that were turning points in teachings about race, even when the church did not reveal an overarching explicit theological direction. For example, the preamble to the 1943 resolution on guidelines for policy on race spoke significantly of a New World Order, signaling that the Episcopal Church thought about a "Christ against culture" social teaching instead of its traditional "Christ in culture" position. The "Guiding Principles Designed to Govern the Church's Negro Work," written by the national staff was adopted by General Convention as instructive for the entire church. These principles, considered at the time quite progressive for a mainstream church, said the church can not tolerate any distinction within itself "which marks our brethren of other races as unequal or inferior." General Convention pledged the church to "set the spiritual and moral goals for society, and to bear witness to their validity by achieving them in her own life."[48]

Likewise, the 1946 General Convention authorized a Bi-Racial Commission and directed that at least 50 percent of its membership should be black, a clear departure from the *noblesse oblige* tradition in Episcopal social policy about blacks. This was a small step toward participatory democracy with whites deciding *alongside* instead of *for* blacks and a module of self-determination for blacks in the church. Nor were pressures from within the church to be overlooked, such as the arrests of the ESCRU prayer pilgrims, which provoked many to question the fairness of the legal system with regard to blacks and how morally accountable it ought to be in light of biblical teachings about racial diversity and fairness.

GCSP modelled perhaps the boldest experiment toward the church's solidarity with blacks and the marginalized in spite of the social class differences and privileges. The controversy over fiscal control and diocesan approval could be looked at, on the one hand, as a responsible act of accountability. On the other hand, it could be seen as a return to the former *noblesse oblige* of a privileged church with status and education, being responsible for the less privileged, thereby exercising control. The controversy about violence in GCSP funded programs remains a continuing question for an establishment-oriented church, since the 1776 War as well as the Civil War demonstrated that the Episcopal Church has supported violence even among kith and kin, when in its own interest as a cultural institution. But the charge against GCSP was that the church supported suspected *black* violence against whites.

In its teachings about affirmative action as a Christian moral principle, the church adapted the theological image of an exemplary agent affirming and modelling a morality for others, even in the midst of a redeemed, sinful world. Interestingly enough, its Teaching Series that was authorized and financed to present the church's tradition and mind, neglected the theological aspect of the church's social teachings about race. Only discrimination in the contemporary scene was dealt with, but little attention paid to the church's pronouncements of the past.

As in other areas of social concern, the Episcopal Church shifted its images and models of the church about race and blacks without much consistency or explicit theological rationale. This may be the church as exemplary model listening to the social context with its own shifting forces, one of the hallmarks in the first social teaching in the nineteenth century. Yet the fact that it is still newsworthy in the Episcopal Church when a black gets elected bishop or rector of a white parish signifies that the 1943 goal has not become normative and requires restatement from time to time as a goal for Christians in matters of race.

Notes

1. *An Account of the Endeavors used by the Society for the Propagation of the Gospel in Foreign Parts, To instruct the Negro Slaves in New York, together with Two of Bp. Gibson's Letters on the Subject* (London: n.p., 1727), p. 27.

2. Quoted in Stiles B. Lines, "Slaves and Churchmen: The Work of the Episcopal Church Among Southern Negroes, 1800–1860" (Ph.D. dissertation, Columbia University, 1960), p. 171.

3. Quoted in Roland Foster, *The Role of the Presiding Bishop* (Cincinnati: Forward Movement Publications, 1982), pp. 27-8.

4. See Angela Davis's analysis of class and racism in the early feminist movement, particularly the mixed reactions and opposition to Sojourner Truth by feminist leaders at the 1851 Women's convention in Akron, Ohio, where Sojourner Truth gave her famous "Ain't I a Woman?" speech. Davis, *Women, Race and Class* (New York: Vintage Books, 1983), pp. 46-86.

5. *Journal of the General Convention, 1865,* pp. 310, 312. See also E.F. Hening, *History of the African Mission of the Protestant Episcopal Church* (New York: Stanford and Swords, 1850; reprint ed., Freeport, NY: Books for Libraries Press, 1971).

6. W.J. Cash, *The Mind of the South* (New York: Alfred A. Knopf 1946), p. 56.

7. *Journal of the General Convention, 1868,* p. 370.

8. For a description of blacks within the Episcopal Church before and after the Civil War, see George Brown Tindall, *South Carolina Negroes, 1877–1900* (Columbia, SC: University of South Carolina Press, 1952), pp. 194 ff; R.E. Hood, "From a Headstart to a Deadstart: The Historical Basis for Black Indifference Toward the Episcopal Church, 1800–1860," *Historical Magazine of the Protestant EpiscopalChurch* 51 (September 1982): 269-96; J. Carleton Hayden, "After The War: The Mission and Growth of the Episcopal Church Among Blacks in the South, 1865–1877," *Historical Magazine of the Protestant EpiscopalChurch* 42 (December 1973): 403-27.

9. Lines, "Slaves and Churchmen: The Work of the Episcopal Church Among Southern Negroes, 1800–1860," p. 240.

10. *Journal of the Convention, 1877*, p. 491. For a description of the free black in the South and in Episcopal churches, see Ira Berlin, *Slaves Without Masters: The Free Negro in the Antebellum South* (New York: Vintage Books, 1976), pp. 284-315.

11. The word takes its name from a Revolutionary War colonel, Charles Lynch of Virginia, who had established a vigilante court to deal with Tory loyalists and criminals by fining and whipping them.

12. John Turner, et. al., *The Ku Klux Klan, A History of Racism and Violence* (Montgomery, Ala.: Southern Poverty Law Center, 1986), p. 27.

13. *Pastoral Letter of the House of Bishops*, A.D. 1886, pp. 12-3.

14. To understand what black denominations themselves did for the emancipated slaves in the South, see Clarence E. Walker, *A Rock in a Weary Land: The African Methodist Episcopal Church During the Civil War and Reconstruction* (Baton Rouge, LA: Louisiana State University Press, 1982).

15. *The Pastoral Letter of the Bishops to the Clergy and Laity*, October 22, 1895, p. 10.

16. *Journal of the General Convention , 1904*, p. 274.

17. "Pastoral Letter," *Journal of the General Convention*, 1919, p. 507.

18. *Journal of the General Convention, 1934*, p. 476.

19. *Journal of the General Convention, 1943*, p. 573.

20. *Journal of the General Convention, 1943*, p. 467.

21. *Journal of the General Convention, 1949*, p. 164; *The Living Church* 119 (August 14, 1949), p. 9.

22. *Pastoral Letter issued by the House of Bishops Assembled in General Convention*, September 19, 1952, p. 6.

23. *Journal of the General Convention, 1952*, p. 279.

24. Ibid., p. 277.

25. David J. Garrow, *Bearing the Cross: Martin Luther King, Jr., and the Southern Christian Leadership Conference* (New York: William Morrow, 1986), p. 12.

26. For a thorough account of King's emergence and tenure as the leader of the civil rights movement, see Taylor Branch, *Parting the Waters: America in the King Years, 1954–63* (New York: Simon and Schuster, 1988), pp. 143–205.

27. "Proposal for the Formation of the Episcopal Society for Racial and Cultural Unity," n.d. Papers of the Reverend John B. Morris. (Mimeographed.)

28. *The Pastoral Letter issued by The House of Bishops*, October, 1958, p. 5.

29. Ibid., pp. 6-7.

30. Ibid., pp. 7-8.

31. Quoted in the ESCRU *Newsletter*, September 17-29, 1961, p. 3.

32. *The Convention Daily*, Official Newspaper of the General Convention, September 19, 1961; The *New York Times*, September 14, 1961.

33. *Journal of the General Convention, 1961*, pp. 419-20.

34. On a sculpture in tribute to civil rights victims of mob violence in the South, of forty people memorialized thirty-two were murdered in Mississippi and Alabama. *Free At Last: A History of the Civil Rights Movement and Those Who Died in the Struggle* (Montgomery, AL: The Civil Rights Education Project, The Southern Poverty Law Center, 1989).

35. This is now Title I, Canon 16 in the church's *Constitution and Canons*.

36. Seth Cagin and Philip Dray, *We are not Afraid: The Story of Goodman, Schwerner, and Chaney and the Civil Rights Campaign for Mississippi* (New York: Macmillan, 1988), pp. 440-1.

37. *Church and Society Social Policy of the Episcopal Church*, Executive Council and General Convention, December 1967-April 1979 (New York: The Executive Council of the Episcopal Church, n.d.), p. 234.

38. *Journal of the General Convention, 1967*, p. 2.

39. *Church and Society Social Policy of the Episcopal Church*, December 1967-April 1979, p. 218.

40. The name was changed to Coalition for Human Needs (CHN) in 1976. However, CHN revived some of the original funding criteria of GCSP and added new ones.

41. Ibid., p. 232.

42. Ibid., p. 237.

43. Ibid., p. 238.

44. William Julius Wilson, *The Declining Significance of Race* (Chicago The University of Chicago Press, 1978).

45. *Church and Society Social Policy of the Episcopal Church*, Executive Council, February 1891-April 1982 (New York: Episcopal Council of the Episcopal Church, n.d.), p. 50b.

46. Executive Council of the Episcopal Church, Resolution at meeting May 18-20, 1988, Minutes of the council. (New York: Executive Council of the Episcopal Church, n.d.) p. 41.

47. Another event which shocked the Episcopal Church and changed its momentum was the murder of Jonathan Daniels (1939–65), a seminarian at the Episcopal Theological School, Cambridge, Massachu-

setts, who was murdered by a deputy sheriff in Lowndes County, Alabama. Daniels, who worked with ESCRU, was gunned down in daylight as he waited to buy a soda in a local grocery. The deputy sheriff was found not guilty.

48. *Journal of the General Convention, 1943,* p. 326.

Chapter 6
Pictures of an Exhibition: Episcopal Social Teachings III

Marriage and Family

Christian marriage is the place to understand sexuality in Episcopal teachings, and sexuality is to be understood within marriage. That is, sexuality has its theological content within the doctrine of marriage and family. Premarital and extramarital sex are excluded as expressions of neither. As a moral teaching viewed in modern times, it sounds like a "hard saying" "out of joint" with a secular emphasis on the sovereignty of individual autonomy and private choice in matters and style of family and sexual identity. Public discourse about sexuality in the late twentieth century has been dominated by the vocabularies of psychology, biology, sociology, and the political claims and critiques of feminists, homosexual men and women, transsexuals, single parents, and young urban professionals cohabiting and having babies without what Christian tradition calls "the benefit of matrimony."

Even the officially authorized Church's Teaching Series says the Episcopal Church cannot "claim to have a single 'Christian model' for family life," since there are so many competing claims with their own authority in the world today. Such competing claims reveal the enormous state of flux in the area of family and sexuality in a social climate with less restrictive values and practices. Hence in recent years, a battle royal has ensued in religious discourse and at church conventions about what Scripture, tradition, contemporary claims, and changing life styles say about family and sexuality. All sides aim to further theological dialogue and rethinking about the Christian tradition and its adaptation in a religiously diverse society. Concepts like *sexual oppression, patriarchy, male chauvinism* are heard frequently as Christians discuss these volatile and emotion-laden issues and as single-issue politics become increasingly a part of national and religious debate.

The Episcopal Church's sources for its teachings about marriage and family (community), until recently, were largely the Prayer Book liturgy and its rubrics about Holy Matrimony and the legacy from the Church of England, which reflect traditional teachings. This continued to be so throughout the nineteenth century, in spite of assaults on monogamous marriage as a role model for human community by Marxists and some early feminists. Both criticized monogamy as gender and class oppression by males who both shape and dominate a privileged society. "The first division of labor is that between man and woman for the propagation of children," wrote Friedrich Engels. "The first class oppression coincides with that of the female sex by the male."[1] Feminists pointed out that the rise of the middle class in the towns and cities of the United States in the aftermath of the Revolutionary War, led to the separation of home and family from work and money in urban commercial circles. As a result, although middle class ladies continued their domestic chores, such were devaluated as real work because no money was produced:

> Home and family became the emotional receptacle for all the sentimental values and feelings middle-class men increasingly felt inhibited from exhibiting. In symbolic terms a wife came to be seen as her husband's 'better half'; she embodied the purity, spirituality, and goodness which his life in business lacked. . . . They tried to regain this aspect of themselves through women.[2]

Such critiques, however, failed to distract the church from its support of monogamy, possibly because American culture and intellectual thought never took to Marx and Marxists the way that European intellectual and political circles did. Nor was it likely, given the social-class structure of the Episcopal Church in the late nineteenth century, that such a milieu would have become normative for Episcopal social thought, the emerging Social Gospel movement notwithstanding. In fact, the church only regularized monogamous marriage as the Christian norm canonically in 1868, which is rather late. Prior to that, it had relied only on a 1808 General Convention resolution forbidding divorce. In that resolution, remarriage was not permitted, except on grounds of adultery or desertion by one of the partners. This position reflected both

Catholic and Reformation doctrines of marriage. The Reformation continued the Catholic tradition that validly married partners in the eyes of the church (which had sole jurisdiction over marriages in the West from the eleventh century onward) could only be granted *a mensa et thoro*, a declaration that no marriage existed, if no consummation had taken place.

At the 1868 Convention, a proposed canon to regularize marriage included this tradition; to be remarried otherwise risked being denied entry to the sacraments. But this did not satisfy a majority of the deputies because many wanted to add incest as a cause for divorce; however no consensus emerged. So in the final text, the church linked marriage and family. In 1877, a canon was passed saying it was against Christian tradition for two people to marry "otherwise than as God's word doth allow." The canon retained a uniquely American idea at the time about the "innocent party" in a divorce, a concept instituted earlier in the church. This was a distinct break with the tradition in the Church of England. At first this canon and its teaching applied to clergy and laity alike. But a revision in 1904 restricted only clergy from remarrying.

Thus, marriage yoked with family became the theological context for teachings about fulfilled, mature sexuality. The actual first Episcopal study of the American family was the report of the Commission on Family Life in 1916, mandated to study family life in order to determine Christian moral teachings about the family and life styles, including marriage.

However, the Western cultural assumptions that lie behind the church's teachings about what constitutes Christian marriage became apparent at the 1888 Lambeth Conference. The bishops debated "the subject of polygamy of heathen converts" in Africa, which was as a violation of the law of Christ.[3] Calling polygamy a tradition of "religious fanatics," the Episcopal Church, possibly also thinking of Mormon polygamy in the West, adopted Lambeth's statement. It urged its clergy and laity to help eliminate the practice in the United States. Another hundred years passed before Lambeth rescinded this teaching about polygamy as an option for Christians in Africa at its 1988 conference. At that time African bishops protested the Western cultural assumptions about Christian marriage in the African experience and Lambeth revised its 1888 teaching: "The Conference upholds monogamy as

God's plan, and as the ideal relationship of love between husband and wife; nevertheless recommends that a polygamist who responds to the Gospel and wishes to join the Anglican Church may be baptized and confirmed with his believing wives and children. . . ."[4]

In their 1892 Pastoral the Episcopal bishops hailed the family as the "root germ" of the church and society:

> When the family is wrecked, neither Church nor State is worth preserving. The hearth of the home is the sacred altar, at last, of all religion, all law, all loyalty, and all order. . . . The awful sacredness of home, the one man and the one woman, who are not two but one, whose union is a great mystery, like the union of Christ and His Church.[5]

Personality and identity develop properly only within the community of the family. Indeed, the inner relations of the Godhead itself is a primordial model for the human family: "It is a thing so divine that Almighty God reveals Himself under a family name. He is a Father; the Godhead Itself there is Father and Son; He has a household in heaven and earth, a great family and many children."[6]

Little more was said about marriage and the family until the 1922 report of the Joint Committee on Home and the Family. The doctrine of the Holy Trinity as the primordial model for the Christian family was reaffirmed:

> Whatever attacks the home is a menace to the national life. God has set the sacred names: 'Father,' 'Mother,' at the center of His commandments. . . . The home is the circle drawn close around [Christ]. The Church is the larger circle including many homes. The State is the largest circle including all mankind. This is not man's arrangement but God's appointment. Pollute the source and the whole stream will be unclean. . . . Church and State are built on the family.[7]

The perpetuation of the human race is the most significant purpose of marriage, continued the document. Marriage is an act of cooperation centered in God's will to continue humanity. "[Marriage] is not an end in itself, but the divinely appointed agency whereby God's will may be fulfilled in giving life, protection and proper rearing to the young of the human species." The divine model of the Blessed Virgin and Child is affirmation of the sanctity of motherhood. Christ himself is the foundation of Christian marriage:

> Christ at the marriage altar, Christ on the bridal journey, Christ when the new home is set up, Christ when the baby comes, Christ when the baby dies, Christ in the pinching times, Christ in the days of plenty, Christ when the wedded pair walked toward the sunset gates, Christ when one is taken and the other left, Christ for time, Christ for eternity—this is the secret of happy home life.[8]

Divorce was dismissed as a "malignant cancer," to be opposed with the "plain, continuous training of the people in the nature and obligations of Christian marriage."

In the conventions of 1922 and 1925 birth control was addressed. The 1922 Convention adapted a teaching from the 1920 Lambeth Conference that Christians are not to use artificial means for avoiding or frustrating the conception of children. It constitutes a serious threat to the "future of the race" and to society in general:

> Boys and girls must be taught as early as possible that the highest purpose of marriage is the perpetuation of the race, involving the begetting and education of children for the work of the world. . . . It is not an end in itself, but the divinely appointed agency whereby God's will may be fulfilled in giving life, protection, and proper rearing to the young of the human species.[9]

The 1925 Convention also reaffirmed the Lambeth teaching and added that birth control is a "menace to family life" that allows the "self-indulgent to feel that their personal, selfish desires are in harmony with what passes for altruistic propaganda."[10]

At the same time, the 1922 Convention also supported mental health as a criterion both for Christian marriage and for birth control. It called for federal and state laws to regulate "the marriage of those who are physically or mentally defective" and to restrict reproduction among such, which leads "to an increase of misery or crime."[11] This reflected a growing interest in *eugenics* (Gk.= "wellborn") at the time, a branch of science founded in 1883 by the British physician Sir Francis Galton (1822–1911), during the flood of Darwinian theories about social progress and survival of the fittest.

Eugenics means promoting or hindering the reproduction of genetically fit or unfit persons by manipulating certain social and genetic factors, like matching parents with "superior" intelligence and good looks or preventing the socially and mentally unfit—criminals, alcoholics, beggars, the homeless, prostitutes, the mentally ill, epileptics—from propagating offspring. Galton's objective was to create a mentally superior and physically fit race (something the Nazis in Germany later tried to do in the twentieth century). In fact, an institute for racial studies was established in Munich, Germany, in 1910, and Galton was its honorary president. In the United States his most devout disciple was Charles B. Davenport (1866-1944), who created the Eugenics Record Office in Cold Spring Harbor on Long Island, New York.[12]

Three areas in twentieth century America most influenced by eugenics were: (1) sterilization laws, which permitted the feeble-minded, insane, epileptics, drunkards, prostitutes, and drug addicts to be sterilized; (2) immigration laws that were based on the assumption that since the Nordic races by hereditary were more intelligent than other races, numbers of immigrants from Nordic countries were higher than those admitted from non-Nordic countries; and (3) the birth control movement, led by Margaret Sanger (1883–1966), founder of the National Birth Control League, who advocated increasing the low birth rate among the privileged and educated social classes and decreasing the high birth rate among the poor and uneducated classes. The logical conclusions of this "science" was the race ideology of the Nazis in Germany and the Ku Klux Klan in the United States.

In 1925 the Episcopal Church reaffirmed its support for eugenics. After a debate at General Convention on the issue of marriage between those deemed mentally fit and those deemed mentally unfit, the Convention voted to send the report of the Joint Commission on Family Life (which supported restricting such marriages) to every bishop and cleric. This conferred a particular authority on the contents and implicitly sanctioned its recommendation that clergy and laity work for a federal study on marriage between "persons of low mentality and infected with communicable disease" because of the suffering and crime caused by marriages between such people.[13]

In 1927, the U.S. Supreme Court joined the eugenics fray with a majority decision favoring sterilization to restrict reproduction by retarded persons. The famous jurist Justice Oliver Wendell Holmes wrote the majority opinion upholding a Virginia compulsory sterilization law in *Buck v. Bell*. Carrie Buck and her mother, both severely mentally retarded, were sterilized under Virginia law because Carrie's baby daughter was judged by the state to be "mentally unfit":

> It is better for all the world, if instead of waiting to execute degenerate offspring for crime, or to let them starve for their imbecility, society can prevent those who are manifestly unfit from continuing their kind. The principle that sustains compulsory vaccination is broad enough to cover cutting the Fallopian tubes. . . . Three generations of imbeciles are enough.[14]

In spite of some of the atrocious experiments with birth control and eugenics practiced by the Nazis in Germany, the church remained largely silent during the 1930s and 1940s about this issue. By the 1960s, the church's mind about the purpose of Christian marriage and its relationship to family life had changed radically. In 1961, General Convention adopted teachings forwarded by its Joint Commission on Human Affairs. Citing the Encyclical Letter of the 1958 Lambeth, the commission said:

> Although it is clearly a primary obligation of Christian marriage that children be born within the supporting framework of parental love and family support, it is not to be held from this that the procreation of children is the sole purpose of Christian marriage. Implicit within the bond between husband and wife is the relationship of love with its sacramental expression in physical union.[15]

This signaled that, not only had the purpose of marriage been drastically revised, but also teachings about the Christian family and the morality of birth control. Restrictions on bringing the fetus to full term were sanctioned under the rubric of "family planning". Birth control was permitted if both partners agreed to it and if it was "secure from the corruptions of sensuality and selfishness."[16]

The concept of "family" underwent slight but significant modification at the 1976 Convention and in a 1978 resolution of Executive Council. General Convention approved the 1976 report of its Joint Commission on the Church in Human Affairs that raised critical questions about the traditional meaning of marriage and family as the basis of Christian life and society: "There is a rapidly growing consensus that traditional marriage and family life are simply two possible options among many for the ordering of our sexual and social lives."[17] Indeed, the marriage vows themselves were questioned: "Committing ourselves to others in marriage until death do us part violates the first rule of adaptive survival behavior which is keeping open as many options as possible. It is also . . . probably bad for the human species."[18]

In 1978, the Executive Council endorsed the statement from the National Conference of Episcopalians that met in Denver November that year as significant for church teachings. The document affirmed the family as the foundation of society, but thought the church's basic assumptions about the family must be reexamined:

> The theology, myths, liturgy, history, and culture which affect our family values need evaluation. Some of our past may be causal to some of today's family stress.[19]

In 1961, abortion was rejected as morally unacceptable as a means of birth control. Programs of population control in developing countries were supported, provided they did not include abortion or infanticide. Yet, six years later, in 1967, the church came full circle and approved reform of abortion laws. This revision may have been influenced by the 1965 Supreme Court *Griswold v. Connecticut* decision and changes in states that liberalized their abortion laws. *Griswold* struck down a Connecticut law that made it a felony for a married couple to practice birth control, saying the law was an invasion of privacy guaranteed by the Constitution even in the bedroom. (In 1973, the Supreme Court would shatter all precedent with its controversial, landmark *Roe v. Wade* decision: the right of personal liberty guaranteed in the Fourteenth Amendment extends to the right of privacy as a fundamental right, which allows a woman to abort without undue interference by the state except under certain conditions prescribed by the court. Nevertheless, cautioned the court, "the privacy right involved cannot be said to be absolute [or] that one has an unlimited right to do with one's body as one pleases. . . .")

The bishops at the 1967 Convention condemned "abortions for

convenience" as inconsistent with the church's teaching about the sanctity of human life. At the same time, they recognized legitimate theological differences within the church about when human life actually begins. Abortions could be a matter of choice for Episcopalians under certain conditions, except for some morally unacceptable reasons: aborting (1) because of social embarrassment or inconvenience; (2) an illegitimate fetus; (3) when the expectant mother is younger than fifteen years old; (4) a difficult pregnancy; and (5) because financial problems would make it difficult to raise the child. However, the final text that was approved by both houses of Convention failed to include these conditions. The church supports abortion-law reform regarding the termination of pregnancy, provided that a decision to abort was made within proper moral safeguards, such as: (1) endangerment of the mother's physical health; (2) strong certainty that the baby would be "badly deformed in mind or body"; (3) pregnancies resulting from rape and incest. It allowed there might be other reasons for abortion, but said they were considered so grave that the parties ought to counsel with a priest and even consider the sacrament of penance before making a final decision.[20]

That General Convention also favorably commended some modern medical technology, such as genetic engineering and test-tube babies, noting that research in these areas will continue and advance "with or without the blessing of the Church." At the same time the church was entreated to provide some ethical teachings in this area because the professionals would be looking to the church for guidance in these areas. This position was a slight irony, since modern medical research and medical ethics have their own worldview and dynamics that proceed apace usually without giving attention to church social teachings or ethics, the occasion of the first test-tube baby being an example.

The pro-choice teaching about abortion under certain conditions continues to be the official mind of the Episcopal Church. A definitive statement was issued both in 1976 and 1982 that reaffirmed the 1967 teaching about the termination of a pregnancy only under certain conditions. At its 1988 General Convention, the church again endorsed this teaching. However, for the first time, it drew a distinction between a legal right and a moral obligation:

. . . in this country it is the legal right of every woman to have a medically safe abortion, [but] as Christians we believe strongly that if this right is exercised, it should be used only in extreme situations.21

Hence, abortion for a Christian is not solely a legal right but rather a moral undertaking *in extremis* as a last resort. This is a moral qualification similar to the conditions prescribed for using the rite of extreme unction (now called the anointing of the dying). Indeed, the church urges alternatives to abortion, such as bringing the child into the world and raising it or putting it up for adoption or handing it over to another member of the family for rearing.

However, the church drew back from supporting abortion legislation as the civil community's resolution of the moral issues: "Legislation concerning abortion will not address the root of the problem," although such legislation would continue despite the church's opposition or ambivalence. Church teachings about abortion do not permit unconditional choice by the mother or even by both father and mother at all times, as some wish to claim. Furthermore, other methods of family planning, such as artificial insemination of male semen for procreation, external fertilization, and intrauterine implantation of ova in the woman, are unequivocally repudiated. However, some other new genetic technologies, like "in vitro" fertilization that "enable parenthood for those who are prevented from pregnancy," thus providing "a child to an otherwise childless marriage, and both members of the couple are party to the conception,"22 are morally acceptable. Other technologies like using prenatal sex selection to decide whether to abort a fetus in order to correct "cosmetic" abnormalities are repudiated as moral options for Christians. 23

Sexuality

Human sexuality as a separate theme in social teachings was first systematically dealt with by the Episcopal Church in 1967, although it was touched upon in the 1922 report on family life. Some scholars say sexuality in the United States has moved through several phases: from the eighteenth century that focused on the family for procreative purposes, through romantic ideas about personal intimacy of the nineteenth century, to the twentieth century, where traditional discretion about sexual intimacy is considered a sign of inhibition and being "in the closet" as opposed to "being honest," and where sex has become a commodity to be marketed and commercialized.

The major event in the postwar years that challenged all ideas about sexuality, including theological concepts, was the sex-change surgery in the early 1950s. This came to public attention because an American, George Jorgensen, who, because of U.S. laws, travelled to Denmark for the first sex-change surgery. He subsequently became Christine Jorgensen and the new term *transsexual* joined the vocabulary of sexuality. Ethicists, psychologists, and theologians alike were jolted as they tried to fit this new phenomenon of human species into traditional concepts. Followed shortly by a sailor in England who became April Ashley and by others, transsexuals all echoed Jorgensen's protest that throughout his/her childhood and adult life they always felt "like a woman trapped in a man's body." This radical shift in understanding sexuality, occurring amid other rapid changes during the 1960s in society's emphasis on individual autonomy versus communal mutuality, had a telling effect on the cognizance of sexuality and sexual morality. One result was that sexuality and morality became matters purely of private choice, personal identity, erotic pleasure, and political liberation, often subject to no restraints or accountability. The teaching that sexuality and sexual morality carry social and communal responsibilities lessened once the hegemony of marriage as the context for fulfilled sexuality was diluted and abandoned. This amounted to a "loss of face," to use an oriental expression, for traditional sexual morality—a loss compounded, at least for middle class people and mainstream Protestant churches, by the feminist assault on marriage and family as signs of oppression and repression for women.

In addition, during the 1960s and 1970s, largely through the media and the feminist movement, sexuality was identified with gender. And through the gay liberation movement, at times it was interpreted as *sexual preference*, an expression of gay autonomy and private choice with its own subculture. Hence, a cornucopia of ideas about the concept of sexuality thrives, fueled by the competing vocabularies of psychology, psychiatry, sociology, biology, power politics, and theology.

In 1967, the church's Joint Commission on Human Affairs identified such times as "signs of confusion" within the secular community as well as the church community. It pleaded for a revision in the church's teachings about sexuality:

> The complex, sometimes referred to as the 'New Morality,' reflects changes in practice and attitudes in sexual behavior of which the Church must be keenly aware. . . . The traditional and often stereotyped attitudes of the Churches may no longer provide adequate guidance for people today.[24]

Toward that end, the commission singled out Gen. 1:27 as the basis of the church's teachings about sexuality: "male and female created he them."

But the report's authors said this text and the context in which it was written had less to do with the sexual act and more to do with dynamics of personal growth and sexual maturity in our male and female relationships. The church's attitude should be changed to focus on relationships of forgiveness and avoidance of chastising or ostracizing "those who have suffered from censure or other consequences of their behavior." Additionally, they urged support for "those who are honestly seeking to find solutions to the problems posed by the pressures of our society." The church was summoned to mobilize for change in civil laws that are repressive toward certain sexual groups, identified as a *minority* by the commission.

General Convention responded to the commission by approving a resolution stating that humankind is sexual by nature, which is a gift of God's creation. Also, the government should regulate only those areas of sexuality that have to do with the protection of society at large; otherwise sex and the practice of it should be a matter of private moral choice. Further studies were authorized "to determine the attitude of the Church with respect to birth control, contraception, sterilization, illegitimacy, divorce and remarriage, pre-marital, post-marital, and extra-marital behavior, sexual behavior of single adults, homosexuality and prostitution."[25]

Nonetheless, the church continued to hold that family life and sexuality mature and are properly fulfilled within Christian marriage, a position it reaffirmed even during internal and external pressures through the gay rights movements in the late 1960s. One outcome of the early conflicts about sexual identity between homosexuals and religious circles was the founding of a separate church for homosexuals in 1968 by a Pentecostal minister, Troy Perry: the Universal Fellowship of Metropolitan Community Churches (MCC). Many in the homosexual community applauded this idea because of their experience and perception of unending oppression and lack of support in all churches. As one lesbian wrote in a bittersweet tone during the 1970s.

> Woe to the lesbian who finds her 'mate' in the church and wants to express her love as openly as her heterosexual friends express theirs. Suddenly she is an outcast and must be removed immediately from any responsible position. . . . Instead she must keep her affectional preference wholly separate from her church life, only rarely sharing those experiences with her lover or, if both are in the same congregation, being absolutely circumspect when in others' presence.[26]

Around the same time, homosexuals in mainstream churches began to spawn unofficial gay caucuses as support groups: Integrity, the national Episcopal caucus, founded in 1976 by an admitted homosexual layman, Louis Crew, and his companion, after they were asked to withdraw from a parish because of their suspected homosexual life style; Dignity, the Catholic gay caucus; similar ones in the Methodist, Presbyterian, Reformed, and Lutheran churches. Many mainstream denominations, reacting to critiques of the homosexuals community about traditional teachings, commissioned studies of the biblical and doctrinal teachings about sexuality and homosexuality. Some were done by the Episcopal Church, the United Methodist Church, the Reformed Church, the Presbyterian Church, the United Church of Christ (UCC), and the Catholic Church. The academic community made its own contribution in 1975 by establishing the first scholarly journal devoted solely to the subject, the *Journal of Homosexuality*, which included articles, book reviews, and extracts from recent court cases.

When the gay movement and its sympathizers began pressuring the Episcopal Church and other mainstream churches to revise their teachings and tradition about ordaining self-identified homosexuals and those with a homosexual orientation to their ministry, these churches also reexamined the meaning of ordination. The National Council of Churches (NCC) in March 1975 responded in a statement urging civil rights for homosexuals, but revised the wording in its final text to exclude ordination for fear of offending some of its supporting churches. The Southern Baptists in 1976 urged their local congregations "not to afford the practice of homosexuality any degree of approval through ordination, employment or other designations of a normal life style." [27]

The Episcopal Church also resisted ordaining practicing homosexuals to the priesthood. Its 1976 General Convention said homosexuals are children of God like all other people with the same needs for the church's love, acceptance, and pastoral care and society's equal protection under civil law. But it refused to admit homosexuals to ordination. A resolution prohibiting bishops from ordaining "practicing" homosexuals was passed and a study of sexuality, particular contemporary life styles, housing, employment, and education with regard to homosexuals' rights was authorized. The study was assigned to the Joint Commission on the Church in Human Affairs, which was mandated to complete its study by the next General Convention in 1979.

In January 1977, the Episcopal Bishop of New York, Paul Moore, Jr., opted to defy this mind of the church and the Christian tradition regarding homosexuality by ordaining a self-identified lesbian to the church's priesthood. Claiming personal knowledge of many ordained homosexual clergy already in the active ministry of the Episcopal Church, the bishop praised the ordinand for "courage and compassion in her identification with the so-called gay community." He further justified his defiance under the general rubric of love and compassion, noting that "Jesus himself was not afraid to love anybody he felt like loving, and that included just about everyone except the Pharisees." [28] A motion of censure against the bishop failed in the House of Bishops, but the Executive Council later that year asked that no more practicing homosexuals be ordained until the church had reached a consensus about the issue at its forthcoming General Convention in 1979.

The 1977 Pastoral Letter reaffirmed the traditional model of Christian marriage as the context for true sexuality as male and female and for family:

It is clear from Scripture that the sexual union of man and woman is God's will and that this finds holy expression within the covenant of marriage. Therefore this Church confines its nuptial blessing to the union of male and female. It is likewise clear that in ordination, this Church publicly requires each ordinand to fashion his or her personal life after Christ as an example to the faithful.[29]

(The continued strength of this teaching about sexuality was reflected even in an amendment to a 1982 Convention resolution on pornography: "Sexual union is a Holy Bond of commitment and fidelity between man and woman through the blessing of the Holy Estate of Matrimony." Any circumstances or unions that equate human sexuality with "temporary pleasure, . . . promiscuity, prostitution, and degeneracy" were said to be contrary to the Christian understanding of human sexuality.)[30]

Accordingly, because homosexuality does not fall within this understanding of sexuality and holy matrimony, the 1977 Pastoral said that ordination was not appropriate for an "advocating and/or practicing homosexual person," since ordinands and priests are to be examples to the faithful.[31] Likewise, the 1979 Pastoral read, while homosexuals have a claim on the church's pastoral care, nevertheless the church upholds "the traditional Christian standards of marriage, fidelity, chastity and loving responsibility as binding on us all in our use of God's gift of sexuality." And although the bishops differed in their personal opinions about homosexuality, they were quite unequivocal that "most of the church cannot accept a homosexual liaison as an alternative lifestyle in the Christian and biblical tradition."[32]

The 1979 report from the Human Affairs and Health Commission to General Convention focused on the plurality of views about sexuality in the Bible. At the same time, it also reaffirmed the social responsibility attached to sexuality. Acknowledging that sexuality is not a primary issue in Scripture, nevertheless, its authors asserted that the Bible generally teaches that sex is basically good:

The Bible provides examples of the good use of sex—as an expression of love, family and friendship, and examples of the misuse of sex—as in infidelity, breaking up family love, regarding people as things as in the case of prostitution, etc. The basic problem of sex, therefore, is not sexual, but ethical and religious.

Furthermore, they noted that biblically such practices as adultery, prostitution, promiscuity, and homosexuality (probably pederasty) are considered immoral, not because they have to do with sex. Rather, these practices violate personal integrity, family fidelity and love, social responsibility to others, and reflect "an idolatrous obsession with sex...or are seen as deleterious to the family and/or to the structure and quality of society."[34]

The doctrine of creation and the biblical covenant form the theological setting for Christian judgment about the worth or unworthiness of different sexual acts. (The commission seemed unclear about whether sex means an act between two people for erotic and pleasurable satisfaction, or sexuality involving gender, personhood, and identity.) Homosexuality, continued the report, is a mixture of the known and the unknown in professional scientific studies. The document concluded with the following social teachings about human sexuality that were approved by the church:

1. Sex is intended for procreation and family life, thereby furthering the welfare of society and the church.
2. Sex is an expression of love apart from producing babies.
3. Sexual activity can be judged good or bad depending on how it expresses well-being and love.
4. For the Christian, all norms must be measured and informed by scripture and "Gospel love," thus adultery and promiscuity are violations of these standards.

The commission, however, failed to carry out the second part of its mandate, namely, to offer a position on the ordination to the ministry of self-identified, practicing homosexuals. Instead, it recommended that, since the fundamental question for ordained clergy ought to be whether the person can lead a life "which is a wholesome example to Christ's flock," homosexuals able to conform to this expectation ought not be barred from ordination. Nor should any church legislation treat homosexuality as an absolute barrier to ordination. But the church rejected this position, agreeing instead to affirm "the traditional teaching of the Church on marital fidelity and sexual chastity as the standard of Christian morality,"[35] thereby barring any one unable to conform to this doctrine. This teaching is the current mind of the Episcopal Church, even with some dissent.

The standing critique by the homosexual movement has been

that the exclusivity of traditional Christian doctrine about marriage prohibits recognition and acceptance of homosexual partnerships as analogous to Christian marriage. In speaking to this critique, the 1982 General Convention reaffirmed marriage between man and woman as the Christian model for family and sexuality. At the same time, it expanded the meaning of *family*: the church "affirms the family under God *in its many forms* [italics added] as the basic foundation of society and church."[36] Parishes were charged to study the

> means of revitalization of the sacramental and redemptive qualities of marriage...counseling, advice, and spiritual support for prospective partners in the sacrament . . . continuing parish support for the married pair; guidance in childbearing and rearing.[37]

Much public support for homosexual rights was gained in the popular culture through the film media in the 1980s, such as "Victor, Victoria" and "Tootsie," both released in 1982. In 1986, however, much of this was eroded by a sharply divided Supreme Court (5-4) in *Hardwick v. Georgia*. The majority ruled that the constitutional right of privacy does not extend to homosexual acts, such as sodomy, when forbidden by state law. A distinction was made between choices considered essential for heterosexual lifestyles, such as marriage, conceiving a child, carrying a pregnancy to term, and homosexual acts:

> Even if the conduct at issue here is not a fundamental right, respondent asserts that there must be a rational basis for the law and that there is none in this case other than the presumed belief of a majority of the electorate in Georgia that homosexual sodomy is immoral and unacceptable. This is said to be an inadequate rationale to support the law. The law, however, is constantly based on a notion of morality.[38]

The enormous state of flux in the church and culture about sexuality and family was further complicated by a controversial 1987 report from the diocese of Newark, New Jersey, entitled "Changing Patterns of Sexuality and Family Life." The model of the church, said the document, should be that of an "open-ended, searching" community rather than a defined community. It proposed that the church approve alternative life styles in addition to monogamous Christian marriage: (1) adults who choose to live in common law marriage, that is, as unmarrieds; (2) adults who choose not to marry or remarry after a divorce or death; and (3) homosexual lovers who live together or who say that they are "married" as a couple. The report, admitting that the church needed criteria for testing alternative life styles, proposed the following: (1) the relationship should be "life-enhancing" for both partners; (2) the relationship should be grounded in sexual fidelity and avoid promiscuity; and (3) the relationship should be grounded in love, support and benefit for the couple and those to whom they are related.[39]

The Newark document furthered the Anglican model of *consensus fidelium* in defining social teachings in contrast to the Roman model of *magisterium ordinarium*. That is, as awkward and as untidy as it might appear, the Anglican model relies on arguments, counter-arguments, and dialogue from various sources within the respective dioceses and the larger human community until an authoritative consensus is reached. But even that consensus is subject to revision and critique by the same process.

For example, the Standing Commission on Human Affairs and Health that had the mandate of providing the church with a clear statement about sexuality and sexual ethics at the 1988 General Convention, initiated a series of articles on sexual ethics in the national newspaper, *The Episcopalian*.[40] The first article by the commission itself complained of the discrepancy between the church's teaching that sex is to be practiced only within the bonds of Christian marriage and the rejection of this teaching by young people:

> With an anticipation of death in one's 30s, waiting until age 25 to marry would not be sensible. One tended to enter marriage shortly after puberty. Those generations of people would never understand our culturally imposed separation between puberty and marriage which now stretches from 10 to 15 years. . . . Can we then take this ancient injunction from its different context and apply it in the complexities of our world?[41]

However, General Convention in 1988 chose to maintain the church's traditional teachings about sexuality and to press for further study of the issue in dioceses.

Oddly enough, the Church's Teaching Series contradicted the bishops and General Convention, saying "We cannot even claim to have a single 'Christian model' for family life," since there are so many competing claims in the world today, which it proceeds to describe and criticize.[42] However, such a claim ignored exiting documents about family life and sexuality. The series may disagree with the teachings and may certainly offer a critique, but it is neither theologically nor pastorally responsible to state that the Episcopal Church does not have a model for family life.

In summary, Episcopal social teachings about the family and sexuality can be described as follows:

1. The Christian model for sexuality is marriage and the family, meaning male and female vowing lifelong partnership and devotion to each other in Holy Matrimony, and the producing of children (if possible or desired) to strengthen this partnership and perpetuate the larger community. The family is the most basic unit for preserving and furthering civil society, although since the 1980s, a consensus no longer exists about how inclusive or exclusive the institution "family" is to be understood with single parents, extramarital live-in arrangements, and elderly widows and widowers living alone.

2. Abortion as a means of birth control and family planning is condemned. Abortion and the termination of pregnancy are moral options for Christians only under certain conditions: (1) the mother's physical health is endangered; (2) strong conclusive evidence that the offspring will likely be "badly deformed" in body or mind; (3) pregnancies resulting from rape or incest. Other reasons for terminating a pregnancy or undertaking abortion may be considered, but Episcopalians should seek the counsel of a priest before a final decision. Hence, the church quite firmly rejects the argument that abortion is an absolute civil right of the woman carrying the child and hers alone. The church says that for Christians, abortion is not an unconditional autonomous right without moral consequences. Abortion is always an extreme action to be undertaken only under certain conditions and with some priestly counsel.

3. Modern scientific and medical technologies such as genetic engineering, "test-tube babies," and "in vitro" fertilization can be undertaken by Christians with good conscience. But applying prenatal sex selection technologies as the basis for an abortion is roundly condemned.

4. The biblical doctrine of creation is the theological basis for a Christian concept of human sexuality, in which the church's view about gender is grounded. Sexuality is not to be confused with the sexual act or "making sex" or "sexual preference." Sexuality is a gift from God, whose fulfillment is to be found in Christian marriage. Any circumstances or unions that equate human sexuality with "temporary pleasure . . . , promiscuity, prostitution, and degeneracy" violate the Christian concept of sexuality.

5. Homosexuals are children of God endowed with God's image like all other people, who share the benefits of the church's attention, pastoral care, and love as well as equal protection under the civil laws like all other citizens. Homosexuality, however, does not fall within the church's concept of Christian sexuality nor homosexual unions within Christian matrimony. For this reason, a practicing or "advocating" homosexual cannot be ordained to the ministry of the Episcopal Church, since this would not conform to the model of Christ as an example to the faithful.

6. Marital fidelity and sexual chastity are the standards for Christian morality and the sex act.

7. Sex is to express mutual love between partners, to afford them pleasure within the marital bond, and to procreate and further family life within the church and the civil community. Adultery and promiscuity fall outside these norms and thus are unacceptable as a proper Christian understanding of the sex act.

Commentary

The continued controversy about the meaning of sexuality and the drastic changes in the social climate about private choice as the arbiter of truth in all matters of sexual morality ensures a "no win" answer to this explosive issue regardless of the position adopted by a person or the church. Moreover, the climate in which such discourse occurs is increasingly influenced and shaped by changing medical technologies, psychotherapy models in pastoral care that are replacing the traditional concept of the care of souls, theonomous-like claims of psychology, psychiatry, and sociology in the civil and religious communities. So at best opinions in this area can only be transitory and risky. This is especially the case in the United States, where surveys show that most Americans still believe religion to be solely a private and individualistic matter devoid of any kind of membership in a religious community or subject to accountability to or intervention by the religious community.[43]

The great flux in cultural attitudes about self-expression and discretion regarding sex, sexual morality, and sexuality during the 1960s and 1970s, induced by reconfigurated openness, permissiveness, and alacrity in discussing and doing sex, diminished or removed previous inhibitions and responsibility. At the same time the excessive number of divorces and court decisions about "palimony," which decided that under certain conditions a live-in mistress was entitled to compensation as a form of alimony from the man, sped up the erosion of teachings and cultural attitudes about the permanence and exclusivity of the marital bond. This corrosion was assisted by the print and film media, the "pill," the critique by the homosexual "gay and proud" liberation movement, and the feminist movement among some women.

At the same time, society has been sensitized to injustices inflicted upon homosexuals and tolerance of their subcultures. Most large cities, for example, allow "Gay Pride Day" or "Gay Liberation Day" parades and activities as a part of their urban ritual, which would not have been possible before "gay rights" became a political and moral issue. In addition the availability and inexpensiveness of "the pill" and other contraceptives, peer and media pressure to use them, legalized abortion, and new pop culture celebrities have joined to remove or lessen fears and risks about engaging in sex outside of marriage, accidental pregnancies and unwanted babies.

This new morality has been most apparent in the age group wanted by all churches as future legatees of their teachings and traditional sex morality: the teenagers and young adults. Studies have shown that traditional codes have largely crumbled among this age group, which on the whole thinks sex and sexuality to be a private matter and choice for individuals without the intervention either of parents or secondary institutions like the church and school. For example, a study showed the percentage of unmarried girls between the ages of fifteen and nineteen admitting to having had sexual intercourse with boys had increased from 28 percent in 1971 to 44 percent in 1982. Additional studies have confirmed that well over 50 percent of teen-agers say they have usually engaged in sex before their eighteenth birthday. Moreover, teenage pregnancies not only are very widespread, but are also no longer taboo in the general public. It is estimated that over 1,000,000 teenage girls get pregnant every year: 400,000 of them have abortions. Hence, traditional social teachings about abstinence before marriage by both males and females have gone the way of all flesh under the pressure and influence of pop culture, instant self-gratification, "me too" fulfillment without social responsibility or limits.

The issue of *sexual orientation* or *sexual preference* has also brought another dimension to contemporary discourse about sexuality. These terms, frequently used interchangeably, have been created largely for the benefit of men and women in the homosexual community and subculture. They intend to express a nonheterosexual alternative to masculinity and femininity as an identity. They also have been politicized in order to influence legislation ending discrimination and legal abuses against homosexuals. One of the first cities to incorporate this term into law was San Francisco in 1978. Its city council passed an ordinance banning discrimination in housing, employment, and public accommodations based on "sexual preference."

However, the proposal that homosexuality as an expression of one's sexuality or sexual preference within the context of life-long fidelity and faithfulness in a same-gender partnership is analogous to Christian matrimony and partnership often begs the question about community, at least according to church teachings about community within matrimony. It is very difficult to separate homosexuality from its many practices and erotic covenants and subcultures accepted by many homosexual communities as entirely permissible under an ethic of individual autonomy and private choice of life style. Many of these covenants, from the perspective of church teaching about bonding and community, can be termed nihilistic and selfish. Such practices frequently tolerated under the rubric of homosexuality include preoccupation with isolated and mutual masturbation and exhibitionism, sadomasochistic sex (bondage, bodily violence, gadgets, Nazi and police uniforms), scat (Gk.= *skatos*, "dung" or "excrement"), pederasty, anal sex with fists ("fisting"). Such may be accepted as proper "sexual orientation" within the homosexual subcultures. Yet the church quite rightly questions the relationship of such practices and codes in light of its own teachings about Christian sexuality and community.

In a series of articles on sexuality and "the sexual revolution" of the 1960s and 1970s, James Nelson proposed that several significant changes have taken place since those tumultuous years, when shorthand for declining intimacy and the abandonment of social taboos and discretion in personal erotic behavior was called "liberation."[44] First, he says, a shift has occurred from theologies of sexuality to "sexual theologies." Human experience rather than church teachings and the Bible has become the primary means for perceiving God and faith. The feminist and the homosexual liberation movements have contributed to this through the media, which in turn has informed and influenced the wider public.

Second, the tradition of dualism between body and spirit that shaped so much of the church's view of sexuality and sex has corroded. Sexuality is now understood as intrinsic to the encounter between humanity and divinity, whereby in traditional teachings, erotic behavior was separated from the divine and therefore from God.

Third, the perception of sexual sin as wrong sexual acts has changed to sexual sin meaning separation from "our intended sexuality." This grounds sexuality in the doctrine of creation rather than in a series of acts, such as sexual violence, sexual perversions, promiscuous sex, pornography, and wife-battering.

Fourth, sexuality has changed from being a private issue to being a public and personal issue, as shown in the churches' willingness to discuss abortion, birth control, sexual abuse, prostitution, AIDS and other sexually transmitted diseases.

The question of interpreting the biblical texts—what academics call the hermeneutical issue—is not a new problem, of course, even in the area of sexual ethics. But the 1988 report of the Standing Commission on Human Affairs may have repeated the same error of nineteenth century liberalism, namely, seeing Jesus Christ largely as a teacher in a particular history rather than as the revealed Word of God preceding, acting in, and following all of history with its past, present, and future eras. If Jesus Christ is primarily thought of as a teacher and if Scripture in the life of the early Christians was primarily an account of axioms and moral principles, then biblical teachings can be viewed largely as examples of certain accidents occurring in that particular history and culture. Such a position runs the risk of trivializing the credibility of God's revelation in Jesus Christ as Christ revealed the new life and the new way in God to all, Christian and non-Christian alike. The event of the Christ and the message of the Christ are one. Theologically, Jesus in the first century cannot be separated from Jesus Christ in Scripture nor the early church separated from Jesus Christ, the complete revelation and Word of God then, now, and in the future. This claim about universal truth dwelling in Jesus Christ extends to Jesus' message about sexual ethics as well. "I am the way, the truth, and the life. No man cometh to the father but by me." (John 14:6)

Therefore, while it is important to understand the context of Jesus's message, it is also important not to *contextualize* his teachings in order to disregard or trivialize them when they do not appear in accord with such neo-Enlightenment cultural values as personal autonomy and absolute private choice. Nor must the canons of modern psychology, sociology, biology, unlimited sexual freedom (even with the AIDS epidemic), and civil religion become the media for defining theologically Christian revelation about community and sexuality. This is not to argue for a biblical legalism. Rather it is a plea to hold both the church and the culture accountable to a revelation that Christians know in Scripture, which is to be witnessed in the life and tradition of the church. It is clear that the church is mandated to interpret that revelation and tradition to various cultures and in changing times at all times. The human family and sexual identity have been public rather than private issues certainly since the nineteenth century raised critical questions about the economic, biological, and psychological infrastructures of human formation and the human community, such as marriage and the family. And the church understands that it must utilize insights discovered by other disciplines asking these critical questions. But it need not abandon its vocabulary and theological methods in doing so.

However, a much deeper theological issue is at stake in the question of the standing commission (and some bishops) about the timeliness and relevance of Christian sexual ethics, often summarily dismissed as "ancient" and therefore "not up to date." This issue has to do with the very person and work of Jesus Christ as light of light, true God of true God, and Lord of lords at the beginning, center, and end of our very existence (including our sexuality). The issue is whether our identity in and obedience to Christ include boundaries, even in sexual ethics. In this respect, Nelson claimed incorrectly that the church had allowed Victorian middle-class conduct to privatize sexuality. Christian doctrine about marriage and sexuality always stressed communal tasks. Community was not restricted to procreation and extension of the race, although at times both were frequently overemphasized. Rather the significance of community in sexuality has to do with creation itself and the link between the creator and the created in male and female, body and soul, in genital sexual pleasure as well as making babies.

Most especially, the communal nature of sexuality undergirds our humanity. "Male and female created he them," says a creation narrative (Gen. 1:27). In Christian doctrine, humanity means a partnership of male and female that is a divine gift revealed at creation itself. Humanity reflects a primal partnership, even though marred by sin. Autonomy and private beliefs about our sexuality, sexual behavior, and sexual orientation held up as private theonomous claims on God or as compassion without ethics can easily become a form of inhumanity. As the ethicist Philip Turner has wisely noted:

If sex is understood as primarily a form of conversation intended for the mutual benefit of autonomous holders of rights and duties, . . . it is not difficult to think of sexual engagements as being *limited* in duration and as appropriate with more than one partner at a time. After all, we can carry on a number of conversations at once, we can limit their duration and intensity, and we can hold conversations for a number of different purposes.[45]

This primal communal character of humanity, expressed most profoundly in marriage and sexual intercourse, can be seriously endangered and lost under the imprimatur of individual autonomy, private pleasure, and genital sex (whether bisexual, heterosexual or homosexual). Loss of the communal nature of sexuality means a loss of our bonding to fellow-humanity. As Karl Barth noted, human beings saying "this is my private affair" or "that is none of your business" usually results in their isolation without fellow-humanity, which is then inhumanity.[46]

Notes

1. Friedrich Engels, *The Origin of the Family, Private Property and the State*, trans. Alec West (New York: International Publishers, 1970), p. 129.

2. Carol Hymowitz and Michaele Weissman, *A History of Women in America* (New York: Bantam Books, 1978), p. 65.

3. Davidson, *The Five Lambeth Conferences*, pp. 133-5.

4. *The Truth Shall Make You Free: The Lambeth Conference 1988*, pp. 220-21.

5. *Pastoral Letter of the House of Bishops, A.D. 1892*, pp. 10-11.

6. Ibid., p. 12.

7. *Journal of the General Convention, 1922*, pp. 697-8.

8. Ibid., p. 703.

9. Ibid., p. 702.

10. *Journal of the General Convention, 1925*, p. 577.

11. *Journal of the General Convention, 1922*, p. 114.

12. See James F. Childress and John Macquarrie, eds., *The Westminster Dictionary of Christian Ethics* (Philadelphia: Westminster Press, 1967), pp. 209-10; *New Catholic Encyclopedia* Vol. 5 (San Francisco: McGraw-Hill, 1967), pp. 627-9.

13. *Journal of the General Convention, 1925*, p. 578.

14. Caleb Foote, Robert J. Levy, and Frank E.A. Sander, *Cases and Materials on Family Law* (Boston: Little, Brown, 1976), pp. 547-8.

15. *Journal of the General Convention, 1961*, p. 548.

16. Ibid.

17. *Journal of the General Convention, 1976*, p. AA-155.

18. Ibid., p. AA-157.

19. *Church and Society: Social Policy of the Episcopal Church*, December 1967-April 1979, p. 332.

20. *Journal of the General Convention, 1967*, pp. 307-9.

21. *Journal of the General Convention, 1988*, pp. 683-4.

22. *Journal of the General Convention, 1982*, pp. C-158.

23. Ibid.

24. *Journal of the General Convention, 1967*, p. 22.4 Appendix.

25. Ibid., pp. 492-3.

26. Nancy E. Krody, "Woman, Lesbian, Feminist, Christian," *Christianity and Crisis* 37 (May 30 & June 13, 1977): 132.
27. Ibid., p. 121.
28. *New York Times*, January 24, 1977.
29. *Pastoral Letter to the Church from the House of Bishops*, October 1977, p. 3.
30. *Journal of the General Convention, 1982*, p. C-154.
31. *Pastoral Letter to the Church from the House of Bishops*, October 1977, p. 3
32. *A Pastoral Letter from the House of Bishops*, October 1979, p. 2.
33. *Journal of the General Convention, 1979*, p. AA-129.
34. Ibid., p. AA-130.
35. *Journal of the General Convention, 1982*, p. C-153.
36. *Journal of the General Convention, 1982*, p. C-153.
37. Ibid., p. C-156.
38. *New York Times*, July 1, 1986, p. A15.
39. In 1988, two public decisions expanded the traditional concept of family. (1) The City Council in San Francisco in May 1988 recognized homosexual and unmarried heterosexual couples as a "family" with regard to insurance claims and rental contracts, provided they registered with the city as "domestic partners, who have chosen to share one another's lives in an intimate and committed relationship." In 1989, this was rejected by the voters of the city. (2) In July 1988, New York State's highest court (Court of Appeals) ruled that a homosexual couple living together under certain conditions for a period of time could be considered a "family" under New York City's rental laws.
40. See *The Episcopalian* (February through May 1987).
41. *The Episcopalian*, February 1987, p. 6.
42. Earl H. Brill, *The Christian Moral Vision* (New York: Seabury, 1979), pp. 107-10.
43. In Gallup Polls for 1957, 1978, and 1988, 76-78 percent of Americans (three out of four) believed one could be a good Christian or Jew without attending church or a synagogue. The highest percentage (84 percent) was college graduates, who are also a large constituency in Episcopal parishes and lay leadership.
44. James B. Nelson, "Reuniting Sexuality and Spirituality," *The Christian Century* 104 (February 25, 1987): 187-90.
45. Philip Turner, *Sex, Money & Power* (Cambridge, MA: Cowley Publications, 1985), pp. 57-8.

46. Karl Barth, *Church Dogmatics*, *(The Doctrine of Creation)*, III/2, trans. Harold Knight, *et. al.* (Edinburgh: T.&T. Clark, 1960), p. 251.

Chapter 7
Pictures of an Exhibition: Episcopal Social Teachings IV

Economic Issues

At its 1988 General Convention the church established the program Ministry of Community Development and Economic Justice with funding of $250,000. The objectives resembled those of GCSP of the 1970s: a ministry "directed to community-controlled economic development programs of the disadvantaged," with particular attention paid to land, housing cooperatives, worker-owned businesses, and community-oriented credit unions. *Land* was understood to mean land-use in cities and in rural areas where farmers were losing their land through the acquisition strategies of the huge agribusiness firms. *Housing* referred to the policies of the federal government in the 1980s, which eliminated federal incentives and subsidies for low- and moderate-income rental units and houses, thereby discouraging private industry from investing in such housing because of its unprofitability.

Likewise, this program addressed the issues of factory closings, which had destroyed some communities and marginalized others, and dwindling jobs in manufacturing industries, which historically provided the unskilled and the undereducated the opportunity of upward mobility. Generally, the church was trying to deal with the rapid technological advances in industry and corporations by paying attention to what some called "the throw away people": those lacking marketable skills or sufficient education to cope in less labor-intensive manufacturing and service industries.

American society, business, industry, and American churches have been forced to pay more attention to the global aspect of economic competition and the increasing dependence of the U.S.

economy on the resources and labor of the developing, poorer countries, the so-called Third World, for our standard of living and comforts. The Brandt Report (officially, the *Report of the Independent Commission on International Development Issues, 1980*), commended at the 1982 General Convention, used the terminology North (Europe, North America, Japan, South Africa, Australia) and South (the developing poorer countries mostly in the Third World) to characterize the economic global divisions. These divisions have serious economic and geopolitical implications for the haves (the North) and the have-nots (the South). Hence, the Episcopal Church was also beginning to understand itself as an *American* denomination concerned about the moral consequences of the United States global and geopolitical aims as the leading economic power in the North.

The Brandt Report emphasized the link between world peace and the economic order:

> While the prevention of nuclear war remains the first ambition of disarmament, 'conventional' (non-nuclear) weapons account for 80 per cent of all arms spending. In fact all the wars since the Second World War have been fought with conventional weapons, and in the Third World. . . . The major powers sell weapons mainly to suit their own foreign policy or to maintain regional balances, rather than benefit their economies. . . .[1]

As the 1982 General Convention resolution said, this report reminded the church of the urgency to address the issue of a just world economic order and the link between huge defense spending and poverty in the Third World.[2] Concern for the effect of the U.S. industrial-military complex on other social problems had been expressed several times before by the church in its statements about peace and military spending. But now the church dealt critically with the moral issues arising from the massive economic force of this complex on the economies and social programs of the United States and the Third World. The reverse side, of course, was sensitivity to the fact that many jobs and communities in the United States depended on defense contracts, military spending, and sales to the military community.

As previously noted, the Episcopal Church first voiced views about economic issues in the report of the Joint Commission on Relations of Capital and Labor, created in 1901. The theological model at that time was borrowed from Anglican social thought as well as the church's own self-understanding as one of the guardians of civil morality: the church as reconciler or arbitrator among opposing camps with different economic interests. The vision was one favored by F.D. Maurice and other Christian Socialists in the Church of England: the restoration of a Christian brotherhood among all classes in society, where each class, mindful of its duty and responsibility for the sake of civility in society, would cooperate with each other. This view persisted even through the First World War. The 1916 Pastoral boldly asserted that the church, because of our common humanity in Jesus Christ, has the "capacity for universal brotherhood."[3] And at the end of the war the 1919 Pastoral claimed, "In the strife between Capital and Labor neither the one nor the other can have a background of certainty on which to proceed without the aid of the Church." It is Christian laity as employer and employee, who can move the economic order toward "neighborliness, friendship, and brotherhood."[4]

But the church also began to address the glaring differences in the distribution of wealth and working conditions in America, particularly during the early twentieth century Social Gospel movement in most mainline Protestant churches. At that time, the standard schedule for workers in manufacturing was a swing-shift of seven eleven-hour days one week followed by seven thirteen-hour nights the next week. Paid vacations and hospitalization did not exist. The usual two holidays given the workers (without pay) were Christmas and July Fourth. At the same time, executives and managers in these industries received large salaries and benefits many times the wages of the workers, while working under more humane conditions. Indeed, it was not until 1923 that industry, under pressure from the government, agreed to an eight-hour day and a six-day work week.

At its 1913 General Convention, the church noted the inhumane structures in the corporate world and labeled them "destructive" to workers. Managers should support business organizational structures that "will genuinely elicit personal initiative and self-respect of the workman and give him a definite, personal stake in the system of production to which his life is given."[5] Christian principles for a just economic order are always related to the advancement of social justice and include the following: (1) equitable distribution of wealth; (2) the elimination of poverty; (3) a just and fair return to the worker for his work; (4) time for personal development and recreation by the workers; and (5) financial benefits for the workers from improved productivity in a business.[6]

Apart from this action, most of the teachings about economic issues during the 1920s were found in Pastoral Letters rather than in actions of General Convention. The 1922 Pastoral meekly moved toward thinking theologically about the economy. The fundamental Christian principle of economic and social justice is the primacy of human values even in corporate culture: "The end of business is not primarily profit but human welfare and the common good." Nevertheless, even this principle can be realized through "cooperation in service for the common good, in place of unrestricted competition for private or sectional advantage."[7] Also at General Convention that year the church adopted a "Social Service Creed" that included under "Christian principles" (1) a minimum wage; (2) extra wages above the minimum to allow the worker minimum living comforts, even if it meant less preference for profits and property rights; (3) cooperation between employer and employee; (4) industrial democracy; and (5) collective bargaining. Under industrial democracy, the creed noted that workers in a factory ought to have some voice in the management and production of the factory. "The worker of today is rightly seeking self-expression and self-determination in industry, as well as a livelihood from industry."[8] In a milder final document, this last point was omitted, but social justice, human dignity, and the need of the strong to help the less-strong were affirmed as the mind of the church.

The 1929 Pastoral after the Great Depression bewailed the general malaise and genuine crisis in the civil community:

> An acquisitive society . . . stands bewildered in the presence of a crisis precipitated, not by earthquake, droughts, floods or any physical catastrophes, but, apparently, by the competitive profit-seeking principles, upon which, it has been hitherto assumed, general prosperity is based. . . . The Church cannot advocate a particular method, but we call upon the employers in our communion to labor for a plan, or plans, which shall coordinate production and consumption, ensure continuity of employment and provide security of income to the workers of this nation.[9]

At the same time, the bishops also were sensitive to the global interdependence of western economies, most of which had been also gravely affected by America's Great Depression:

The mountains and seas which once separated nation from nation have lost their meaning, and in an area no longer divided into separate compartments, racial and economic barriers to intercommunication are doomed. . . . No international relations can be stable which are not universal in their scope.[10]

In 1931 a report by the Committee on National and World Problems spoke to the issue of jobs and economic security in the American economic system. The report challenged the prevailing Leibniz-like view that society was made up of individual monades (which really was a playback of Victorian ideology about rugged individualism): "It is becoming increasingly evident that the conception of society as made up of autonomous, independent individuals, each free to seek his own ends, is as faulty from the point of view of economic realism as it is from the standpoint of Christian idealism."[11] From a Christian ethical position, interdependence existed between all members and classes in American society and indeed globally. Hence, job and economic security was to be a priority on behalf of the poorer members of the human community, even in the crisis of the Depression.

By 1933 the bishops were boldly calling for a *new economic order* in their now famous Davenport Pastoral. Sketching the new order in quick brushlike strokes, they wrote:

No mere reestablishment of an old economic order will suffice. Christ demands a new order in which there shall be a more equitable distribution of material wealth, more certain assurance of security for the unemployed and aged, and, above all else, an order which shall substitute the motive of service for the motive of gain.[12]

Possibly, as a Christian alternative to President Roosevelt's National Recovery Act (1933), the bishops with some whimsy proposed the cross: "For us the Cross stands as the symbol of a world recovery act. It demands that we become world recovery agents who dare to carry the Cross."[13]

The following year the bishops went further and endorsed the right of workers to organize trade unions and to bargain with employers. They emphasized the special concern of Christ for the poor and underprivileged, saying that even though Christian civilization had produced economic inequities, they were departures "from the right principles enunciated by Christ."[14] However, the bishops were not concrete about the content of these "right principles." They also reaffirmed the Maurician idea of a partnership between labor and capital as exemplary of Christian brotherhood.

By 1937, the idea of a new economic order was heard no more. Most of the principles in the 1922 "Social Service Creed" were reaffirmed as all of Europe was in chaos because of German aggression and labor-capital strife and strikes everywhere. The church's national department of Christian Social Service submitted a fairly dauntless document, announcing that the gospel's message is at the same time a social mandate. What finally passed Convention was a milder substitute text called "Affirmation of Christian Principles." In it social justice, individual dignity, and the duty of the strong to assist the weak were affirmed, while class warfare, intolerance, and barriers preventing harmony were decried.

Attention to economic issues after the war focused mostly on unemployment rather than structures and forces within the U.S. economy that caused unemployment. The 1949 report of the Joint Commission on Social Reconstruction, set up to advise and alert the church about pressing social and economic matters, failed to mention economic issues at all. In its 1952 report the commission spoke of existing trade barriers in the United States leading to economic discrimination, but neglected to provide any theological rationale as to why this policy ought to engage Christians or Episcopalians. It also commended the Four Point program of the government that offered technical and financial assistance to developing and under-developed countries, but again failed to provide any reflection on even the economic issues at stake in that a program.[15] (In 1958, it was renamed the Joint Commission on the Church in Human Affairs.)

At its 1949 General Convention, the church amended a proposal creating a Joint Commission to Study Work in Industrial Areas to be instead a Joint Commission to Survey Problems of Missionary Work in Industrial Areas, which was not funded until the 1952 Convention. Its primary purpose was to educate and develop a strategy for attracting blue-collar workers to the Episcopal Church. Its reports examined various economic issues and social conditions more precisely than those of the previous Commission on Social Reconstruction. In its first report in 1955, the commission encouraged active solidarity between the unions and the church: "A passive Church will never win the militant worker. The union is fighting . . . for all kinds of things that make for a better community. As the Church fights militantly for these goals, it finds itself fighting side by side with the labor union."[16] At the same time, the church could be the instrument for bringing managers and unions together:

> Both saint and sinners are to be found among men who punch time clocks and among men who do not. The Church fights for the conversion of everyone, worker and manager alike, neither praising or condemning any man on the basis of his membership in either group.[17]

(In 1961, the commission proposed that the church undertake a theological study of work conditions and leisure among workers in industrial areas. General Convention failed to pass it.)

Economic issues as a part of the church's social ministry moved in a new direction in 1967: a proposed review of church investments in corporations and banks doing business in southern Africa. In 1970, the House of Bishops (without the House of Deputies concurring) said, "The Church must express responsible stewardship in the investment of its wealth."[18] They asked for an Executive Council committee to examine church investments in southern Africa and a Ghetto Investment Committee to review the church's investments in minority-owned banks and businesses in order "to improve the economic well-being of minority and poverty groups located in both urban and rural areas within the United States."[19] Executive Council established the committees.

The 1970s saw a more reflective church prepared to be more aggressive in carrying out its mission as a participant in the economic system of the United States. Its actions could be called a "Christ as transformer of culture" position. This new assertiveness began with a 1971 report from the Executive Council's Committee on Social Criteria in Investments (its name was eventually changed to the Committee on Social Responsibility in Investments). SRI monitored (and still does) the national church's investments. Each of its actions was (and continues to be) authorized by Executive Council at its regular meetings. The committee acknowledged the church's considerable financial influence as a shareholder in many American corporations and owner of substantial investments. Ownership has social and theological significance for stewardship and social justice: "What has not always been so obvious is the necessity for this Church to use its economic power for Godly purposes in the framing of a more just and equitable society which respects and enhances human dignity while preserving the only inhabitable environment we possess."[20] The church must insist on criteria other than maximizing profits to measure benefits gained from its investments. Toward this end, the church must

> use our power as shareholders to influence the social policy aspects of corporate decisions. . . . If we, the Church, are indifferent to the responsibilities of ownership regarding our own securities, we forfeit the right to expect the individual to be a responsible steward of his possessions.[21]

The Executive Council authorized the first proxy vote of the Episcopal Church in light of this new social teaching to be cast at the annual meetings of General Motors, Kennecott Copper, and American Metal Climax. The latter two companies had copper mines in Puerto Rico that were viewed as ecologically endangering the environment as well as the health and welfare of Puerto Ricans.

In a 1982 resolution on "Moral criteria," the coupling between economic benefits and profits in U.S. corporations and our affluent life-styles and stewardship in the environment was addressed because of an increasing scarcity of natural resources. The church said the communal "common good" was abused by many corporations, especially those whose factories move from communities whose economic and social welfare has depended on those factories, resulting in economic and social disorientation. Common good in this context means (1) optimal employment of people in a community; (2) equitable wage standards for all employees; (3) support of collective bargaining; and (4) support of measures that help stabilize communities.[22] Common good also includes the idea that management's unavoidable social responsibility is a moral as well as a business task: "That such decisions avoid increasing the concentration of power and wealth as inconsistent with both biblical teachings about justice and American democratic traditions."[23]

The church expanded its idea of community in another 1982 resolution on "Jubilee ministry." Christian ministry includes a *joint discipleship* [italics added] with the poor and the oppressed wherever they are to be found.[24] An interlocking relationship exists between society's poor and the church's ministry in the parishes and several agencies. Jubilee ministry was therefore, not only a program but also a concept and criterion to mark the church's entire future ministry. To program this concept, the office of Jubilee ministry was "to challenge and confront the [church's] members . . . to understand the facts of poverty and injustice, encouraging them to take an active role in meeting the needs of poor and oppressed people and in the struggles against the causes of such suffering."[25]

For the Episcopal Church to establish "struggles of the poor" as the ethical norm in its core teaching about mission and ministry was very different from its understanding of the role of the poor at the beginning of the twentieth century. At that time in earlier social teachings, militancy by the poor and the workers toward self-determination was considered a breach in the social contract and concept of natural harmony intended between capitalists and workers. While the church frequently spoke of greed motivating many of our economic structures and values, resulting in an inequity of possessions and wealth, even then the ills of society were linked solely to industrial relationships. As late as 1934, the bishops wrote in their Pastoral with full self-confidence: "We hold that the recognition of a partnership relationship between employer and employee is required not only by principles of Christian brotherhood but as a policy insuring the largest measure of economic satisfaction to all concerned."[26]

The late 1970s and 1980s, however, witnessed a revised model for ministry that engaged the economic forces and structures perceived as shaping poverty and promoting oppression, although a systematic social and theological analysis of those forces and structures failed. The 1979 General Convention, for example, declared that as Scripture reveals God's unswerving commitment to the poor and outcasts and calls the church to make no peace with oppression in any form, "the Church can claim obedience to its Lord who came as One who preached good news to the poor, deliverance to the oppressed . . . only as it continues His ministry in the world."[27] Parishes and clergy were implored to model such a ministry in communities ruined by oppressive economic forces that cause further injustices to the poor. The task of the church was to coalesce with others to defeat or at least reform radically such forces.

The 1982 Labor Day Pastoral Letter written by the Coalition of Urban Bishops, though unofficial, did provide a theological treatment of these forces and free-market ethics. Human labor is the way men and women continue to participate in God's creation and thus help build the kingdom of God, declared their Pastoral. The "kingdom of God" in this context is "the good community which establishes justice and peace among men and women and nations."[28] Any inequality that impedes or distorts this purpose of labor—such as the widening gap between the wealthy and the poor, the haves and the have-nots, racism, discrimination against women, corruption, and exploitation is not to be tolerated by the Christian.[29]

This inextricable link between labor and the building of the kingdom obliges the church to address three significant issues: First, workers have the right to organize trade unions in light of the fact that one class owns property and the means of producing goods and services while another social class must sell itself and its labor to the class controlling the capital and means of production: "We reject any notion that one class of people can be trusted to hold the interest of another class of people in higher priority than their own self-interest."[30] Second, alternatives to our traditional pattern of corporate ownership by shareholders and management must be devised and the market ethic esteeming competition and the maximization of profits must be examined. Third, the church ought to put its resources at the side of the marginalized uprooted communities where economic dislocation has occurred. Furthermore, they urged democratic control of corporate resources and structures as an alternative to existing corporate hierarchical structures.

Finally, the urban bishops urged the church to be an active participant in influencing and reminding the economic system that for the Christian justice is the measuring rod for testing the effect of economic structures on human dignity and the human community. While they were not as precise in their understanding of justice in terms of traditional ethical concepts, such as commutative justice, distributive justice, and social justice, nonetheless, they were quite clear about justice as the guiding norm in the economic order in this country.[31]

In one sense the economic justice program at the 1988 Convention provided programmatic tender for some of the theological and social visions in the Urban Bishops' Labor Day Pastoral. That program also highlighted a trend in the Episcopal Church and other churches during the 1970s and 1980s, namely, a reassessment of stewardship over God's creation and in the economy as part of our Christian vocation—a concept that actually came out of the Protestant Reformation.

Thus, chief characteristics of Episcopal social teachings on the economy can be described as follows:

1. Capitalists and labor as a part of the same divine creation are intended to live and work together in cooperation for the cause of community rather than opposition: "toward neighborliness, friendship, and brotherhood."[32]

2. Enhancement of human dignity and protection of the individual spirit are to be of supreme concern in establishing working conditions and economic structures: "The end of business is not primarily profit but human welfare and the common good."[33]

3. The elimination of poverty and the conditions causing poverty is a God-given priority that ought to be a chief good in the economy and the church's ministry in all its forms. Empowerment and liberation of the poor by the poor with the assistance of the church is a social priority of the church.

4. The right of workers to organize trade unions and to bargain with employers about wages, benefits, and conditions that deny or distract human dignity and damage the human spirit is essential to the Christian view of the U.S. economic community.

5. Social justice cannot be separated from economic issues.

6. Work and labor are God-given means intended for furthering God's creation and his kingdom.

7. Social responsibility and action to advance social justice for all, protection of workers and economically dislocated communities, and protection of the environment are to be priorities of modern corporate management along with strategies for making money, improving production, and investments. Ownership in corporations through stocks carries moral responsibility for Christians and Christian institutions such as churches, which is to be witnessed in concrete action, such

as proxy voting, boycotts (if necessary), and consultations with the corporate world.

Commentary

The Episcopal Church, like other American mainstream churches, has reexamined ethics and the economic order under the theological rubric of stewardship over and in God's creation. Stewardship in creation includes not only environmental issues largely raised by corporations and government policy, but also the economic benefits of creation for all people, nations, and local communities. This has been largely a legacy from the Protestant tradition.

Martin Luther (1483–1546), for example, taught that nature and its benefits such as food, minerals, and other natural resources, are gifts from God to be gratefully received and responsibly enjoyed by humanity. Our labor replenishes and is a means of educating ourselves about our God-given stewardship. Because stewardship is a gift from God, its authority and sovereignty are relative and not absolute. That is, the creation does not belong to humankind, although Luther esteemed private property as a concept and means for organizing the created order.

John Calvin (1509–64), living in sixteenth century Geneva with all its commerce and trade has had the most lasting influence on America's economic spirituality. In contrast to Luther, who was familiar mostly with an agrarian economy fueled by small towns and rural areas, Calvin set out to understand the call of the Christian life amid urban affluence and mercantilism. He, like Luther, was not opposed to private property and the acquisition of private wealth. A carryover of what some call Calvin's "commercial spirituality" has been what the German sociologist Max Weber named the Protestant Ethic. Weber held that Calvinism was most influential in shaping the work ethic and accumulation of private and corporate wealth in the United States. However, Calvin himself taught that the accumulation of wealth was not against God's word, provided it was obtained through honest work and served the greater communal good; that is, social responsibility is always a duty of those accumulating private wealth. This connection between spirituality and commerce also carried over to other countries where Calvinism prevailed, such as England, Scotland, the Netherlands, and parts of France.

Episcopal economic social teachings have steadily focused on individual dignity and working conditions in a system rewarding what the church many times has labeled competition and unbridled selfishness for a few. Since its first report about the economy, the Episcopal Church has raised serious questions about our esteem of autonomy and individualism, given the injustices and inequalities evident in the larger community. At the same time, the church has shown a consistent concern about a central issue in a consumer society such as the United States, namely, does the acquisition of wealth and possessions have limits?

This issue is not recent, arising because of the millions earned by individuals in Wall Street through junk bonds, ill-gotten gains, and illegal insider deals. The relationship between the accumulation of unbridled wealth in the business world and its social responsibility to the larger community has engaged U.S. churches since the industrial revolution in the nineteenth century. The economist Milton Friedman, from the side of the conservatives, denies that ethics ought to be a concern of business. He argues in his book *Capitalism and Freedom*:

In [a free economy] there is one and only one social responsibility of business—to use its resources and engage in activities designed to increase its profits so long as it stays within the rules of the game, which is to say, engages in open and free competition, without deception or fraud. . . . Few trends could so thoroughly undermine the very foundations of our free society as the acceptance by corporate officials of a social responsibility other than to make as much money for their stockholders as possible. [34]

Another economist, Arthur Okun, however, who admits the implicit conflict in our social contract between the claims of a democracy (equal rights and justice for all citizens) and the ethics of a capitalist economy (rewards for the accumulation and maldistribution of wealth by a few) notes:

American society proclaims the worth of every human being. . . . Yet at the same time, our institutions say 'find a job or go hungry,' 'succeed or suffer.' They prod us to get ahead of our neighbors economically after telling us to stay in line socially. They reward prizes that allow the big winners to feed their pets better than the losers can feed their children. [35]

The church has wrestled with this duality between political claims and market ethics, both of which are foundational to our social well-being and historical self-esteem, by speaking about private wealth and its effect on social justice in U.S. society. It has particularly focused on the issues of unemployment, the dislocation and shutting-down of factories in communities dependent on the factories for its social and economic well-being, and the poverty in cities. GCSP was conceived to focus and mobilize the church for action against poverty and for self-determination, only to be aborted by various forces within the Episcopal Church after a short life.

Jubilee ministry, established in the late 1970s, and the economic justice program, established at the 1988 Detroit General Convention, are the latest programs rejoining these issues. The entire ministry of the church, say its social teachings, is to give first priority to ministry with and among the poor and to economic justice. But as Okun wisely reminds us about the dominating role the market plays in American society:

> The marketplace transgresses on virtually every right. Money buys legal services that can obtain preferred treatment before law; it buys platforms that give extra weight to the owner's freedom of speech; it buys influence with elected officials and thus compromises the principle of one person, one vote. The market is permitted to legislate life and death, as evidenced, for example, by infant mortality rates for the poor that are more than one and one-half times those for middle-income Americans.[36]

The tensions between economic issues and the social claims of biblical teachings have been debated by Christians since St. Clement of Alexandria (150–215) wrote *The Rich Man's Salvation* in the third century A.D. Trying to accommodate the hard demands of Jesus in the parable of the rich young man in Mark 10:17–31 (cf. Matt. 19:16–26; Luke 18:18–30) to the wealth and affluence of Alexandria, Clement determined that Jesus was really talking about the interior life and not external riches. Riches provide us an opportunity for fellowship among different classes and the means for doing good by helping one's neighbor, he said. Jesus in these texts teaches absolving the heart of the desire for wealth that blinds us from seeing the good that wealth can do for others:

For he who holds possessions . . . as the gifts of God; and ministers from them to the God who gives them for the salvation of men; and knows that he possesses them more for the sake of the brethren than his own; and is superior to them, not the slave of the things he possesses . . . is able with cheerful mind to bear their removal equally with their abundance. This is he who is blessed by the Lord, and called poor in spirit. . . .[37]

Yet the economic teachings of the Episcopal Church (and also the Catholic bishops) have been weakest in their failure to examine critically some of the basic tenets of the market ethics at work in the U.S. economy and corporate culture. Such a failure or oversight suggests acquiescence as an extension of civil religion, a posture no doubt derived from its descendance as the established church in England and its being a mainstream church in America. This is reflected, for example, in the piety and theology of the Episcopal Church's liturgy. In the Prayer Book service for Evening Prayer, for instance, instead of praying for a person as in England (the sovereign), the Episcopal Church prays for the state. While this alternative was made because of the political situation after the Revolutionary War and the subsequent separation from the Church of England, at the same time it demonstrates a piety and theological view supportive of preserving and maintaining the order and fabric of the nation-state.

A crucial feature in maintaining any state's fabric is a productive economy that provides the goods, services, and jobs needed for a healthy and thriving civil community. The U.S. economy is structured around the concept of the "free market," whose moral and ethical foundations were laid by the Scottish economist Adam Smith (1723–90), author of *The Wealth of Nations* (1776). Smith sacralized raw self-interest as an important driving force for prosperity and a high standard of living in a capitalist society: "It is not from the benevolence of the butcher, the brewer, or the baker, that we expect our dinner, but from their regard to their own interest. We address ourselves, not to their humanity but to their self-love, and never talk to them of our own necessities but of their advantages."[38] Thus, self-love and self-interest are vital foundations of free market morality and our economic system, although Smith naively thought that competition among capitalists would be a "check and balance" on self-interest getting out of hand: The merchants will treat each other well because of their own mutual self-interest and welfare, which, in turn, will benefit the consumer. Therefore, the exercise of some self-control by the players in the economic community will benefit the entire civil community.

With the advent of the modern U.S. corporation in the nineteenth century, this morality continued as a motivating force in the *laissez-faire* business world, evidenced in the "robber barons" and their companies. But through the growing complexity of the corporation and multinational conglomerates in the twentieth century, not to mention leverage and managerial buy-outs, and through the emergence of modern corporate management, which for the sake of efficiency has relieved the proprietor and shareholders of day-to-day concern, self-interest has become more impersonal and abstract as acquisition, mergers, take-overs, and growth became important concepts in business vocabularies and strategies. Market ethics have created what can be called the corporate culture: the day-to-day values, vocabularies, rules, rituals of recognition and self-esteem, and space of the business world that generate their own power structures and establish their own sovereignty and ethical norms. Often the only check on this culture and its morality is the law, but law and ethics are not the same.

These rules, rituals, and norms have a telling influence on corporate and personal behavior and thinking, people's lives and leisure, professional advancement, and the environment of its players. Furthermore, because many of these free-market rules and rituals have been accepted as a given by mainstream churches and conservative fundamentalist churches alike—as well as by the influential televangelists—a synthesis between religious codes and free market ethics about wealth and possessions has occurred. Moreover, many identify these market ethics as a cornerstone of the American concept of freedom and liberty—*Novus ordo seclorum* (the new order of the ages)—and therefore are woven into our very fabric of order and meaning of democracy.

At the same time, many aspects of market ethics have been identified as Christian ethical principles, such as equating freedom of choice with free will, benevolence and welfare by government with Christian compassion, individualism with the equivalent of freedom of conscience. Such is illustrative of Niebuhr's "Christ of culture" theological position. Parts of the market ethic

that have been largely accepted by liberal mainstream and conservative religious churches in America are:
1. Maximizing profits as the necessary "bottom line" in corporate culture for the benefit of the shareholders;
2. Freedom of choice based on alternatives in a vast variety of consumer products;
3. Competition and individual and corporate aggressiveness as necessary for survival, efficiency, and profits;
4. Concentration of wealth and power as incentives for ambition and creativity;
5. Consumerism and self-indulgence in the marketplace as a foundation of liberty ("one can never have enough");
6. Ownership of property as a natural political right and sign of achievement and blessing (but also a means used to exclude certain racial and religious groups);
7. Tolerating a talented elite and the exclusion of most women and minorities from positions and private associations necessary for moving through corporate culture;
8. Toleration of poor people and inequities as a natural given in the system;
9. Believing that God blesses those who have much and helps those who help themselves economically;
10. Love and concern for fellow human beings beginning with love of self and looking out for "number one."

Identifying these hallmarks in corporate ethics is not to say *ipso facto* that they are evil. They establish credibility and veracity in the corporate community. Church social teachings engaging these aspects of market ethics may gain a hearing and credibility in the business world. Otherwise, such teachings may be dismissed as idealistic or unrealistic in terms of the actual forces and powers constituting corporate morality and culture.

The single-most theological motif in Episcopal economic social teachings has been the nature of community under American and international economic conditions and structures. Even if not always explicit, in more recent times the church has steadily challenged the idea of *laissez-faire* individualism within the civil community and the enrichment of some over against the impoverishment of others. As the ethicist Philip Wogaman (with Episcopal bishops and Catholic bishops no doubt agreeing) said about the Christian priority when examining economic issues:

The same Jesus who taught that we should pray for 'our daily bread' also said that we do not live 'by bread alone.' One shorthand way to express this is to say that economic production is a necessary condition to every other priority but that it is not a sufficient condition. It is a necessary base for everything else. . . . We cannot avoid more careful consideration of *what* is to be produced and *how* it is to be produced and *for whom* it is to be produced.[39]

Notes

1. *North-South: A Program for Survival. The Report of the Independent Commission on International Development Issues under the Chairmanship of Willy Brandt* (Cambridge, Mass.: MIT Press, 1980), pp. 119-20.
2. *Journal of the General Convention, 1982,* p. C-141.
3. *Journal of the General Convention, 1916,* p. 403.
4. *Journal of the General Convention, 1919,* p. 508.
5. *Journal of the General Convention, 1913,* p. 122.
6. Ibid.
7. *Journal of the General Convention, 1922,* p. 544.
8. *Ibid.,* p. 378.
9. *Pastoral Letter,* Adopted by the House of Bishops, September 10, 1931, p. 3.
10. Ibid., pp. 6-7.
11. *Journal of the General Convention, 1931,* p. 544.
12. *Pastoral Letter,* Adopted by the House of Bishops, November 9 1933, p. 5.
13. Ibid.
14. *Pastoral Letter,* Adopted by the House of Bishops, October 23, 1934, p. 7.
15. *Journal of the General Convention, 1952,* pp. 585-7.
16. *Journal of the General Convention, 1955,* pp. 370-1.
17. Ibid., p. 370.
18. *Journal of the General Convention, 1970,* p. 252.
19. *Church and Society Social Policy of the Episcopal Church,* December 1967-April 1979, p. 335.
20. *Church and Society Social Policy of the Episcopal Church,* December 1967-April 1979 (New York: The Executive Council, n.d.), p. 367.
21. Ibid.
22. Resolution 58A, *The Blue Book of the Committees, Commissions, Boards, and Agencies of the General Convention of the Episcopal Church,* September 1982, pp. 125-6.
23. Ibid., p. 125.
24. *Journal of the General Convention, 1982,* p. C-95.
25. Ibid.

26. *Pastoral Letter*, October 23, 1934, p. 7.

27. *Journal of the General Convention, 1979*, p. C-135.

28. *Labor Day 1982, A Pastoral Message from the Coalition of Urban Bishops* (Photocopied.), p. 1.

29. Ibid.

30. Ibid., p. 2.

31. Ibid., p. 3.

32. *Journal of the General Convention, 1919*, p. 508.

33. *Pastoral Letter*, Adopted in Portland, Oregon, in *Journal of the General Convention, 1922*, p. 544.

34. Milton Friedman, *Capitalism and Freedom* (Chicago: The University of Chicago Press, 1962), p. 133.

35. Arthur Okun, *Equality and Efficiency: The Big Trade-Off* (Washington, D.C.: Brookings Institution, 1975), p. 1.

36. Ibid., p. 22.

37. Quoted in Martin Hengel, *Property and Riches in the Early Church*, trans. John Bowden (Philadelphia: Fortress Press, 1974), p. 75.

38. Adam Smith, *An Inquiry into the Nature and Causes of the Wealth of Nations* (1776; reprint, New York: Collins 1937), p. 14.

39. J. Philip Wogaman, *Economics and Ethics: A Christian Inquiry* (Philadelphia: Fortress Press, 1986), pp. 60-1.

Chapter 8
The Authority of Social Teachings: Do They Have Teeth?

Even though the Episcopal Church has social teachings about peace and war, race, family, sexuality, and the economy, the larger question is, so what? Are these teachings authoritative for clergy and laity? If so, in what way? What, if anything, is expected in terms of conformity? Is the issue of obedience or conformity even an appropriate question for a church in American culture with its deeply imbued belief in the individual conscience as the final arbiter for believing and acting?

What about the equally deeply felt issue of individualism, personal autonomy, and private beliefs, captured so well in the Eisenhower motto, "I don't care what you believe as long as you believe something"? In other words, are these teachings binding as "official" references only when addressing social and political matters in public, that is, for public relations? Are they to be guidelines on equal terms with other sets of moral guidelines from which the individual Episcopalian may choose to govern his or her private conduct and thinking? Are these social teachings expected to have any priority for and influence on the very existence, being, and behavior of Episcopalians in society? In other words (to use a colloquial expression), do they have any teeth?

Given the current state of anarchy and confusion within the Episcopal Church regarding morality and ethics, complicated by many single-issue constituencies inside and outside the church, *authority* is no doubt a most illusive concept. Endowed with a legacy of episcopal governance, on the one hand, and a tradition of synodical governance, on the other, the Episcopal Church has sometimes dealt with the issue of authority more rhetorically or without always probing deeply its content and meaning for church teachings (and doctrines) in a changing culture where individual autonomy has become more like a divine right in the marketplace.

For example, during the nineteenth century Tracterian controversies in the Episcopal Church, when the 1844 General Convention was asked to judge the authority of the Oxford Movement's revisions of Anglican theology by renouncing it, the church declined, saying instead

> the Liturgy, Offices and Articles of the Church [are] sufficient exponents of her sense of the essential doctrines of Holy Scripture, and the Canons of the Church afford ample means of discipline and correction for all who depart from her standards. . . . [The] Church is not responsible for the errors of individuals, whether they are members of this church or otherwise. [1]

Yet some 140 years later, the 1985 General Convention claimed authority in matters of doctrine when it agreed to strike the *filioque* ("and [from] the Son) from the Nicene Creed—subject to the approval of Lambeth Conference.

Authority continues to intrigue the Anglican Communion as well. It has been discussed and debated constantly from the very first Lambeth Conference in 1867. Lambeth's 1948 statement on authority, considered the best statement of consensus on the question, dealt with the issue of what is authoritative in the worldwide Anglican Communion with its several autonomous national churches. Authority is both *singular*, that is, from a single divine source: God's revelation in Jesus Christ, and *manifold*, which the document calls "dispersed authority," that is, a mutual checks and balance (to borrow a term from constitutional law) built within the very concept of Anglican authority and the exercise of it.

In 1964, General Convention passed a resolution on "Levels of Authority within the Church." Four levels are authoritative for the church that operate under the overall authority of Scripture, both creeds, the *Book of Common Prayer*, and the Constitution and Canons of the Episcopal Church:[2] (1) resolutions, statements, and actions of General Convention, "which speak for the Church, to the Church, to the world"; (2) statements from the House of Bishops expressing the mind of its chief pastors; (3) the Presiding Bishop and the Executive Council acting between General Convention meetings; and (4) the officers and staff of the Executive Council implementing decisions of the Executive Council in "areas where General Convention has not acted." The resolution cautions, however, that the last level is not to be considered on the same level as the previous three. "The Church in so speaking rests upon the authority given to it by the Lord Christ."[3] In more recent years both the World Council of Churches' Faith and Order Commission (1967) and the joint Anglican-Roman Catholic International Commission (ARCIC: 1976, 1981) have also studied Anglican authority.

As the 1964 statement noted, the Christian tradition itself has sources of authority that are definitive. These include (1) biblical authority, which contains all that is necessary for salvation, the unique account of God's revelation in Jesus Christ, the author and finisher of our faith. This is the most fundamental authority, as the bishops of the Church of England reaffirmed during the controversy about views of the resurrection by the Bishop of Durham, David Jenkins:

> This faith in Christ's Resurrection is the faith of every member of this House. On the question whether, as a result of this divine act of resurrection, Christ's tomb that first Easter Day was empty we recognize that scholarship can offer no conclusive demonstration; and the divergent views to be found among scholars are reflected in the thinking of individual bishops. But all of us accept: first, that belief that the tomb was empty can be held with full intellectual integrity; secondly, that this is the understanding of the witness of Scripture which is generally received in the universal Church; and thirdly, that this House acknowledges and upholds this belief as expressing the faith of the Church of England and its historic teaching.[4]

Moreover, there is (2) creedal authority, which, according to the Chicago-Lambeth Quadrilateral—the formulary establishing the minimal foundations for Christian unity for Anglicans—is "the sufficient statement of the Christian faith." It is not clear, however, how self-evident this "sufficient statement" is both to the church and to the believer.

A third source of authority is (3) tradition, that is, the legacy of doctrine, dogma, and institutions inherited from earlier General Councils, patristic and Reformation theologians that have shaped much of what we preach, teach, and pray today. Another is (4) liturgical, found for the most part throughout the Anglican Communion in the *Book of Common Prayer*, even with its variations. In recent years, however, it has become increasingly difficult to affirm that there is even a commonly understood Prayer Book among Anglicans, be it in English or some other language.

Finally, especially for Americans with a history of revivalism and pietism, there is (5) the authority of personal experience and private conscience: "Let your conscience be your guide." This is the American appeal to personal autonomy in which the individual as the final arbiter can be relied upon to pick and choose his or her own authority. The English theologian Stephen Sykes of Cambridge University (now Bishop of Ely) says reliance on personal judgment is also theologically a fundamental part of the Anglican understanding of "dispersed authority." Citing article six of the Thirty-nine Articles on Holy Scripture containing "all things necessary for salvation," Sykes observes that the article also says the person can be relied on to discern what is to be "believed as an article of faith, or be thought requisite of necessary for salvation."

> It means that whatever machinery a church may devise for making decisions, and with whatever spiritual powers this machinery may adorn itself, at the end of the day the people of God have the means of judging, independently if need be, whether or not the truth is being upheld.[5]

The authority of social teachings in the Episcopal Church is complicated by the fact that the category *social teachings* is not a clear concept within its historical and institutional consciousness, Pastoral Letters, standing commission reports, General Convention resolutions and memorials. *Authority* in its teachings, unlike the Roman Catholic church, has to be inferred based on the authoritative character of the sources from which these teachings have been drawn. The 1964 statement on authority supports this inference.

But then, what about the authority of *personal experience*, so highly esteemed in American history and society. This authority frequently creates conflicts and irritations for Episcopalians when they also hear such traditional terms as *obedience* or *conformity* with regard to the authority of the church's social teachings in matters of conduct and thinking. "Who says so?" is frequently the reaction of most parishioners (and clergy). For many, even the phrase the *authority of the church* rings authoritarian and dogmatic, producing immediate resistance to counter what they interpret as a threat to their "freedom of choice," even in matters of church doctrine and social teachings.

Social *policy*, on the other hand, found in statements and mandates for programs, conveys a different kind of authority from social *teachings*. Frequently a budget and staff are provided by General Convention to initiate social action or to implement the church's response to particular social and political conditions. Both the budget and staff visibly institutionalize social policy and provide for its monitoring. The more focused Executive Council speaking and acting in the constantly changing social arena in America and elsewhere has the effect of sharpening the identity of the Episcopal Church in the public square, but raises new questions about authority when its implementing of church teachings and policy conflict with the authority of private conscience. And new players have appeared on the "public square" with the rise of fundamentalist and charismatic claimants that frequently reshape the rules of the debate, making it all the more important for Episcopal social teachings to have authority and some theological grounding and content.

Also, Episcopalians themselves engaged in the marketplace and public discourse are asking more for authoritative biblical and theological foundations undergirding church positions on social issues such as nuclear arms; feminist issues; economic issues; the increasing racial and cultural conflicts, tensions, and diversity; the gap between the haves and have-nots in America, the industrial nations, and the Third World. Such issues and others highlight the need for theological integrity in the social pronouncements of a church that insists it is a "bridge church" between the Catholic and Protestant traditions.

That Roman Catholics and Eastern Orthodox in ecumenical discussions continue to raise questions about the character of authority within the Anglican/Episcopal tradition, in spite of official formularies addressing this matter (such as those from ARCIC), signifies that Episcopal theological identity is still unclear, at least to other churches in the catholic tradition. The identity issue has become more diffused for mainstream churches because of an inclination to blur differences for the sake of dialogue and inclusiveness. But even an identity that rests on the authority of Scripture as the place containing everything necessary for salvation means boundaries (e.g. Matt. 18:23-35, 2 John), as do teachings whose core authority is the revelation of God in a particular person called Jesus Christ who claims total obedience: *"I am the way, the truth, and the life"* (John 14:6). Allegiance to such an authority means allegiance to a unique and distinct revelation of God which obliges a distinct morality and responsibility that can also play a role in public discourse in a pluralistic society.

Such a morality and ethics have to be reexamined frequently, since the context and the conditions under which the allegiance is affirmed and exercised change from age to age. At times Christian ethics may share common goals with other ethical codes; at other times, a limit or boundary may set off Christian and, by extension, Episcopalian teachings from other moralities and positions. As George Bernard Shaw reputedly said about the tyranny of living without boundaries: the definition of hell is having to do what you want to do. The question is what is the particularity and boundaries of authority of Christian social teachings within a diverse, multicultural society that maneuver between the Sylla of a Savior who demands obedience to his commandments and ordered life within a community, and the Charybdis of a national heritage that counsels final obedience to private conscience and personal experience of Jesus Christ as Lord and Savior?

For the sake of some coherence and consensus in the social fabric, a secular vocabulary to reduce conflict about and between the authority of private codes of ethics in America's diverse society exists. This civil morality includes such concepts as *plurality, tolerance, freedom of choice*. These have often been baptized and sacralized in the church's theology as *freedom, comprehensiveness, ordered liberty, freedom of choice, inclusiveness, reconciliation*. Yet at the same time, it bears repeating that boundaries or limits or even exclusion have always been necessary for the Christian faith to distinguish its message and morality, even from the prevailing civil morality. The blurring of Christian morality and social teachings by civil morality is not a new force in religious life, as we have seen both in the early church and in the German churches during the 1930s. But it endangers the "cutting edge" and forcefulness of distinctive Christian social teachings in public discourse as a possible catalyst of transformation in a changing society. Some branches of the church still claim boundaries and exclusions, as the Alliance of Reformed Churches in their 1982 declaration that South African apartheid is not only against the

Word of God but also a heresy. It may be that because the Episcopal Church moves often in many directions without a focused theological rationale or anchored position in its social teachings that its power for transformation as an institution in the public forum is totally dependent on the private conduct of its adherents.

A review of the place of authority within Anglican tradition and the purview of the bishops sitting at Lambeth Conferences would not necessarily deal with the concrete issues of authority at stake in the Episcopal Church in the United States. For neither its clergy nor its laity generally identify with the collective tradition of Anglicanism (except possibly during royal weddings and appearances by the Archbishop of Canterbury). The authority of Episcopal social teachings therefore has to be examined within the tensions of the American national ethic of individual autonomy and the church's modified congregationalism. As already noted, the Pastoral Letters claim a binding authority upon the entire church. They are the place where social teachings were first articulated. Beginning with the first Pastoral Letter in 1808 to the 1820 canon requiring that they be read to the congregations, Pastorals have had a particular influence and authority in the life of the church. At the Baltimore General Convention of 1808 the bishops' wrote that their Pastoral was a means of addressing issues of doctrine, worship, discipline, and "a holy life and conversation."[6]

In 1820, after a brief time of the entire House of Bishops writing Pastoral Letters, the canons were revised to support their presumed authority by requiring that the Pastoral Letter be read during morning worship to the entire congregation (this, even in its amended form, which permits it to be distributed instead of being read still holds in the Episcopal Church). The earliest example of the Pastoral Letter (1862) announcing explicit social teachings affirms this intent quite clearly both in method and content:

They look to us, their chief Pastors, . . . to give them the support and comfort of our approbation, if we think they have rightly judged the great question of duty to the Government in the present struggle. . . . Whatever the Apostles of Christ were inspired by the Holy Ghost to teach the Church; the Ministers and Stewards of that Church are bound to illustrate and *enforce* [italics added], for instruction of her members. 'All Scripture is profitable for doctrines, reproof, correction, and instruction in righteousness.'[7]

Part of the problem about authority in Episcopal social pronouncements may have to do with a historical ambivalence about the authority of the episcopate. In Episcopal Church history the authority of the clergy and the laity was enhanced through the rector, the vestry, and diocesan standing committees, which diminished the traditional authority of the episcopate. They also affected the presumed authority of social teachings for congregations and parishioners. The absence of bishops and the need for day-to-day management in the parish churches of the colonies strengthened the authority of the lay vestry in America far beyond its parent in England.[8] In fact, in America the laity so dominated the governance of local parishes that the vestry selected its minister, raised money for his support, and gave him life tenure in the parish unless he did some moral indiscretion. The vestry's authority as the legal corporation in the parish established congregationalist autonomy early on, especially in such southern colonies as Virginia (1607) and Maryland (1632), among the oldest. On the other hand, this fiercely defended diocesan "states rights" concept was not unrelated to the checks and balances built into the synodical authority of Episcopal national and diocesan conventions. At the end of the Revolutionary War, some 400 local fiefdoms were operating as parishes rather than as 400 parishes under the jurisdiction and authority of diocesan bishops.

Initially suspicious of episcopal jurisdiction (with the exception of Connecticut), several founding dioceses hedged and conditioned the authority of bishops before and after the Episcopal Church's first national synod in 1785. Maryland, for example, in 1784, passed a resolution saying that the duties and authority of a bishop only differed from those of other priests by bishops having the authority to ordain, confirm, and preside at synods and conventions. But even the bishop's ability to select candidates for the ministry required the concurrence of the Standing Committee or the diocesan convention in Maryland. In Virginia, its first bishop-elect, David Griffith, was just barely elected at the diocesan convention in 1785 because of opposition to the concept of bishop. However, the diocesan convention refused to sign his testimonials. He died before he could be consecrated, and James Madison became the first bishop.

Political conditions had much to do with suspicion about bishops and episcopal authority. At the First Continental Congress in 1774 in Philadelphia, those proposing bishoprics were also among the most militant pro-British representatives. Even the Reverend William White (1748–1836), rector of Christ Church, Phila-delphia, and one of the first bishops in the Episcopal Church, wrote in his famous *Case of the Protestant Episcopal Church in the United States of America* that the continued life of Anglicanism in postwar America could best be carried out by independent Episcopal congregations free to choose whether to participate in state or national organizations. Any kind of national church should be a federation of parishes upward instead of from an episcopate downward. White resisted even using the word *bishop* or *episcopate*, preferring instead to speak of a "superior order." Furthermore, he proposed that there be no central authority, only authority deemed official and authoritative through the consent of clergy and laity meeting together as equals and voting on the matter.

At the same time there was wide latitude among American Anglicans about the authority of the *Book of Common Prayer* over against the liturgies of other colonial churches, even in colonies where the Anglican Church was established. According to William Sweet's *Story of Religion in America*, about 3100 "religious organizations" were in America at the end of the 1776 war, with about 1000 in each region: New England, the South, and the Middle colonies. In most of these regions, creeds and sacraments bred suspicion of popery, thus they were frequently omitted, except in New York, New Jersey, and New England, where the concept of High Church had some standing.[9]

Another factor in the problem of authority in the church's teachings is the Declaration of Independence: "All men are created equal with certain inalienable rights. . . ." This document is a basic tenet in American democracy and culture; it also provides the sacred ground for American civil religion, even if it did exclude all Indians and slaves at the time. Few bishops (other than Henry Hobart) were likely to question this belief about authority during the early formation of a nation and an identity. Likewise, few bishops could expect obedience from clergy and laity in the young, rebellious United States of America. Nevertheless, the Episcopal Church acknowledged first informally and then formally the peculiar authority of the episcopate in Pastoral Letters, historical suspicions to the contrary.

The internalization of authority in church teachings will always remain a problem in post-Enlightenment, industrialized society that stresses individual critical thought and private conscience. Hence, resolving conflicts between personal codes of ethics and the church's code of social teachings is unlikely to be done by any one method. It is obvious, however, at least from the thinking of the bishops in their Pastoral Letter of 1862, that the Word of God compelled them to speak to the church at large about social issues. Social teachings based on Scripture could reprove, correct, and instruct members of the church and the church itself in righteousness:

> Whatever the Apostles of Christ were inspired by the Holy Ghost to teach the Church; the Ministers and Stewards of that Church are bound to illustrate and *enforce* [italics added], for instruction of her members. 'All Scripture is profitable for doctrines, reproof, correction, and instruction in righteousness.'[10]

Within the American context, the authority of this instruction in righteousness may have to take "a diverse path in righteousness." This does not necessarily mean a reductionism or relativism because "all cats are gray" in a multicultural society and church wishing to honor private judgment. Rather, this "diverse path in righteous" is best described in the language of the Inter-Anglican Theological and Doctrinal Commission:

> [T]here is indeed a 'sovereign' truth, something beyond our fashions and fancies, but it is to be known in the continuation of active encounter. . . .

> What is essential, then, in the processes of interpretation by which the church makes judgments is an attitude which is analogous to—and may even be a part of—the repentance which the Lord called for in all of his disciples. That the Scriptures speak in a variety of social situations and cultural contexts is a sign to us that the risen Christ and the Kingdom which he represents are indeed the transcendent horizon of every human society and culture. . . . The church grasps the Scriptures and is grasped by its Lord not apart from the challenges and dissonances which pluralism occasions, but in the repentance which these call for and make possible.[11]

Notes

1. *Journal of the General Convention, 1844,* p. 60.
2. Standing commissions and joint commissions of General Convention, for example, are mandated "to study and make recommendations to the General Convention on major subjects considered to be of continuing concern to the Church." *Constitution and Canons for the Government of the Protestant Episcopal Church in the United States of America,* Adopted in General Convention, 1789–1982 (New York: for the General Convention, 1982), p. 13.
3. *Journal of the General Convention, 1964,* pp. 312-3.
4. *The Nature of Christian Belief: A Statement and Exposition by the House of Bishops* (Cincinnati, Ohio: Forward Movement Publications, 1986), pp. 37-8.
5. Stephen W. Sykes, *The Integrity of Anglicanism* (London: Mowbray, 1978), p. 91.
6. See Appendix A.
7. *Pastoral Letter of the Bishops of the Protestant Episcopal Church in the United States of America . . . in St. John's Church, New York* (New York: Baker & Godwin, Printers, 1862), p. 8.
8. See Frederick V. Mills, *Bishops by Ballot: An Eighteenth Century Ecclesiastical Revolution* (New York: Oxford University Press, 1978).
9. See Mullin, *Episcopal Vision/American Reality,* about the theology of High Church in New York.
10. *Pastoral Letter of the Bishops of the Protestant Episcopal Church,* October 17, 1862, p. 8.
11. *For the Sake of the Kingdom: God's Church and the New Creation* (London: Anglican Consultative Council, 1986), pp. 48-9.

Appendix A
First Pastoral Letter of the Episcopal Church Bishops

A

PASTORAL LETTER

TO THE

MEMBERS

OF THE

PROTESTANT EPISCOPAL CHURCH

IN THE

UNITED STATES OF AMERICA,

FROM THE

HOUSE OF BISHOPS OF SAID CHURCH,

ASSEMBLED IN

GENERAL CONVENTION,

AT BALTIMORE,

MAY, 1808.

New-York:

PRINTED BY T. & J. SWORDS,

No. 160 Pearl-Street.

1808.

A

PASTORAL LETTER

From the House of Bishops of the Protestant Episcopal Church to the Members of the same.

BRETHREN,

BEING assembled in General Convention, with the Clerical and the Lay Deputies of our communion, we embrace the opportunity of addressing you on its concerns.   But before we proceed to the subjects of advice contemplated by us on this occasion, we lift up our hearts to the Father of mercies; thanking him for our being in possession of all that we esteem necessary for the professing of his holy and eternal truth.   And while we ascribe this benefit to his unbounded goodness, we recognize in it the truth of the promises made to the Church by her divine Head, of being with her to the end of the world.

It is within the memory of many of you, that when these States, in the course of divine Providence, became elevated to a place among the nations of the earth; and when, in consequence, our congregations, planted under the jurisdiction of the Church of England, were withdrawn from it, they had no longer any common centre of union; being not only without an entire Ministry, but severally in a state of separate independence, inconsistent with the Catholic principles which they had inherited from their founders.   Under these circumstances there was required no small measure of faith, as well in the integrity of our system, as in the divine blessing on any endeavours which might be begun, to elevate us above those apprehensions which described the continuance of our communion as problematical, if not to be despaired of.

From correspondence in some instances, and from personal communications in others, it soon appeared that there was at least so much attachment to the religious principles of our Church, as ought to prevent our considering of her cause as desperate. The correctness of this sentiment became confirmed, by connections speedily created, of our Churches, until then detached from one another, on terms which contemplated the perpetuating of the communion, with all the distinguishing properties of the Church of England. And the unanimity with which this was accomplished, afforded a pleasing presage of whatever else we now gratefully remember.

We were, however, without that order of the Ministry, which we had learned from Scripture and primitive antiquity, to be essential to the due conducting of ecclesiastical concerns; and to the clothing of others with authority to preach the word and to administer the sacraments. The effects of this had become conspicuous, during the war then recently ended; in the course of which the greater number of our congregations had become deprived of their Ministers, without opportunities of replacing them. Matters were approaching to the extreme in which the voice of a duly authorized ministry would not have been heard within our walls. And what deepened the gloom of the prospect, were the restraints laid on our former ecclesiastical superiors, by the establishments under which they held their stations; and which, unless removed by authorities to which we could not with propriety apply, might prevent them from extending to us that aid, which, it was presumed, their Christian charity would otherwise dispose them to bestow.

Under these circumstances, recourse was had to the Archbishops and Bishops of England, who best knew the

nature of any civil impediments in their way, and were the
best judges of the means expedient for the removing of
them. . That we now address you in our official characters,
is an evidence of the success of the application.   And it
ought not to be noticed in this place, without the record of a
debt of gratitude to the Prelates of England generally, and
to their lately deceased venerable Primate* in particular, who
exerted all the influence of his high station, to accomplish
the wishes of this Church ; and who, at last, carried them
into effect, with a deportment which endeared his character
to those who received the succession from his hands.   While
we thus do justice to the source to which we principally
looked in consequence of past habits and a sense of past
benefits, it is with pleasure we acknowledge a similar debt
of gratitude to the Episcopacy which, in Scotland, survived
the Revolution in that country in the year 1688.   Although
the succession from thence derived is now incorporated with
that obtained from England, yet we retain a sense of the
benefit, and offer up our prayers for the perpetuity and the
increase of the Episcopal Church of Scotland.

Even when the succession had been obtained, there was
far from being a certainty of combining our Church
throughout the Union.   An important step for the accomplishing of this, was the uniting in a common Liturgy.   And
although there was reason to believe that the Liturgy of the
Church of England was substantially acceptable to us all ;
yet there were some parts of it utterly inconsistent with the
new relations in which we stood ; while, in regard to the rest,
there was room for considerable difference of opinion, on
points confessedly within the sphere of human prudence.
The case was full of difficulties ; which were at last removed
by that consent in all things necessary, and that temper of
concession in matters subjected to discretion, which led to

* The Most Rev. John Moore, D. D. late Archbishop of Canterbury.

the establishment of the Book of Common Prayer, now the standard of the public worship of our Church.

There remained a work, in itself more fruitful than any hitherto noticed, of discord and dissent. Our Church had not made a profession of Christian doctrine, with a reference to the points on which it has been contradicted, by what we conceive to be dangerous error. It is true, that the Articles of the Church of England, except the parts of them abrogated by the Revolution, might still be considered as binding on Churches, which had been founded on a profession of them. There was, however, wanting an explicit declaration to silence all doubt, in regard to their binding operation. And this, although a matter encumbered with much embarassment, was at last happily effected.

Whatever labours, and whatever cares there may have been bestowed for the accomplishing of the objects stated in this address, there must have been an ample compensation for them, in an observation of their effects. These are, indeed, far short of our wishes, and of what should still be the object of our endeavours: yet it must be confessed that there has not only been an arresting of the state of decline which threatened a dissolution; but such a religious prosperity in many places, and such a prospect of it in many more, as are at once a reward of zeal and an incentive to it. By communications made to us from the Church in several States, in obedience to the 11th Canon of the last General Convention, we have been favoured with a more satisfactory view of this subject than had been before possessed by us. While we record this, we take occasion from it to express our expectations that similar reports will be more generally transmitted to the next triennial meeting. For we have to lament that the communications exacted by the said canon, have not been universal; owing, perhaps, to its not having been sufficiently made known; or, perhaps, to there not having been sufficiently understood the object of it. We are not to learn how far such returns must be, from an exact measure of the power of godliness. Yet, where there is a growth of the profession of religion, there is occasion for charity to hope, and even ground in human nature to justify the belief, that there must be, in some proportion, an increase of its holy influence over the heart.

While we look back with gratitude on the blessings of Almighty God vouchsafed to our communion, it is for the purpose of a due improvement of them that we now present them to the view of its members; and, for the accomplishing of this, we invite their attention to the resulting considerations, as they affect *doctrine—worship—discipline*—and the end of all, an *holy life and conversation.*

In regard to *doctrine;* although it would be foreign to the design of this address, to display to you the whole body of Christian Truth, as affirmed in the Articles of our Church; yet we think ourselves called on by the occasion, to refer to some points; the contrary to which are the most apt to show their heads, among persons calling themselves of our communion. For the guarding of you, therefore, against that great danger, we affectionately remind you, that whatever derogates from the divinity of our blessed Saviour, or from the honour due to the Holy Spirit, with the Father, and with the Son, divine; that whatever detracts from our Lord's sufferings on the cross, as a propitiatory sacrifice for sin; that whatever supposes man in himself competent to his salvation, or to any advance towards it, without the grace of God going before to dispose him to the work, and concurring with him in the accomplishment of it; also, that whatever describes the favour of God in this life and the happiness which he offers to us in another, as the purchase of human merit, or any thing else than of the free grace of God in Christ, and through the merits of his death; still, in connection with its end, which is the bringing of us to be holy in heart and in conversation; in short, that whatever is in the least degree infected with the poison of the recited errors, was intended to be guarded against by our Church, in her decisions in regard to doctrine.

We are not ignorant of the prejudices which represent all ecclesiastical decisions on these and the like points, as the arbitrary acts of man, interfering with the word of God, revealed in Scripture. And we are ready to acknowledge that, did this charge lie, the matter censured would be not only presumptuous in itself, but especially inconsistent in a Church which has so explicitly declared her sense, that the Scriptures contain all things necessary to belief and practice. Let it then be understood, that we disclaim all idea of adding to the word of God, or of its being infallibly interpreted by any authority on earth. Still, it lies on the Ministers of the Church to open to their flocks the truths of Scripture, and to guard them against interfering errors. What then is the making of a declaration of the sense of the Church, but her doing that as a social body, which must be done by her Pastors individually; although, as may be supposed in some instances, not with due judgment and deliberation? It is evident, indeed, that this does not answer the objection, in another shape in which it meets us—the supposed hardship laid on those who are otherwise minded, than as the standard may have prescribed. Still, the Church exercises in this matter no power, but such as must be exercised by every Minister, in his individual capacity, under the danger of great abuse ; the effect of there being always the interference of discretion, and sometimes that of passion. To go no further than to the few evangelic truths which have been referred to : there is no faithful Minister of Christ who will endure the denial of them, in a Church under his pastoral care, and in circumstances in which there shall be no authority superior to his own, for the remedying of the evil, and not exercise that authority, within its reasonable limits, in order to defend his flock from errors. Thus, there would and ought to be accomplished by the individual, in the event of the silence of the Church, what she has rescued from arbitrary will, and made the subject of deliberate law.

While we exhort all to sustain the evangelic truths found in the Articles, as deduced from Scripture and attested by the earliest ages of Catholic Christianity, we would particularly impress on the Clergy, not only a sufficient frequency in professedly stating to their hearers the same truths, but also to manifest their salutary influence on all the other subjects of their public administrations. We are aware of the interference of this advice with the opinion that mere morals are the only suitable topics of discussion, and the only ends of exhortation, in discourses from the pulpit. Far be from us the thought of assigning to morals, considered as comprehending not only a correct course of conduct, but an holy state of heart, a subordinate rank in the scale of Christian endowment. For what is morality, thus defined, but " the living godly, righteously and soberly in this present world," which an Apostle has pronounced the very end for which " the grace of God, bringing salvation to all men, hath ap- " peared?" But when we take in connection with the subject, the depravity of the human heart; when we recollect the influence of this, wherever the Gospel is unknown, as well on the theory of morals as on practice ; and when there are many evidences before our eyes, how little there is in the world adorned by the attribute of moral virtue, in any other association than as embodied with, and growing out of the high and leading sense of Revelation, we suppose a fallacy in every modern scheme of religion, which professes to make men virtuous without the motives to virtue supplied to them in the Gospel; and we think, that, in every endeavour of this sort, in which infidelity is not avowed, we discover it in disguise.

Let there not be thought an objection to what we advise, in the unreasonable conduct of those, who, in their zeal for unprofitable speculation, lose sight of every practical use for which Christian light has been bestowed. We believe that from this there have arisen many errors, and much mischief. But we are so far from admitting it to be a reasonable cause of dispensing with the matter of our present exhortation, that we perceive, even in the errors the nearest allied to the truths of Scripture with which they are confounded, a motive to the laying of a due stress on these truths.

We shall say no more on the present branch of this address, except to assure our brethren of every description in the Church, that as, according to our judgment, any preaching, falling short of what is here held up, is not that which the Gospel calls for; so, according to our experience, neither is it of any considerable use. It has but little effect on the morals of society; still less in the excitement of piety; and least of all, in enlarging the bounds of the kingdom of the Redeemer, which is established on quite another basis, and has always been extended by quite other means.

When we bring before you, Brethren, the subject of *public worship*, you will of course suppose that it is principally with a view to the devotions, which, with an extraordinary degree of harmony and much previous deliberation, have been constituted our established Liturgy.

Independently on the admirable prayer prescribed by our Lord himself,* there is no fact equally ancient, of which we are more fully persuaded, than that the having of pre-

---

* The Lord's Prayer is given to us by St. Luke (chap. xi. 2.) under the injunction—" When ye pray, say"—which is evidently language expressive of the appointment of a form. But the construction has been thought to sustain an abatement of its force by the words in the parallel place of St. Matthew (chap. vi. 9.)—" After this manner pray ye." There is, however, no difference of sense in the two places. The Greek word ἅτως, translated " after this manner," may be rendered " thus;" that is, " in these words." For that either of the two phrases would have expressed the meaning, appears from chap. ii. 5, of the same Evangelist. When Herod had demanded of the Sanhedrim,—" Where Christ should be born," they made answer—" In Bethlehem of Judea; for thus [ἅτως] it is written by the Pro-

scribed devotions is a practice that has prevailed from the earliest origin of our religion.   We mean not that there were the same forms of prayer in all Churches; but that every local Church had its rule, according to the suitableness of time and place, and under the sanction of the Episcopacy of the different districts.   And we are further persuaded that the Christian economy in this matter was no other than a continuation of the Jewish, as prevailing in that very worship which was attended on, and joined in, by our blessed Saviour and his Apostles.   This is a mode of worship that has been handed down to us through the channel of the Church of England; and we suppose that we may affirm, as a notorious fact, its being acceptable to our communion generally.

But if this feature of our system is to be retained, we cannot but perceive that the order of divine service must be directed, not by individual discretion, but by public counsel. If, on the contrary, this principle is to cease to govern, we know of no plea for deviation tolerated in any Minister, which will not extend to the indulgence of the humour of every member of his congregation.   For this is a necessary result of that property of our ecclesiastical system, which contemplates the exercises of prayer and praise as those of a social body, of which the Minister is the leader.

If there should be in any a rage for innovation, it would be the more deplored by us, from the circumstance that it often originates in the affecting of an extravagant degree of animal sensibility ; which, it must be confessed, will not be either excited or kept alive by the temperate devotions of our prescribed Liturgy.   There are but few prayers handed down to us in the New Testament : If, however, any who may be advocates of an enthusiastic fervour would duly con-

phet." Then they go on to repeat the Prophet's words—" And thou Bethlehem, in the land of Judah, art not the least among the princes of Judah : for out of thee shall come a Governor, who shall rule my people Israel."

template the spirit that animates these prayers, they would not, we think, undervalue those of the Church, as though they were uninteresting to the best affections of the human heart.

It is impossible that there should be composed forms for public use, and yet that individuals should not perceive instances in which, according to their respective habits of thinking, the matter might have been more judiciously conceived, or more happily expressed. It is, however, evident that this; far from being prevented, would be much increased, by removing the subject from the controlling authority of 'the Church, to that of her Ministers, in their respective places. The cause of the supposed evil is an imperfection in human affairs, to which they will be always liable; and a temper to accommodate to it is an essential circumstance of a worthy membership of society, whether civil or religious. The dissatisfaction alluded to may affect either circumstantials, or the essence of the established Liturgy. If it apply to the former, submission of private opinion is one of the smallest sacrifices which may be exacted for the maintenance of order. But if any should lightly esteem the service, from the opinion, that it is below the dignity of the subjects comprehended in it, and unequal to the uses which prayers and praises point to, we have so much to oppose to such a sentiment, in the sense of wise and holy men of our communion in former ages, still shining as lights to the world in their estimable writings; so much, also, in the acknowledgment of judicious persons not of our communion, both in past ages and in the present; and so much of the effects of the habitual use of the Liturgy, on the tempers and on the lives of persons, who, in their respective days, have eminently " adorned the doctrine of their God and Saviour," that, if we spare an appeal to the modesty of the complainants, we are constrained to make a demand on their justice; and, in the name of all true members of our communion, to insist on being left in the secure possession of a mode of worship, which has become endeared to us by habit and by choice. It is on this ground that we consider every Churchman as possessing a personal right to lift up his voice against the intermixture of foreign matter with the service; rendering it such, as can never be acceptable to the same judgments, or interesting to the same affections.

In regard to any license which may be taken of another kind, that of varying words or phrases, for an accommodation to the reader's ideas of correct expression; to any Minister who may be tempted to this fault, we intimate, that it has the effect of subjecting him to the imputation of a species of levity, which breeds contempt. Certainly, every consideration which should relieve him from the charge of error, would proportionably expose him to that of vanity. But, whether it be error or vanity, the fault of wanton irregularity is attached to it.

Under the operation of the sentiments which have been delivered, we should be especially grieved to hear of any Ministers, that they make the services of the Church give way to their own crude conceptions. We call them such, because it may be expected, from experience of former times, that a practice so irregular in itself, would be generally found in those who have the most moderate share of the knowledge and the discretion, qualifying for a judicious exercise of the authority thus arrogated. While we earnestly admonish all Ministers against this assumption of a power not committed to them, we also exhort the laity to avoid encouragement of the delinquency should it happen, and, much more, inducement to it. We know that the most intelligent and best informed lay members of our communion, if this license should be obtruded on them, would disapprove of it; and, if they did not complain in public, would mourn in private. Even of those who, in any way, might countenance the irregularity, we should hope that they either did not know or did not recollect the sacred promises which would be hereby broken. And, on the whole, we announce, both to the Clergy and to the laity, our utter disapprobation of the irregularity here remarked on; calling on every one of them, in his place, to give his aid to the guarding against the evil, both by persuasion and by every other temperate expedient provided by the Canons of the Church.

We cannot be on this subject without lamenting, that, of a service in itself so full of edification, a considerable proportion of the due effect should be defeated, in consequence not of disapprobation or dislike, but of neglect of joining in it, as in heart, so likewise audibly and in the prescribed postures. We pray you, Brethren, not to impute what we say on this point to a zeal for mere decorous appearance. We do not, indeed, hesitate to acknowledge, even of this, that it is a laudable object of endeavour. But the matters on which we have laid a stress are supposed by us to be considerably connected with the devotion of the inward man. It is one of the properties of social worship, that, of those engaged in it, every one may excite and receive excitement from the others. And, indeed, when we open the uses of such worship, in order to demonstrate the reasonableness of its being required, this is the point on which the weight of the argument principally rests. If the present view of the subject be correct, the omissions complained of reach much deeper than to the deforming of the service, and disclose to us how much there may be imputed to this cause, of the entire neglect of it by many. And even if the other only were the consequence, it ought to have great weight; especially since, if the omission were defensible, the service has been constructed on a mistaken plan, which occasions its excellency to be in a great measure lost sight of, in the inconsistent manner of the performance.

There is another department of our religious worship necessarily left in some measure to discretion, which we know to be much abused in many places, and have reason to believe to be so in many more, not intentionally, either by Ministers or by their congregations, but probably to the dissatisfaction of both, yet too patiently endured by them. What we allude to is the manner in which there is sometimes conducted the otherwise pleasing and edifying exercise of Psalmody. In this line there are employed persons who, being regardless alike of godliness and of decency, presume to set themselves in contrariety to all the uses for which alone the art of music can with propriety display its charms within the house of God. Thus, there are outraged the feelings of all devout persons ; and not of them only, but of all who entertain a sense of consistency and propriety. On the ratifying of the Book of Common Prayer, an endeavour was made to give a check to this enormity, by the Rubric preceding the Psalms in metre. We desire to recal the attention of the Church generally, and of the Clergy in particular, to the provisions of that Rubric. And we further recommend to all those who have the appointment of performers in the musical department, that, if possible, none may be appointed in whom there are not found a visible profession of religion, in alliance with an irreproachable conversation. But if, in any instance, it should be thought that the profession must of necessity be dispensed with, let it at the most be in favour of persons who are not capable of dishonouring the worship of Almighty God, and of disgusting those who join in it: for this is a censure which we do not hesitate to lay on the conduct which has been referred to.

From worship we proceed to *discipline*. And here we wish our clerical and our lay brethren to be aware, as, on one hand of the responsibility under which we lie ; so, on the other, of the caution which justice and impartiality require. The Church has made provision for the degradation of unworthy Clergymen. It is for us to suppose that there are none of that description, until the contrary is made known to us, in our respective places, in the manner which the Canons have prescribed: And if the contrary to what we wish is in any instance to be found, it lies on you, our clerical and lay brethren, to present such faulty conduct; although with due regard to proof ; and, above all, in a temper which shows the impelling motive to be the glory of God and the sanctity of the reputation of his Church.

While we are not conscious of any bias, which, under an official call, would prevent the conscientious discharge of duty, we wish to be explicit in making known to all, that we think it due to God and to his Church, to avoid whatever may sanction assumed power, however desirable the end to which it may be directed. We have at least as weighty reasons to restrain us from judging without inquiry, and from censuring without evidence of crime. These are ends to which men of impetuous spirits would sometimes draw. But we would rather subject ourselves to the charge of indifference, however little merited, than be the mean of establishing precedents, giving to slander an advantage, against which no innocence can be a shield; and leaving to no man a security either of interest or of reputation. Although we have no reason to complain, that sentiments in contrariety to these prevail among us to any considerable extent, yet we freely deliver our sentiments on the subject, in order to give us an opportunity of calling on all wise and good men—and we shall not call on them in vain—to aid us in resisting, wherever it may appear, that mischievous spirit which confounds right and wrong, in judging of the characters and of the rights of others.

We should not discharge our consciences, could we be on this part of the subject, without declaring unequivocally our hope, that the time will come, when there shall not be acknowledged, even as nominally of our society, any person of an immoral life and conversation. We are not unapprized of the property of the Christian Church, stamped on it by the hand of its holy Author, that it was to comprehend the opposite characters of good and bad until the appointed time of an eternal separation. But this, as is evident, relates to the hearts of men, which cannot be known to one another. Every notorious sinner is a scandal to the Church of Christ; although he may be less guilty in the sight of God than some hypocrite, whose depravity lies concealed within her pale. Still it must be acknowledged, that there is no Christian work more full of embarrassment, than the one here referred to: And we freely confess that it were better left undone for ever, than to be accomplished at the expense of the violation of impartiality, much more of the gratification of malice. Still, the presenting of this object to your view is what the integrity of the Christian economy requires of us. Until it can be brought about, let us at least fence the table of the Lord from the unhallowed approach of every ungodly liver. And while we address this admonition especially to our brethren of the Clergy, we rejoice in the conviction that there is no part of their duty which they can execute, if it be done with a good conscience and with prudence, to the more entire satisfaction of the people generally: For there are few, perhaps none, disposed to tolerate the profanation of an ordinance, of which there is, on the part of so many, a neglect.

But while we thus admonish our brethren of the ministry to guard against the profanation of the Eucharist, we ought not to lose the opportunity of exhorting them to increase the number of the attendants on it, as by all proper means, so especially, by opening the nature of the Apostolic rite of confirmation, and by persuading to an observance of it. Were it an institution of human origin, we should admire it for its tendency to impress, on persons advancing to maturity, a sense of obligations resting on them, independently on their consent, in this ordinance voluntarily given. But we remind our brethren, knowing that they agree with us in the opinion, that it was ordained and practised by the Apostles of our Lord and Saviour Jesus Christ ; and that in the ages immediately subsequent to the age of the Apostles, it was one of the means of exciting to the sublime virtue which adorned them. Let us remember that the same grace, first given in baptismal regeneration, is increased and strengthened by confirmation. And let us extend the use of this holy and Apostolic rite, as one of the first principles of the Christian Religion, and a great mean of leading on towards that perfection of Christian morals, which is its object.

When we look back on the subjects of this address, we find ourselves impelled, by their united force, to direct our attention to an object deeply interesting to us, as members of the Episcopal Church, of the Catholic Church at large, and of civil society, with a due regard to its prosperity and its peace. What we mean is the taking of our share of the work of extending Christian preaching and worship to the States recently risen, and to these still rising, within our Federal Republic. It is an effect of the civil privileges which we enjoy, and of the honourable exertions which they prompt, that useless forests become changed to cultivated fields, and that the reign of science and civilization supplant that of ignorance and barbarism. But this will be far from an addition to the stock of human happiness, if, on such improvement, there be entailed the effect of a population let loose from the restraints of religion ; without which, the most estimable refinements of society only make men the more ferocious and the more mischievous to one another. We have, however, no considerable apprehension that this will be the result. The progressive property of the kingdom of the Redeemer, stamped on it by his own unerring hand ; and, harmonizing with this, the consent of prophecy, as well under the Law as under the Gospel, make us believe the contrary : And, on the ground of the designs of Providence, disclosed in Scripture, we look forward to the time when, over the whole extent of the regions beyond us, there shall ascend to Heaven the incense of evangelical prayer and praise ; and there shall be presented the peace-offering of the commemorative sacrifice of the passion of the Redeemer. But while we rejoice in all suitable means conducted with a view to this end, under any systems, not so agreeable as we suppose our own, to the word of God, we are urged to an extension of the latter, by every consideration which is an evidence to us of its superior usefulness. If, in reference to those regions spoken of, there be wanting any further inducement to a compliance with this Gospel call, we may remind you of some extravagances which we have heard of as there prevalent ; assuming the name of the religion of Jesus, but alien from its blessed nature ; and tending, as we presume to say from observation of the same cause, and its effects more within the spheres of our observation, eventually to increase that infidelity, which wages open war on whatever piety holds sacred, and which is covertly pernicious to whatever humanity has reason to esteem. During the present session, our minds have been much impressed by a sense of what is due from us to our western brethren, and especially to those of them professing themselves of our communion. We wish to extend to them the Episcopacy and the celebration of the worship of this Church: And we invite all our brethren now addressed to aid us in the accomplishment of these objects; and, until it shall be found practicable to avail themselves of any opportunities occurring, to encourage the settlement of suitable Ministers of this, Church, who may be disposed to remove from the elder States, into that vast field of labour. And we further invite Ministers and other members of our communion, who may be already seated in those districts, to aid us in carrying our purposes into effect ; and, in the mean time, if it be practicable, to make such internal organizations as may conduce to it.

But, Brethren, we wish it to be understood, in what we have brought before you, relative to doctrine, to worship, and to discipline, that it is all with a view to *practice*, in order to call on and entreat you, as a religious body, "to walk worthy of the vocation wherewith you are called;" illustrating the evangelic properties of your religious system, in its being seen to be productive of a religious life and conversation. The Clergy in particular, we exhort to remember the holy walking attached to the heavenly designation of their ministry, and with this their own assent, in the promises made by them at ordination, to the responsibility in which they stand. And we remind the laity, that, in respect to the obligation of Christian morals, there is no difference of extent over the different orders in the Church, whatever aggravation there be of delinquency in some, in consequence of the especial obligations which they have assumed.

In thus exciting you to *Christian virtue*, we find ourselves drawn to the contemplating of it, in an alliance with the more conspicuous relations in which the providence of God has placed you.

And, first, when we consider you as citizens, and in relation to the state, we exhort you not to view your character in this respect, as if it were unconnected with Christian obligation; not only that which Christianity enjoins, under all circumstances, of submission to law and government, and of reverence of those who are cloathed with its authorities; but also the temperate exercise of the rights provided for by the liberal genius of the constitutions under which we live. It is a property of the course of divine Providence, that there can be no temporal mercy of Heaven, without the attendant danger of its being abused by us, to our moral loss; which should be an admonition to us, in respect to the

civil privileges which we enjoy, not to exert them in such a
manner, as to add to the mass of inordinate ambition, of
fierce contention, and of intemperate revilings, by which we
observe the concerns of the commonwealth dishonoured
and her peace occasionally disturbed. If provision for the
public weal must necessarily open a field, on which the worst
passions of human nature are to display themselves in all
their enormity and outrage, let them be exclusively characteristic of those who live professedly without God in the
world; being as much lost to the forms of piety as they are
strangers to its spirit. Then will they of a contrary character, in the more reasonable exercise of privilege, hold out a
standing protest against the licentiousness which irreligion
begets and fosters, while there will also thus be moderated
the unhappy effects resulting from it. And if, under this
call to an holy care, lying on all professors of Christianity
differing as they do in the forms of their profession, it
should appear of our Church in particular, that her sons, in
proportion to their subjection to the duties of devotion which
she enjoins on them, are also observant of the duties of
which the objects are the peace of society, the safety of the
state, and the faithful administration of law and justice;
there will result from it no inconsiderable presumption, that
their principles bear on themselves the evidences of having
had their origin in divine illumination.

If in your several relative situations of a civil nature,
there be a demand for the forbearance and the charity which
have been recommended, how much more evidently are
the same exacted by your respective standings in the Church
of God; which was founded on a new law of love; and of
which one of the most illustrious properties is the " keeping
of the unity of the Spirit in the bond of peace!" In this line,
also, we blame no man for maintaining his just claims, or
for expressing his opinions on subjects which are within its
sphere. But we blame him, if, in the exercise of these his

rights, he break loose from the restraints of the wisdom from above; of which we are told that it is " first pure, then peaceable, gentle, and easy to be entreated." When in the line of right, and even in that of duty, there is so much of "the wrath of man," which "worketh not the righteousness of God," how much more distant should every Christian keep himself from that contentious spirit which seeks occasion to excite and to foment division; which so conceives of its own privilege to think and speak, as to leave no liberty elsewhere to do the same; and which is impatient of all government, except such as is vested in itself, or which it can over-rule! Be assured, Brethren, of the love of strife, wherever it shows its head, that it falls under that censure of holy writ—" This wisdom descendeth not from above, but is earthly, sensual, devilish." Much more consistent would it be, to deny the existence of the Church of Christ, as a social body, divinely instituted, than to imagine it divested of the properties found to belong to society, in all the variety of its forms; and to suppose that in this instance, although in no other, the individual is left to govern himself, and to incommode others, according to his own opinion or caprice.

While we are thus inviting your attention to the duties attached to your Church-membership, it may, perhaps, be expected that we should dwell on the magnitude of some objects which require expense. But we wave all particular discussion, at the present, of matters of this sort. It is not, however, that we conceive of reasonable pecuniary contribution, as any other than a Christian duty; in the extent, not only of the provisions essential to public worship, but also of those which make it venerable and comely. And, indeed, it is a duty especially incumbent in a country of increasing population, which, of course, frequently exacts contributions for new houses of worship and new provisions for their support. But we put these things out of view, because of a persuasion in our minds, that the true mean of

accomplishing the end, is the possessing of men with an
adequate sense of the uses for which such accommodations
are designed.   For if any one feel the weight of the obligations of Christianity on his conscience, and the enlivening influence of its consolations on his hopes, and, at the same
time, be sensible how much the welfare of civil society and
of families require the restraints on passion, and the incite-
ments to virtue, which the Gospel only can supply, and
which nothing but its authenticity can sustain, there will be
no danger of his hesitating to give of his substance, according as God, in his bounty, may have bestowed on him.
And there is no instance, in which God's protecting and
perpetuating of his Church has been more conspicuously displayed, than in his thus disposing of his professing people to
contribute to her according as her exigences have required.
Yes, Brethren, let us, in the rearing of our spiritual fabric,
reject the untempered mortar of worldly policy and of
passion in every shape which it may put on, and we need not
fear the failure of the outward means, by which Christ's
kingdom is to be made visible on earth ; until it shall exchange its properties in this respect for those of a better
kingdom in the Heavens.

Finally ; in regard to domestic and personal conduct, we
desire to be considered as addressing ourselves to every individual of you in particular, and as admonishing that individual to act under the influence of the Christian name ; to
remember that even so far as the good of the Church is involved in the conduct of its members, no zeal in her cause,
and no apparent services in support of it, can balance the disgrace brought on her by a licentious life ; and yet, that the
responsibility created by a religious profession towards man is
but an image of the higher responsibility, which it increases
towards the King of the whole earth ; who, in the sentence
which he will at last pronounce on the barren and false professor, may well say, with a reference to the inconsistency

between his profession and his practice—" Out of thine own mouth will I judge thee, thou wicked servant."

But we do not dwell on dissuasives from immoralities, which are a disgrace to Christianity, when there is before us the more pleasing duty of inciting you to the graces and to the works by which it may be adorned. It is by the being faithful and affectionate in the relations of husband and wife ; the being kind and provident on one hand, and dutiful and grateful on the other, in those of parent and child ; and the being in the exercise of justice and of mercy from masters to their servants, and of fidelity and obedience from these to them : it is further, by righteous and equitable dealings in all those intercourses with our fellow men in which there are so many temptations of rapacity impelling to wrong, and so much influence of self to seduce to it under the appearance of right; in addition to these things, it is by the being liberal to the poor, in contributing a full proportion to the tax laid by Providence on those who have, in favour of those who want, for the relief of misery in all the variety of its forms ; and, finally, it is by the government of the appetites, those foes of the household, which, unless subdued by religion's all conquering power, breed conflict within, and very often impatient of the restraints of considerations from any other source, break forth into deeds of disorder and big with temporal ruin ; it is, Brethren, by such a discipline in all its branches, that there must be felt the energy of a religion which is described to us as " the power of God unto salvation."

But, Brethren, the only way in which that power can be effectual, is in holiness of heart, under the operation of the divine Spirit, known no otherwise, than by the precious fruits which it produces. Independently on the grace of God, through our Lord and Saviour Jesus Christ, our desires and our pursuits, besides being productive of guilt and misery in their progress, look no further than to the objects of the present world ; the very shadow of which is daily passing away from us.   Whatever elevates our minds with an hope full of immortality, much more whatever prepares us for it by transforming us to the image of him who is "the pattern of all goodness, and righteousness, and truth," can come from nothing else, as we are assured in scripture, than from his own holy influence, which must be cultivated by devotion, and carried into effect by a continual " pressing forward to the mark for the prize of our high calling."

That this grace, freely bestowed on all, may be improved by all, to our comfort in the present life, and to the consummation of our happiness in Heaven, is the fervent prayer of those who fill the Episcopacy of this Church.   And, with this assurance, we commend ourselves to the prayers of all her members.

Signed by order of the House of Bishops, in General Convention, at Baltimore, May 23, 1808,

WILLIAM WHITE, *Presiding Bishop.*

Attested by

JAMES WHITEHEAD, *Sec'ry.*

Appendix B
First Pastoral Letter Dealing with Social Teachings

PASTORAL LETTER

OF THE

BISHOPS

OF THE

𝔓𝔯𝔬𝔱𝔢𝔰𝔱𝔞𝔫𝔱 𝔈𝔭𝔦𝔰𝔠𝔬𝔭𝔞𝔩 𝔆𝔥𝔲𝔯𝔠𝔥

IN THE UNITED STATES OF AMERICA

TO THE

CLERGY AND LAITY OF THE SAME.

DELIVERED BEFORE THE GENERAL CONVENTION,
AT THE CLOSE OF ITS SESSION,

IN

ST. JOHN'S CHURCH,

NEW YORK,

FRIDAY, OCTOBER 17, 1862.

———— • ————

NEW YORK:
BAKER & GODWIN, PRINTERS,
Printing-House Square, opposite City Hall.
1862.

PASTORAL LETTER.

————— ❖◆❖ —————

BRETHREN :

We have been assembled together in the Triennial Convention of our Church under most afflicting circumstances. Hitherto, whatever our Church had to contend with from the fallen nature of man, from the power of this evil world, or the enmity of that mighty adversary who is called by St. Paul "the god of this world," her Chief Council has been permitted to meet amidst the blessings of peace within our national boundaries, and as representing a household of faith at unity in itself. Our last meeting was in the metropolis of a State which has long held a high place and influence in the affairs of our Church and Country. Long shall we remember the affectionate hospitality which was then lavished upon us, and the delightful harmony and brotherly love which seemed to reign, almost without alloy, in a Convention composed of representatives of all our Dioceses ! Never did the promise of a long continuance of brotherly union, among all parts and sections of our whole Church, appear more assuring. But, alas ! what is man ? How unstable our surest reliances, based on man's wisdom or will ! How unsearchable the counsels of Him who "hath his way in the sea, and his path in the mighty waters, and whose footsteps are not known " ! What is now the change ? We look in vain for the occupants of seats in the Convention, belonging to the representatives of no less than ten of our Dioceses, and to ten of our Bishops. And whence such painful and injurious absence ? The cause stands as a great cloud of darkness before us, of which, as we cannot help seeing it, and thinking of it, and that most sorrowfully, wherever we go and whatever we do, it is impossible not to speak when we address you in regard to the condition and wants of our Church. That cause is all concentrated in a stupendous rebellion against the organic law and the constituted

Government of the Country, for the dismemberment of our national Union—under which, confessedly, all parts of the land have been signally prospered and blessed; a rebellion which is already too well known to you, brethren, in the vast armies it has compelled our Government to maintain, and in the fearful expense of life and treasure, of suffering and sorrow, which it has cost on both sides, to need any further description here.

We are deeply grieved to think how many of our brethren, clergy and laity, in the regions over which that dark tide has spread, have been carried away by its flood; not only yielding to it, so as to place themselves, as far as in them lay, in severance from our ecclesiastical Union, which has so long and so happily joined us together in one visible communion and fellowship; but, to a sad extent, sympathizing with the movement, and giving it their active co-operation.

In this part of our address, we do not attempt to estimate the moral character of such doings. At present we confine ourselves to the statement of notorious facts, except as to one matter, of which this is the convenient place to speak.

When the ordained Ministers of the Gospel of Christ, whose mission is so emphatically one of peace and good-will, of tenderness and consolation, do so depart from their sacred calling as to take the sword and engage in the fierce and bloody conflicts of war; when in so doing they are fighting against authorities which, as " *the powers that be*," the Scriptures declare "are ordained of God," so that in resisting them they resist the ordinance of God; when especially one comes out from the exalted spiritual duties of an Overseer of the flock of Christ, to exercise high command in such awful work,—we cannot, as ourselves Overseers of the same flock, consistently with duty to Christ's Church, His Ministry and people, refrain from placing on such examples our strong condemnation. We remember the words of our blessed Lord, uttered among His last words, and for the special admonition of His Ministers—" They that take the sword shall perish with the sword."

Returning to this great rebellion, with all its retinue of cost and sacrifice, of tribulation and anguish, of darkness and death, there are two aspects in which we must contemplate it, *namely:* as it comes *by the agency of man*, and as it comes *from the Providence of God*.

We desire, *first*, to call your attention to it as it proceeds from *the Providence of God*. So comprehensive is that Providence that it embraces all worlds and all nations; while so minute is it that not a sparrow falleth without the knowledge and will of our Father in

Heaven. In its vast counsels, this deep affliction has its place. God's hand is in it. His power rules it. It is His visitation and chastening for the sins of this nation. Who can doubt it? Just as the personal affliction of any of you is God's visitation to turn him from the world and sin, unto Himself; so is this national calamity most certainly His judgment upon this nation for its good. And we trust, dear brethren, we are in no danger of seeming, by such interpretation of our distresses, to excuse, in any degree, such agency as men have had in bringing them upon us. God's Providence has no interference with man's responsibility. He works by man, but so that it is still man that wills and works. The captivities of God's chosen people were, as His Word declares, His judgments upon them for their sins; while the nations that carried them captive were visited of God for heinous guilt in so doing. St. Peter declares that our Lord was "delivered" unto death "by the determinate counsel and foreknowledge of God;" and that, nevertheless, it was "*by wicked hands*" that He was "crucified and slain." Thus we need be under no temptation to diminish our estimate of the present dispensation of sorrow, as coming from the hand of God, for the punishment of our sins, whatever the agency of men therein. It is our duty, as Christians and as patriots, so to consider it, that it may do us the good for which it is sent, and may the sooner be taken away.

It is not possible for us, in this address, to set before you, in detail, or in their true proportions, all the national and other sins which make us, as a people, deserve, and need, the chastisements of a holy God. It needs no Daniel, inspired from on high, to discover them. Surely you must all be painfully familiar with many of them, in the profaneness of speech with which God's name and majesty are assailed; in the neglect of public worship which so dishonors His holy day; in the ungodliness of life which erects its example so conspicuously; and especially in that one great sin for which Jerusalem was given over to be trodden down by the heathen, and the people of Israel have ever since been wanderers and a by-word among the nations, *namely*, the rejection, whether in positive infidelity, or only in practical unbelief, of God's great gift of grace and mercy, His beloved Son, our Lord Jesus Christ, to be a sacrifice of propitiation for our sins, and an all-sufficient and all-glorious Saviour of our souls.

But there is a passage in the Scriptures which is of great use as a guide in this consideration of national sinfulness. It is a warning to the nation of Israel, and found in the eighth chapter of the book of Deuteronomy, as follows : "Beware that thou forget not the Lord thy

God, in not keeping His commandments, and His judgments, and His statutes, which I command thee this day, lest when thou hast eaten and art full, and hast built goodly houses and hast dwelt therein, and when thy herds and thy flocks multiply, and thy silver and thy gold is multiplied, and all that thou hast is multiplied, then thy heart be lifted up, and thou forget the Lord thy God; for it is He that giveth thee power to get wealth. And it shall be, that if thou do at all forget the Lord thy God—as the nations which the Lord destroyeth before your face, so shall ye perish, because ye would not be obedient to the voice of the Lord your God."

Now it was because that nation was guilty of precisely such self-glorying, and such forgetfulness of its indebtedness to God and dependence on His favor, as this warning describes, that the grievous calamities which so fill its history, before the advent of Christ, were brought upon it. And it is because there is so much agreement between this description and the aspect which we, as a people, have presented before God, that we place the passage before you.

Marvellously have we been prospered in every thing pertaining to national prosperity, riches, and strength. God has loaded us with benefits; and with our benefits have grown our ingratitude, our self-dependence, and self-sufficiency, our pride, our vain-glorying, and that sad deficiency, so much felt, in the representative acts and voices of the nation as to all adequate acknowledgment of God and of the Gospel of Christ. Let us mark the words of the prophet Jeremiah: " Let not the wise man glory in his wisdom, neither let the mighty man glory in his might; let not the rich man glory in his riches; but let him that glorieth, glory in this, that he understandeth and knoweth me that I am the Lord which exercise loving-kindness, judgment, and righteousness in the earth."—(Jer. ix.; 23, 24.) How remarkably do these words exhibit our sin as a nation! How seldom, in any thing of a representative character, or any thing that speaks for the nation, especially in the counsels of our chosen rulers, or in the enactments of our legislatures, do we see any such reference to God, as is here required as the basis on which He blesses a nation! How literally have we gloried in our wisdom, and power, and wealth; and said in our hearts, *Our power and our hand have gotten us all these things!*

Dear brethren, can we consider these things, so palpable to every eye, and not acknowledge that we deserve God's anger, and need, for our good, His chastening Providence? Is it wonderful that this tribulation hath come upon us? O, that when thus His judgments are upon the land, the inhabitants may learn righteousness ! We exhort you, brethren, that, as citizens and as Christians, you will take these things seriously to heart. Search and try yourselves, that you may duly humble yourselves under God's mighty hand, and He may, in due time, exalt us out of the present distress. Such a spirit of humiliation, taking wide possession of the people, especially of those who, as members of the Church of Christ, profess to be His disciples—above all, such a spirit appearing among those whose official position makes their words and acts of eminent weight and responsibility in determining the nation's standing before God—would more encourage us concerning the prospect of a happy removal of our national afflictions, a happy future of stability in our civil institutions, and of peace in the whole land, than if many signal victories were given to our honored armies. Let us pray earnestly and constantly for that spirit, which, above all things, is a nation's wealth, and strength, and praise. "The Lord's hand is not shortened," that it cannot thus bless us. "His ear is not heavy, that it cannot hear" us when we seek so great a blessing. He is "able to do exceeding abundantly above all that we ask or think ;" and prayer is the arm that places our wants on His mighty power.

Let us turn now to the other aspect of our great trial; namely, *as it comes from the agency of man.* We deeply feel, dear brethren, how momentous is this portion of our subject, and with what carefulness and charity, and at the same time with what decision and plainness of speech, with what faithfulness to Church and Country, and to those arrayed against us, as well as to ourselves, it becomes us to speak. Gladly would your Bishops avoid a subject so painful. But there is no possibility of avoiding it. Should we keep silence, we should not avoid it. Our silence would speak far and wide, and with a meaning by which we are not willing that our minds should be interpreted. At such an alarming crisis of our national and ecclesiastical union, as well as of our whole welfare, when a voice from such a body, occupying such intimate relations to a wide-spread communion, may be of such importance to the strength of the public counsels, through the guidance of the people of that communion,—should we address you on other topics of less prominence at the present time, and yet keep silence on that one which banishes almost every other from the thoughts of the nation, we should not only neglect an opportunity of usefulness which ought to be improved, and subject ourselves to imputations which we are not willing to bear, but we should inflict a serious injury upon a cause we are bound to aid.

It is the first time this Convention has met since these troubles began. God grant they may be ended long before it shall meet again! Ever since our Church had her Litany, we have been praying for deliverance "from sedition, privy conspiracy, and rebellion." And now that all the three are upon us, and in a depth of scheme, a force of action, a strength of purpose, and an extensiveness of sway such as the world never before saw united for the dismemberment of any government, shall we refuse to tell you in what light we regard that gigantic evil?

We are moved the more to speak, because we believe that you, brethren, desire it of us. You feel bound, by your views of duty, to take a position and manifest principles, too decided to be mistaken, in support of the national Constitution and Government in this day of their peril. Our communion is nobly represented wherever the nation's cause has dangers to brave, difficulties to be surmounted, sacrifices to be made, or sufferings to be borne. In the ranks, and through all the grades of command, our Church testifies her loyalty by the devotion of her sons. Many of them are her choice young men, whom it is hard to spare from works of Christian well-doing at home. Many of them are her Sunday-school teachers. They have gone to her armies, not in any bitterness of feeling toward those who have brought on us this war, but in a ready mind to love their enemies and to do good to those who hate them, as well as out of a well-considered and conscientious conviction of duty to their Country, to their Government, and to God. They look to us, their chief Pastors, especially as we are now gathered together here, to give them the support and comfort of our approbation, if we think they have rightly judged the great question of duty to the Government in the present struggle. Amidst the perils of battle, in hospitals and prisons, under privations and wounds, they feel the preciousness of such comfort. Acknowledging the reasonableness of such desires, we have pleasure in complying with them; not apprehending that in touching on this subject it can with reason be objected that we enter amidst questions with which, as Ministers of Him whose "kingdom is not of this world," we have nothing to do. Whatever the Apostles of Christ were inspired by the Holy Ghost to teach the Church; the Ministers and Stewards of that Church are bound to illustrate and enforce, for instruction of her members. "All Scripture is profitable for doctrine, reproof, correction, and instruction in righteousness." Whatever is contained therein is part of what has thus been "written for our learning"— part of that spiritual provision which you, brethren, are to "read, mark, learn, and inwardly digest;" and which, therefore, God's Stewards must distribute, as varying circumstances · shall make it "a word in season."

Then what say the Scriptures touching the subject before us ? We have no need to go beyond the words of St. Paul, in the thirteenth chapter of the Epistle to the Romans—"Let every soul be subject to the higher powers. For there is no power but of God. The powers that be are ordained of God. Whosoever, therefore, resisteth the power, resisteth the ordinance of God; and they that resist shall receive to themselves damnation."

Now, it is the application of these words to our duties, under present circumstances, of which we have need to inquire, if we would use this portion of Scripture as "a light to our feet." Where, then, do we find those powers and ordinances to which, as "ordained of God," we, recognizing the great truth that "there is no power but of God," are bound, for His sake, to be subject? We answer, IN THE CONSTITUTION AND GOVERNMENT OF THE UNITED STATES. Under them, the people of all the States, now resisting them, were just as much bound to render obedience, when such resistance began, as we, whose allegiance is still unbroken. According to the Scriptures, that resistance, so far from making null and void those powers, is a resistance to ordinances of God still in force; and, therefore, brings His condemnation on those so engaged.

When St. Paul, in direct connection with the words just cited, exhorts us to "render to all their dues, tribute to whom tribute is due, custom to whom custom, fear to whom fear, honor to whom honor," and *that* "not only for wrath, but for conscience' sake ;" we have no hesitation in teaching that the claim to all these duties and manifestations of allegiance and loyalty from us, and from all those States so recently united in rendering them, is rightfully in that Government which is now by force of arms maintaining such claim. The refusal of such allegiance we hold to be a *sin ;* and when it stands forth in armed rebellion, it is *a great crime* before the laws of God, as well as man.

Thus, brethren, your Bishops teach, as official expositors of the Word of God. Less, they believe, they could not teach without unfaithfulness to the Scriptures.

If godly submission to the laws and constitutional rulers of the country should be regarded as a matter of less than the most religious obligation ; if it shall be held a thing of indifference whether the Government, given us in the Providence of God, be obeyed "for conscience' sake," or be overthrown by conspiracy and armed rebellion, without the pretence of any existing and oppressive wrong, or of any wrong for which the remedy might not be found under, and by, provision of that very Government,—then all the horrors, of which such rebellion may be the prolific parent, may at any time be caused, and even intended, without guilt. But, let us hear what the Fathers of our Church, in one of those Homilies which our Articles declare to contain "a godly and wholesome doctrine," teaches on this head. We can well understand it now and appreciate it, as never before. In the Homily "Against Willful Rebellion" we have these wholesome words : "He that nameth rebellion, nameth not a singular, or one only sin, as is theft, robbery, murder, and such like ; but he nameth the whole puddle and sink of all sins against God and man ; against his country, his countrymen, his parents, his children, his kinsfolk, his friends, and against all men universally ; all sins against God and all men heaped together, nameth he that nameth rebellion." In another passage, after speaking of the general miseries of all war, the Homily proceeds with a still darker description : "But when these mischiefs are wrought in rebellion by them that should be friends, by countrymen, by kinsmen, by those that should defend their country and countrymen from such miseries, the misery is nothing so great as are the mischief and wickedness where the subjects unnaturally do rebel * * ; countrymen to disturb the public peace and quietness of their country, for defence of whose quietness they should spend their lives ;" "and, universally, instead of all quietness, joy, and felicity, which so follow blessed peace and due obedience, to bring in all trouble, sorrow, disquietness of minds and bodies, and all mischief and calamities ; to turn all good order upside down ; to bring all good laws into contempt, and to tread them under foot ; to oppress all virtue and honesty, and all virtuous and honest persons ; and to set all vice and wickedness and all vicious and wicked men at liberty to work their wicked wills, which before were bridled by wholesome laws ; to weaken, to overthrow, and to consume the strength of the realm, their natural country, which, by their mischief weakened, is thus ready to be a prey and spoil to all outward enemies."

Such is the testimony of our Homilies against "Willful Rebellion."

The reasons which make this so great a crime are the same which make the constituted authority so indispensable to the very existence of human society. God has invested the magistrate with power, and given him the sword to be borne, "not in vain," because he is His

Minister "*for good;*" because, without him, all the floods of ungodliness would be set free; and the only remedy remaining for all social disorders would be that of force overcoming force, and of cunning overreaching cunning.

We have now, brethren, in strict confinement to the testimony of the Scriptures, ascertained a basis of principle and duty on which we may heartily rejoice in all the active and energetic loyalty with which the members of our Churches, in union with their fellow-citizens, of all classes and conditions, are sustaining the Government in its vast efforts to reinstate the rightful control of its laws, wherever they have been disowned. We bid them never to be weary of that well-doing; and particularly would we say to those who, out of love to their country, and not out of any vindictive exasperation towards her enemies, have gone in our armies, *be of good cheer!* Whatever the dangers you may have to meet, or sufferings to endure, let it be your consolation that you have gone to sustain the power, ordained of God, and which rightfully claims your most devoted loyalty.

And now, we can ask your further attention only to a few concluding words, touching great spiritual interests, which the absorbing claims and the strong excitements of these times endanger. No doubt, dear brethren, you have all been painfully conscious of the powerful tendency of the present anxieties and excitements to draw down your thoughts and affections from daily communion with God; to elevate earthly interests and duties into injurious rivalry with those of the soul and eternity; to carry your minds away on this powerful flood of feeling and active concern for our beloved country, till they become, in a great degree, separated from all earnest engagedness in God's service. With some minds, under divine grace, the tendency of these troubles is to lead them nearer to God; while with others it is to take them away from God, to make His Word less precious, His holy day less sacredly kept, secret prayer less faithfully observed, and less their refuge and consolation; Christian example less decided and exalted.

We desire affectionately to exhort you to increased watchfulness and prayer in consequence of such danger. Let not love of Country make your love to God and your gracious Saviour the less fervent. Immense as is this present earthly interest, it is only earthly. The infinitely greater interests of the soul and of the kingdom of God remain as paramount as ever. We counsel, not that you feel less concern for the former, but that you seek God's grace so to sanctify all its anxieties that it may constantly lead you to Him for refuge, and rest, and peace ; making you only the more earnest to secure, in exchange for this sinful and troublesome world, that inheritance which is incorruptible, that better country where " sorrow and sighing flee away."

And we also charge you, brethren, that you watch and pray, lest during this unhappy strife you should allow any bitterness of spirit to dwell in you toward those who, from whatever cause, have brought on us this war, with its great injuries and calamities, or who are now waging it against us.   To hate rebellion, so uncaused, is duty ; but to hate those engaged therein, is the opposite of Christian duty.   Nothing can release us from the charge of our blessed Lord to love even our greatest enemies; do good to them that hate us, and pray for such as despitefully use us and persecute us.   In this temper of mind let us be followers of Him who, when *we* were enemies, died for us.

We are pained to learn, from the reports of committees of our General Missionary Society, to what extent the means of pursuing their great work have suffered by reason of these times.   We are aware how much of the contributions of our people have gone to the relief and consolation of our brethren who, in exposing themselves to the dangers of battle for our defence, have fallen under wounds or sickness.   We rejoice in all that is done for them ; and it is a vast relief from the horrors of this war to see what a spirit of self-denying and devoted benevolence has appeared all over the land, in men and women of all conditions, banding them together in labors of love, or scattering them abroad over the field of suffering, on errands of compassion and tender ministration to our sick, wounded, dying soldiers. God be praised for all this !   It goes far to comfort us in the great tribulation.   But the claims of the kingdom of God are not diminished.   The calls for the labors of men of God to preach the Gospel in destitute places are as loud as ever.   And we believe that while the ability of many to contribute of their substance to the missionary work has been greatly impaired and almost taken away by our national troubles, that of many others is not so diminished or so drawn upon by objects peculiar to these circumstances that they may not enlarge their gifts to the work of missions, and greatly supply what is lacking by the disability of others.   We pray them, and all our brethren, seriously to review their duty in this respect.   The missions in Africa and China are afflicted at the prospect of being painfully reduced for want of means to sustain them as they are.   In the domestic field, the absence in missionary stations of the labors of the Minister of the Word and Sacrament, is even a greater evil in such times than when no great national affliction carries its sorrows and clouds into every village of the land. Let us seek God's blessing upon our country's cause, by seeking to promote His kingdom and righteousness in all our borders.

But it is not merely for the support of our missionary work that we are concerned at this time. The ability of many a faithful parish Minister to continue his labor of love among a people beloved, is greatly endangered at this time for lack of the most slender pecuniary support; so that by the additional cause of Ministers feeling it their duty to see to the spiritual wants of our soldiers and taking service as chaplains in the army, we are increasing the number of vacant congregations to an alarming extent. We must therefore exhort our brethren to take heed and to do their utmost in their several parishes, that the blessing of a settled Minister be not lost for lack of the needed pecuniary support. If such privation, in ordinary circumstances, be of great detriment; much more is it so in days of affliction such as we have never known before. Never was it so important to all individual, domestic, and social interests, for the light of every household in a day of darkness, and the strengthening of every heart in a season of manifold burdens, that the lamp of the sanctuary should be trimmed and burning; that the precious " comfort of the Scriptures," through its appointed Messenger, should not be removed; that the soothing, purifying, governing, elevating influences of the public means of grace, under the hand of God's Minister, should be regularly enjoyed in the congregation. But if such cannot be the privilege, then we exhort vacant congregations that instead of forsaking the assembling of themselves together, as if, because they have no pastor, they could have no worship, one with another, they will take advantage of the great privilege of having our Book of Common Prayer, whereby a Church without a Pastor may still have its public worship and the Word of God, in purity, in fitness, and in power. Meet together regularly, brethren; have the Morning and Evening Prayer, and some approved published sermon, read by one of your number. You will thus have much to enjoy, though not all you need and desire. Lose it not, because you cannot have more.

And now, praying a merciful God and Father soon to restore to our beloved country the blessings of peace, under the banner of our honored national Union, and with our wholesome laws and righteous liberties more than ever strengthened, defended, and established; praying that those who have sought to depart from us may speedily and happily be reunited with us in the bonds of Christian, as well as national, fellowship; and that all bitterness, and wrath, and anger, and clamor, and evil speaking may be put away from us and them " with all malice;" that we may "be kind one to another, tender-hearted, forgiving one another even as we hope that God, for Christ's sake, hath forgiven us," we affectionately "commit you to God and the word of His grace." May the blessing of God so abide on you, beloved brethren, in all your families and congregations, that "your faith may grow exceedingly," "that your love may abound more and more," "that you may walk worthy of the Lord unto all pleasing, being fruitful in every good work and increasing in the knowledge of God;" "to whom be glory in the Church, throughout all ages, world without end."

CHARLES PETTIT McILVAINE, D. D., D. C. L.,

Bishop of Ohio,

Presiding in the House of Bishops, *pro tem.*

Appendix C
Second Instance of Episcopal Social Teachings

JOURNAL

OF THE

GENERAL CONVENTION

OF THE

Protestant Episcopal Church

IN THE UNITED STATES OF AMERICA

Held in the City of Boston
From October 5th to October 25th, inclusive
In the Year of Our Lord

1904

WITH APPENDICES

PRINTED FOR THE CONVENTION

1905

The Bishop of New York, from the Commission on the Relations of Capital and Labor, presented the following report:

The Standing Commission on the Relations of Capital and Labor was appointed by the General Convention of 1901, on the motion of the Rev. Dr. R. H. McKim of Washington, and its duties were defined as follows:

First, to study carefully the aims and purposes of the labor organizations of our country.

Secondly, in particular, to investigate the causes of industrial disturbances, as these may arise.

Thirdly, to hold themselves in readiness to act as arbitrators, should their services be desired, between the men and their employers, with a view to bring about mutual conciliation and harmony in the spirit of the Prince of Peace.

The Commission was directed to give an account of its proceedings to the General Convention, and it submits accordingly the following report:

Taking the definitions of our duty in reverse order, we have to say regarding *arbitration* that no request for our services has been received.

We have to confess regarding *investigation* that we have not, as yet, succeeded in studying in common the occasions of current disturbances. We are agreed, however, in the conviction that the causes of the violence of the past three years in Pennsylvania, in Colorado, and in Illinois are not so much economical as moral. The strike commonly begins in distrust. The reason at the heart of it is that the master has as little confidence in the good will of the men as the men have in the good faith of the master. The employer and the employed, separated by our industrial conditions at such a social distance as to make fraternal understanding difficult, make their bargain one with another, under these conditions, not as partners, but as competitors. Where distrust and antagonism are well founded, there is nothing for it, as far as the Church is concerned, except conversion. They who are at fault are to be admonished on the one side against prejudice and passion, and on the other side against covetousness and the sins which proceed from the inordinate love of riches. Where distrust and hostility are unfounded, the Church may afford an opportunity of conference. The capitalist and the laborer are alike sons of the Church. They may not sit in the same seat, or even in the same building; that is largely a matter of locality. But there is as much loyalty to the Church and to the Divine Head of the Church in the one class as in the other. The voice of the Christian religion reaches both capital and labor. The Church helps to remove the moral causes of industrial strife when she brings these different members of her family into better acquaintance.

Beside these duties of arbitration and of investigation, we were charged to study the aim and spirit of labor *organization.*

We perceive, among our clergy and laity alike, much ignorance (frankly confessed and deplored) as to the principles which are involved in the conflicts of the industrial world. At the same time, it is plain that an enlightened public opinion is one of the determining factors of the situation. Every industrial dispute involves three parties—the employer, the employed, and the public; and the public eventually casts the deciding vote. Thus a serious social responsibility rests upon every Christian citizen and more especially upon the Christian Minister.

We suggest, therefore, the following books, as affording an introduction to the study of these matters:

Westcott, " Social Aspects of Christianity " (Macmillan).
Mitchell, " The Organization of Labor."
Drage, " The Labor Problem " (Smith, Elder & Co.).
Peters, " Labor and Capital " (Putnam).

Bull Lectures, 1904, " Organized Labor and Capital " (Jacobs).
Brooks, " The Social Unrest " (Macmillan).
Gladden, " Tools and the Man " (Houghton, Mifflin & Co.).
Abbott, " Christianity and Social Problems " (Houghton, Mifflin & Co.).
Peabody, " Jesus Christ and the Social Question " (Macmillan).
Report of the Anthracite Coal Commission.

We call attention to the analogy between certain offenses of the Union, and like offenses, past or present, of both the capitalist and the church-man.   Thus the employer's black list corresponds to the Union's boy-cott, and both are akin to the major excommunication.   The lockout and the strike are of the same nature, and there is no great difference be-tween such endeavors to employ the argument of famine and an interdict which deprives a people of the blessings of spiritual life.   The question of the closed shop is like the question of the closed State.   Men whose Puritan ancestors strove to maintain a State whose privileges should belong only to members of the Church, ought to be able to understand the struggle of their brethren to maintain a shop in which no man shall serve except a member of the Union.   They may not agree with these brethren, but they ought to appreciate their self-sacrifice.   The laborer has learned from the capitalist to despise order and break law.   He has learned from the churchman to pursue the dissenter with menace and violence.   The recent tragedies in Colorado do not follow at a far dis-tance the massacres which in the sixteenth century ensued upon the withdrawal of Holland from the ecclesiastical union.

While, then, we condemn the tyranny and turbulence of the Labor Union, and call upon the law to preserve the liberty of every citizen to employ whom he will and to work for whom he will, we deprecate the hasty temper which, in condemning the errors of the Unions, condemns at the same time the whole movement with which they are connected. The offenses of the Union are as distinct from the cause for which the organization of labor stands, as the Inquisition is distinct from the Gospel.

In the face of a prejudice and an hostility for which there are serious reasons, we are convinced that the organization of labor is essential to the well-being of the working people.   It is based upon a sense of the inestimable value of the individual man.   " The cause of labor is the effort of men, being men, to live the life of men."   Its purpose is to maintain such a standard of wages, hours, and conditions as shall afford every man an opportunity to grow in mind and in heart.   Without or-ganization the standard cannot be maintained in the midst of our present commercial conditions.

This report is designedly general in its terms, but there is one matter which we are constrained to commend in particular to the consciences of Christian people.   We do not undertake to say how much of the blame of child-labor belongs 'to the employer and how much to the parent, but we do say this: that the employment of children in factories and mills depresses wages, destroys homes, and depreciates the human stock.   Nothing is so important in any community as a human being. Whatever interferes with the proper nurture and education of a child contradicts the best interests of the nation.   We call, then, on Christian employers and on Christian parents to endeavor after such betterment of the local and general laws as shall make the labor of children impos-sible in this Christian country.

In the name of our Common Master we ask the attention and the energy of the Church to the removal of this and other crying evils. Thus shall we assist in setting forward the kingdom and obedience of our Lord and Saviour Jesus Christ.

We offer the following resolution:

Resolved, That the Commission be continued.

> HENRY C. POTTER,
> WILLIAM LAWRENCE,
> CHARLES P. ANDERSON,
> R. H. McKIM,
> GEORGE HODGES,
> C. D. WILLIAMS,
> SAMUEL MATHER,
> JACOB RIIS,
> SETH LOW.

The question being on the resolution contained in the foregoing report, to wit: that the Commission be continued, it was adopted. [See p. 122.]

The Bishop of Western Texas presented the following report of the Committee to whom was referred the Memorial of the Annual Conference of Church Workers among Colored People [see p. 57] :

Your Committee, to whom was referred the above mentioned memorial, beg leave to report that we have read the same with interest, and have considered with care the Canon suggested by the conference. We sympathize deeply with the spirit of the conference, longing to gather more of their race into the fold of the Church, and praying for some modification of ecclesiastical custom to meet the unprecedented conditions which confront them.

But the departure from ancient custom suggested by the memorial is so decided and far reaching, and the practical difficulties to be overcome so great, that we have concluded that it is wise to delay action until we can secure fuller information, and can agree upon some method which will approve itself to the mind and conscience of the whole Church. We therefore offer the following resolutions:

Resolved, the House of Deputies concurring, That a Joint Commission on Work among the Colored People, consisting of five Bishops, five Presbyters, and five Laymen, be appointed, to gather information, to ascertain the mind of the Church, and to propose to the next General Convention such legislation as they may think desirable to meet the conditions.

Resolved, That the Bishops of those Dioceses and Missionary Districts in which the largest numbers of colored people are congregated be requested to bring this matter before their respective Councils and Convocations, with a view to having it fully discussed; and that they transmit to this Joint Commission as soon as may be convenient the action which may be taken by them, together with their own views on the subject.

> J. S. JOHNSTON, *Chairman,*
> JOS. BLOUNT CHESHIRE,
> ROBERT A. GIBSON,
> HENRY Y. SATTERLEE,
> ALEX. MACKAY-SMITH,
> EDWIN S. LINES.

Selected Readings

Chapter 1: WHAT DO SOCIAL TEACHINGS LOOK LIKE?

Abbott, Walter M. *The Documents of Vatican II, With Notes and Comments by Catholic, Protestant, and Orthodox Authorities.* New York: Guild Press, 1966.

Flannery, Austin. *Vatican Council II: The Conciliar and Post Conciliar Documents.* Northport, N.Y.: Costello Publishing Company, 1975.

Fremantle, Anne, ed. *The Papal Encyclicals in their Historical Context.* New York: New American Library, 1956.

Huttmann, M.A. *The Establishment of Christianity.* New York: Columbia University, 1914; reprint, New York: AMS, 1967.

Jones, A.H. *Constantine and the Conversion of Europe.* Harmondsworth, England: Penguin Books, 1972.

Seven Great Encyclicals. Glen Rock, N.J.: Paulist Press, 1963.

Troeltsch, Ernst. *The Social Teaching of the Christian Churches.* 2 vols. Translated by Olive Wyon. New York: Harper & Row, 1960.

Weston, M. Moran. *Social Policy of the Episcopal Church in the Twentieth Century.* New York: Seabury Press, 1964.

Chapter 2: WHAT DO ANGLICAN SOCIAL TEACHINGS LOOK LIKE?

Binyon, Gilbert C. *The Christian Socialist Movement in England.* New York: Macmillan, 1931.

Christensen, Torben. *Origin and History of Christian Socialism 1848–54.* Aarhus, Denmark: Universitetsforlaget, 1962.

Davidson, Randall T. *The Five Lambeth Conferences.* London: SPCK, 1920.

Iremonger, F.A.   *William Temple, Archbishop of Canterbury: His Life and Letters.* London: Oxford University Press, 1948.

Jones, Peter d'A.   *The Christian Socialist Revival 1877–1914.* Princeton, N.J.: Princeton University Press, 1968.

The Lambeth Conferences (1867–1948). London: SPCK, 1948.

Maurice, Frederick D.   *Theological Essays.* New York: Harper & Row, 1957.

Murchland, Bernard.   *The Dream of Christian Socialism: An Essay on Its European Origins.* Washington, D.C.: American Enterprise Institute for Public Policy Research, 1982.

Norman, E.R.   *Church and Society in England, 1770–1970: A Historical Study.* Oxford: Clarendon Press, 1976.

Raven, Charles.   *Christian Socialism, 1848–1854.* New York: Augustus M. Kelley, 1968.

Suggate, Alan M.   *William Temple and Christian Social Ethics Today.* Edinburgh: T. & T. Clark, 1987.

Temple, William.   *Christus Veritas.* London: Macmillan, 1924.

_____ .   *Christianity and Social Order.* London: SPCK, 1976.

Thompson, Dorothy.   *The Chartists: Popular Politics in the Industrial Revolution.* New York: Pantheon Books, 1984.

Wolf, William J., ed.   *The Spirit of Anglicanism: Hooker, Maurice, Temple.* Wilton, Conn.: Morehouse-Barlow, 1979.

Chapter 3: BEGINNINGS OF EPISCOPAL CHURCH SOCIAL TEACHINGS

Hopkins, Charles.   *The Rise of the Social Gospel in American Protestantism: 1865–1915.* New Haven: Yale University Press, 1940.

Chapter 4: WAR AND PEACE

"The Challenge of Peace: God's Promise and Our Response," Pastoral Letter of the U.S. Catholic Bishops. Washington, D.C.: National Conference of Catholic Bishops, 1983.

"In Defense of Creation: The Nuclear Crisis and a Just Peace," Pastoral Letter of the United Methodist Council of Bishops. Nashville, Tenn.: Graded Press, 1986.

"Peacemaking: The Believers' Calling," United Presbyterian Church, U.S.A. New York: Office of the General Assembly, 1980.

"To Make Peace," The Reports of the Joint Commissions on Peace of the General Convention of the Episcopal Church. New York: Office of Peace and Justice, 1988.

Chapter 5: RACE AND RACIAL AFFAIRS

Burgess, John M. *Black Gospel/White Church*. New York: Seabury Press, 1982.

Hayden, J. Carleton, "After the War: The Mission and Growth of the Episcopal Church Among Blacks in the South, 1865–1877," *Historical Magazine of the Protestant Episcopal Church* 42 (December 1973): 403-27.

Hood, R.E., "From a Headstart to a Deadstart: The Historical Basis for Black Indifference Toward the Episcopal Church, 1800–1860," *Historical Magazine of the Protestant Episcopal Church* 51 (September 1982): 269-96.

Jordan, Winthrop D. *The White Man's Burden: Historical Origins of Racism in the United States*. New York: Oxford University Press, 1976.

Walker, Clarence E. *A Rock in a Weary Land: The African Methodist Episcopal Church During the Civil War and Reconstruction*. Baton Rouge, La.: Louisiana State University Press, 1982.

Chapter 6: MARRIAGE AND FAMILY

Turner, Philip. *Sex, Money & Power: An Essay in Christian Social Ethics*. Cambridge, Mass.: Cowley Publications, 1985.

Chapter 7: ECONOMIC ISSUES

Wogaman, J. Philip. *Economics and Ethics: A Christian Enquiry*. Philadelphia: Fortress Press, 1986.

Chapter 8: AUTHORITY

Sykes, Stephen W., ed. *Authority in the Anglican Communion.* Toronto: Anglican Book Centre, 1987.

Vogel, Arthur A., ed. *Theology in Anglicanism.* Wilton, Conn.: Morehouse-Barlow, 1984.

Index

African Methodist Episcopal
Church
See A.M.E. Church 54, 110
American Indians (Native
Americans)
Episcopal Church 68-9, 77
Anglican Social Teachings
(nineteenth century)
industrial problems in 34
on brotherhood 37, 52, 53, 54,
165
on cooperation among classes
37, 52, 54-5
on private property 37, 38, 52
on socialism 37, 51, 52
public policy and 47
relationship to Episcopal social
thought x, 33, 189
social change and 34
the "natural order" in 36, 38
the poor in 35, 44
theological foundations of
36-9, 42,-3, 46-9
Aquinas, Thomas 91
Augustine 86, 91
Authority
"All men are created equal..."
191
1948 Lambeth Conference on
184
and "freedom of choice" 188
and inclusiveness 188
and private codes of ethics
188, 192
biblical 184, 185, 187, 192
conscience 58, 186, 188, 192
constitutional and canonical
184
creedal 184, 185
dispersed 184, 186
liturgical 184, 185, 191

of clergy and laity 190
of General Convention's
standing and joint
commissions 184
of Pastoral Letters 184, 189
of the Church's Teaching
Series 129, 135
of the episcopate 190-1
of the great awakenings 9
of the lay vestry 190
personal experience 186, 188
tradition 185
Baker, Ella 119
Barmen Declaration 82, 94
Barth, Karl 82, 93, 159
Beecher, Lyman 24
Bernier, Francois 101
Birth control (family plan-
ning) 56, 58, 139, 140, 141, 146
Bishop Payne Divinity
School 106, 115
Blumenbach, Johann F. 101
Brandt Report 164
Brown v. Board of Education of
Topeka 116
Buck v. Bell 144
CAIL 71, 74
Calvin, John 174
Calvinism xii, 174
Canons of Hippolytus 91
Cash, W.J. 107
Catholic Bishops' Pastoral Letter
on Peace 25, 86, 95
Cathrein, Viktor 12
Caution, Tollie 113
Chaney, James 121
Chartists 34-5
Christian Social Union
(CSU) 41-2, 53, 74
Christian Socialism
"sacramental socialism" 40-1

and the Lambeth Conferences
42, 53
Christian socialist movement
x, 35, 37, 165
revival of   39, 40, 41-3, 53
theological thought in
revived   41-3
Christian Socialist League
(CSL)   41, 42
Paul B. Bull   42
Chrysostom, John   10
Church Association for the
Advancement of Interests of
Labor
See CAIL
Church Congress   40, 43, 71
Church of the Brethren   92
Church Socialist League   41
Church's Teaching Series   x, 92,
129, 135, 152
Clement of Alexandria   176
Colenso, John Coleman   50
Colwell, Stephen   70
Communism   56, 78, 90, 95, 96
addressed at 1948 Lambeth
Conference   56-7
Companions of the Holy
Cross   74
Confederate Episcopal Church
105
Constantine   6, 8, 11, 91
Courier-Journal (Louisville,
Ky.)   24
Dalcho, Frederick   104
Davenport, Charles B.   140
Davidson, Randall T.   53
Delaney, Henry B.   112
Demby, Edward T.   112
Economic issues
"Affirmation of Christian
Principles" (1937)   168
"Social Service Creed" (1922)
166, 168
1913 General Convention
165
1919 Pastoral   165
1922 Pastoral   166
1929 Pastoral   166

1933 Pastoral (on a new
economic order)   167
1982 General Convention and
Brandt Report   164
1982 Labor Day Pastoral
(urban bishops)   172, 173
and the Social Gospel   165
capital-labor strife   165
Christian principles for a just
economic order   165-6,
167, 172
commitment to the poor
167, 168, 171, 176
committee on national and
world problems (1931)
167
committee on social responsibility in investments (SRI)
169-70
common good as a moral
issue   166, 170
corporations and their
culture   165, 178
first joint commission dealing
with   73-4, 164
free market, ethics of the   179
free market, moral foundations of the   177-8
individual dignity and working conditions   165, 166, 173
investments and social
responsibility   169-70
jubilee ministry, a joint
discipleship with the poor
171, 176
Ministry of Community
Development (1988)   163,
173, 176
profit motive as moral issue
165, 166, 170, 172
stewardship as Christian
vocation in   170
summary of social teachings
on   173
trade unions   167, 169, 172
"Economic Justice for All" (R.C.
Pastoral)   25
on corporations   28

on human labor and employment 26-7, 28
on human rights 26, 27
on the poor and the margin-
alized 26, 28
on trade unions 26, 27
theological principles of 25-7
Eight Hour League 74
Elliott, Stephen 104
Ely, Richard 70
Engels, Friedrich 6, 35, 45, 136
Enlightenment, the 2, 12, 13,
118, 158
Episcopal Peace Fellowship 82
Episcopal Social Teachings
theological foundations of
early 65-6, 84
Episcopal Society for Cultural
and Racial Unity (ESCRU)
117, 119, 120, 121, 127, 128
Fourier, Charles 12
Franco, Francisco 83
Freedman's Commission xiv,
xv, 106, 107
Friedman, Milton 175
Galton, Sir Francis 139
Garbett, Cyril 57
Gladden, Washington 70, 71
Gobineau, Joseph Arthur de 102
Goodman, Andrew 121
Gore, Charles 39, 41, 44
Community of the Resurrec-
tion (Mirfield Fathers) 44
Griswold v. Connecticut 142
Hancock, Thomas 39
Hardwick v. Georgia 151
Harris, Bravid W. 113
Hay, John 68
Headlam, Stewart Duckworth
39, 40-1
Guild of St. Matthew 39, 40,
41, 42
Hines, John 122, 124
Hitler, Adolf 83
Hobart, John Henry xi, xii, 191
Holland, Henry S. 39, 41
Holmes, Oliver Wendell 141
Hopkins, Charles 66

Hopkins, John Henry 105
Howard, Oliver Otis xv
Human rights
1982 Labor Day Pastoral
(urban bishops) 172
addressed at 1978 Lambeth
Conference 58
addressed at 1988 Lambeth
Conference 59-60
Catholic views about 18, 19,
27
Huntington, Frederick D. 71
Huntington, William R. 71
Jehovah's Witnesses 7, 79
Jim Crow laws 109
Joint commissions and
committees
as source for social teachings xiv, xvi
earliest report on dissent and
loyalty to state xv
first joint commission on
social services xvii, 7
function of xvi
on non-combatant Service
81, 83
on peace 85, 86
on relations of capital and
labor xvi, 73-4, 164
Jones, Paul 80
Jorgensen, Christine (George)
145
Kautsky, Karl 6
Kelly, Herbert 44
Society of the Sacred Mission
(Kelham) 44
King, Martin L., Jr. 116, 119,
121, 122, 126
Kingsley, Charles 35, 38, 47, 52
Know-Nothing movement 24
Ku Klux Klan 24, 52, 78, 108,
121, 140
Lambeth Conference
as source for social teachings
xviii
Lichtenberger, Arthur 119, 120,
122
Linnaeus, Carolus 101

Ludlow, John   x, 35, 38, 39, 44,
  47
Luther, Martin   174
Mackarness, J.F.   43
Marcion   90
Marriage and Family
  1961 General Convention   141
  1982 General Convention   143
  abortion   56, 142, 143, 144
  abortion (*Roe v. Wade*)   142
  abortion as a civil right   143-4
  abortion, conditions for
    permitting   143
  artificial insemination   144
  as "root germ" of church and
    society   138
  canonically regularized by
    church   136-7
  commission on family life
    137, 138, 140
  eugenics   139-41
  eugenics and Nazism   140
  family as concept expanded
    141, 151
  first Episcopal commission to
    study   137
  for the mentally unfit   139-41
  gay caucuses in churches   147
  in the Church's Teaching
    Series   135
Marxist critique   136
modern medical technology
  143, 144
polygamy   137
proposed alternatives to
  Christian   151-2
  sexuality fulfilled within
    145, 146, 148, 149, 151
  sources for social teachings
    about   136
  summary of social teachings
    about   153-4
  teenage pregnancies   155-6
Marx and Marxism   11, 20, 34,
  35, 52, 136
Maurice, Frederick D.   x, 14, 34-9,
  44, 47, 48, 49, 52, 165
  "associations"   37

Workingmen's College
  36, 38
McCarthyism   78
Memling, Hans   102
Mennonites   7, 79, 92
Methodist Bishops' Pastoral
  Letter
  on Peace   86, 95
Models of the church
  as advocate   72
  as exemplary in racial issues
    113, 129
  as mediator   72
  as reconciler of opposites
    74, 165
Modeste, Leon   123, 124
Montalembert, Charles   12
Moore, Paul, Jr.   148
Moorhouse, James   44, 51
Morehouse, Clifford   114, 121
Morris, John B.   117, 119
Mullin, Robert B.   xi, xii
Mussolini, Benito   83
Nelson, James B.   157, 159
Neuhaus, Richard   ix
Niebuhr, H. Richard   xv, 9, 10, 39,
  66, 178
Niebuhr, Reinhold   45, 46, 48, 56,
  85, 86
Norman, E.R.   45
Okun, Arthur   175, 176
Origen   10
Owen, Robert   34
Ozanam, Frederic   12
Pan-Anglican Congress   42
Parks, Rosa   116
Pastoral Letters
  1862, earliest Episcopal social
    teaching   viii, 189, 192
  as source for social teachings
    vi, xiii, 189
  canonical authority of   viii, 189
  origins of   xiii, 189
Peace
  "Star Wars"   89
  "To Make Peace" (1982)
    86, 88, 96
  1931 General Convention   85

1934 General Convention   85
1937 General Convention   85
1962 Pastoral   85, 87
1982 Pastoral Letter   87
and conscientious objectors
    88, 89
and just war doctrine   86, 89
and nuclear deterrent
    86, 87-8
nuclear freeze   88, 95
Perry, Troy   147
Pesch, Heinrich   12
Pike, James   115
Plessy v. Ferguson   109
Pope John XXIII   16, 17, 18, 20
Pope Leo XII   13
Pope Leo XIII   1, 2, 11, 12, 13,
    14, 16
Pope Paul VI   16, 20
Pope Pius IX   12, 13
Pope Pius X   2
Pope Pius XI   16, 17
Quakers   7, 79, 92
Race and racial issues
    "Guiding Principles for
    Negro Work" (1956)   117,
    128
    1865 Pastoral   104
    1886 Pastoral   110-11
    1895 Pastoral   110
    1904 General Convention
        (anti-lynching)   111
    1919 General Convention
        (anti-lynching)   111, 112
    1919 joint commission to study
        living conditions   112
    1931 commission on Negro's
        status in the church   112
    1958 Pastoral (on civil
        disobedience)   117-8
    addressed at 1908 Lambeth
        Conference   54
    addressed at 1930 Lambeth
        Conference   55
    affirmative action as a social
        teaching   125
    Bishop of London's letter,
        1727   103, 121, 126
    Bishop Hopkins' support of
        slavery   105
    canons, use of   114, 121
    catechisms and collections of
        sermons for slaves   106
    empowerment as a social
        teaching   125
    feminist movement as
        anti-black   106
    GCSP, demise of   124
    GCSP, social teachings
        undergirding   123, 124
    General Convention Special
        Program (GCSP)   123, 128,
        176
    joint commission on strategy
        (1943)   113
    joint commission to study
        causes of lynching   112
    Presiding Bishop Lichten-
        berger (civil disobedience)
        120
Rauschenbusch, Walter   71
Raven, Charles   35
Rerum novarum
    child labor   14
    labor unions   14
    on Catholic labor associa-
        tions   14
    on social classes   13, 15
    on socialism   15
    role of the state in   13
    strikes   13
Resolutions
    as source for social teachings
        xvii, xviii, 184
Roe v. Wade   142
Roman Catholic social teachings
    Quod apostolici muneris (1878)
        11
    "Partners in the Mystery of
        Redemption" (about
        women)   25
    Catholic social movement   12
    Dignitatis humanae (1965)   17
    Gaudium et spes (1965)
        11, 17, 20, 22, 23
    Mater et Magistra (1961)   16, 20

on cultural diversity   22
on family planning   22
on marriage   21
on racism   22-3
Pacem in terris (1963)   17, 18
Quadragesimo Anno (1931)
    16, 17
Rerum novarum (1891)
    11, 13, 16, 21
role of the state in   13, 17
subsidiarity   17, 19
Syllabus errorum (1864)   13, 23
theological principles of
    16, 17
theological sources of   2
Saint-Simon, C. Henri de   12
Sanger, Margaret   140
Schwerner, Michael   121
Sexuality
    "gay and proud" liberation
        movement   145
    gender and   145
    homosexuality and erotic
        covenants   156
    homosexuals and ordination
        148-9, 150
    joint commission on human
        affairs   145, 148, 149, 157,
        168
    model of the church in
        Newark (N.J.) report, the
        151-2
    "sexual preference"   145, 156
    1977 Pastoral and homo-
        sexual unions   148-9
    1979 Pastoral (homosexuals
        and ordination)   149
    1988 General Convention   152
    addressed at 1988 Lambeth
        Conference   61
    summary of teachings about
        sexuality   146, 150, 153-4
    transsexuality   145
Sherrill, Henry Knox   117, 124
Shuttleworth, Henry C.   39
Smith, Adam   177
Social Gospel, The   70-1, 165
Social teachings

church-type   8, 9, 66, 84, 93,
    127
definition of   1
political goals of church-type
    10
sect-type   5, 7, 9
St. Mark's Church   70, 71
    Workingmen's Club   70
Standing commissions   xiv, xvii
    creation of   xvii
    names of current   xvii
Sykes, Stephen   186
Tait, Archibald Campbell   41, 51
Tarplee, Cornelius   117
Temple, William   34, 42, 44-50
    Malvern Conference on the
        Social Order   46
Tertullian   90-1
Till, Emmett Louis   116
Troeltsch, Ernst   1, 4, 6, 8, 9, 84,
    93
Turner, Philip   159
Tuttle, Daniel   79
United Nations   17
University of the South
    (Sewanee)   114, 115, 120
Von Ketteler, Emmanuel   12
War
    1892 General Convention   77
    1898 General Convention   77
    1916 General Convention   79
    1933 Pastoral   81
    1934 Pastoral   82-3
    1939 Pastoral   83-4
    addressed at 1886 General
        Convention   77
    addressed at 1930 Lambeth
        Conference   55-6, 82, 85, 88
    addressed at 1948 Lambeth
        Conference   57-8
    addressed at 1988 Lambeth
        Conference   60
    ambivalence toward Indian
        wars   77
    and "nuclearism"   95, 96
    and conscientious objectors
        81, 82, 94, 95
    and evil spirits   84

and just war doctrine 91, 93
and nuclear deterrent 85, 95
and pacifism 82, 95
and patriotism 77, 78, 79, 80
and peace movements 83, 88
and social injustices 79, 83
and the Thirty-nine Articles
    91-2
and U.S. aggression 77
and U.S. wars 77, 78, 94
early church teachings about
    90-1
in the Church's Teaching
    Series 92
nuclear arms at 1948 Lambeth
    Conference 57
pacifism among bishops 80

selective conscientious
    objection 95
the peace churches 79
view of the American revolu-
    tionary war 77
World War I and Episcopal
    social teachings 79-80, 81
Westcott, Brook F. 39, 41
White Citizens Councils 78
  See Ku Klux Klan
White, William 191
Williams, Peter xv
Wilson, Bryan 3
Windhorst, Ludwig 12
Wogaman, Philip 179
World Council of Churches
    86, 185